Walker Percy: Novelist and Philosopher

Walker Percy

Novelist and Philosopher

Edited by Jan Nordby Gretlund
and Karl-Heinz Westarp

University Press of Mississippi
Jackson and London

IN MEMORIAM
Walker Percy
1916–1990

Copyright © 1991 by University Press of Mississippi
All rights reserved
Manufactured in the United States of America

94 93 92 91   4 3 2 1

The paper in this book meets the guidelines for permanence
and durability of the Committee on Production Guidelines
for Book Longevity of the Council on Library Resources.

Library of Congress Cataloging-in-Publication Data

Walker Percy : novelist and philosopher / edited by Jan
  Nordby Gretlund and Karl-Heinz Westarp.
     p.   cm.
   Includes bibliographical references and index.
   ISBN 0–87805–487–1 (alk. paper)
   1. Percy, Walker, 1916–1990—Criticism and interpreta-
tion. 2. Philosophy in literature. 3. Percy, Walker, 1916–
1990.
  I. Gretlund, Jan Nordby. II. Westarp, Karl-Heinz.
PS3566.E6912Z96 1991
813'.54—dc20   90–49285
                                              CIP

British Library Cataloguing-in-Publication data available

Contents

Walker Percy   Foreword: Approving or Disapproving Eyes   vii
Karl-Heinz Westarp   Preface   ix
Abbreviations   xv

I. THE NOVELIST

Lewis A. Lawson   The Cross and the Delta: Walker Percy's Anthropology   3

Gary M. Ciuba   Walker Percy's Enchanted Mountain   13

Patrick Samway, S.J.   Two Conversations in Walker Percy's *The Thanatos Syndrome*: Text and Context   24

W. L. Godshalk   The Engineer, Then and Now; or, Barrett's Choice   33

Joseph Schwartz   Will Barrett Redux?   42

II. NOVELIST AND REGIONALIST

Bertram Wyatt-Brown   Percy Forerunners, Family History, and the Gothic Tradition   55

Susan V. Donaldson   Tradition in Amber: Walker Percy's *Lancelot* as Southern Metafiction   65

Jan Nordby Gretlund   On the Porch with Marcus Aurelius: Walker Percy's Stoicism   74

Peggy Whitman Prenshaw   Elegies for Gentlemen: Walker Percy's
The Last Gentleman and Eudora Welty's "The Demonstrators"   84

III. NOVELIST AND EXISTENTIALIST

Marion Montgomery   Kierkegaard and Percy: By Word, *Away from* the
Philosophical   99

Kathleen Scullin   *Lancelot* and Walker Percy's Dispute with Sartre
over Ontology   110

Linda Whitney Hobson   The "Darkness That Is Part of Light":
Lancelot and "The Grand Inquisitor"   119

John F. Desmond   Language, Suicide, and the Writer: Walker Percy's
Advancement of William Faulkner   131

John Edward Hardy   Man, Beast, and Others in Walker Percy   141

Robert H. Brinkmeyer, Jr.   *Lancelot* and the Dynamics of the
Intersubjective Community   155

IV. NOVELIST AND MORALIST

Ashley Brown   Walker Percy: The Novelist as Moralist   169

François Pitavy   Walker Percy's Brave New World: *The Thanatos
Syndrome*   177

William Rodney Allen   "Father Smith's Confession" in *The Thanatos
Syndrome*   189

Elzbieta H. Oleksy   Walker Percy's Demonic Vision   199

Patricia Lewis Poteat   Pilgrim's Progress; or, A Few Night Thoughts
on Tenderness and the Will to Power   210

Sue Mitchell Crowley   *The Thanatos Syndrome*: Walker Percy's Tribute
to Flannery O'Connor   225

Notes   239
Contributors   249
Index   253

Foreword
Approving or Disapproving Eyes

This is to thank the writers of these essays.

I read this collection of critical essays on my work with a peculiar sensation, looking at it sideways and out of the corner of my eye, which is the only way I could do it. I feel somewhat embarrassed to be the subject of these essays, and I confess that most of them made me uneasy. I do not feel like commenting on each of the contributors, as I can't stand to hear or read anything about me—or **by** me, for that matter.

I was invited to come to Denmark to be with this gathering of writers. I hope they understand when I tell them that I would not get within ten thousand miles of the place. It was not that I did not like the writers assembled, but mainly that I could imagine how sick they must have been of Walker Percy. If I had been present, it would have been like Banquo's ghost showing up for the feast, so I had sense enough to stay away—from both the positive and the negative critics. Praise makes me feel fraudulent; I do not know which is more embarrassing, praise or blame.

Reading something about oneself is like being ten years old and talking to a hundred people. Talking or listening is eye play, or fencing: one person you can deal with, with his or her eyes; with a hundred people, you are undefended against ninety-nine. Approving or disapproving eyes are equally hard to handle. With the one, it is a case of uneasy satisfaction—Thank God he/she has not found me out. With the other, it is dismay. Found out! Oh Lord, what to do?

Reading one's own work is even worse, the only honest reaction is, Dear God, I could have done this better. At any rate, when all is said and done, one writes. Why? Why bother if you don't have to? Almost any other job pays better. Here's the secret all good writers share: writing comes from boredom. After all the horrors of the whole bloody business, the writing and being written about, in the end one is always stuck with oneself and paper and pencil. What to do?

It works out so: bored as any sensible man must be these days in this God-forsaken mad world, finding oneself Scripto in hand, three-ring binder paper virginal, one might as well set down a sentence or two, acutely mindful of how easy it is to make a fool of oneself with two sentences, and knowing for a fact that 98 percent of the galleys one receives do just this: one does it. So it comes to pass that one writes a sentence or two, each as invulnerable as a Sherman tank. Then, sometimes, one thing leads to another.

One would as soon do one thing as another, but it is too much trouble to get a bunch of ornery writers to write about something, and then get them together; an enterprise as vast and complex as General Lee's laying out the strategy for the Battle of Seven Days. I doubt that I will ever want to get within range of such a gathering. But it is not inappropriate that this symposium was in Denmark. I know no other writer, living or dead, who owes more to "the great Danish philosopher and theologian," as Binx Bolling called Søren Kierkegaard. So, though I did not participate, I had invoked the shade of the Great Søren and was there in spirit with him. (Do Danes know that Søren Kierkegaard is the greatest philosopher-writer of the past two hundred years?)

I am sure that my fellow writers will understand both my dismay and my gratitude. Writers are held to be a nutty lot by normal people. This may or may not be true. In this case I felt both nutty and grateful. Thanks, fellow nuts.

Walker Percy
Covington, Louisiana
9 February 1990

Preface

In a 1966 interview Walker Percy explained his position as novelist and philosopher: "I think of myself as being more in the European group than the American or Southern. I use the fiction form as a vehicle for incarnating ideas, as did Jean-Paul Sartre and Gabriel Marcel. I long ago decided that my philosophy is in the vein of the existentialist, as theirs were. Both said that fiction is not just recreation. In my case, it is the embodiment of ideas of both philosophy and psychiatry into a form through which the reader can see a concept which otherwise might not be recognized" (*Con.*, 9). To the two fields of knowledge mentioned by Percy himself we must add his medical education and his extended studies in language acquisition and general linguistics. Percy discussed his convictions both in his scholarly essays and in the many interviews he gave, but they are most imaginatively fleshed out in the protagonists of his novels. His characters are wayfarers on a quest for the true self which can be reached only by suffering the throes of indirection.

Percy's decision to present his philosophical ideas not only in scholarly treatises but as integral parts of his novels accounts for the high level of learning and complexity in his fiction. Walker Percy's philosophical fiction has puzzled many readers, who have found his writings a sometimes excruciating challenge. The present volume is a comprehensive contribution to a deeper understanding of Percy's work and will be of help to the scholar and the general reader alike. Contributors from the United States and Europe approach Walker Percy from many different angles and bring the most recent results of their research to bear upon the multifaceted Percy universe. The essays contained in this volume deal with Percy's entire oeuvre, including his last novel, *The Thanatos Syndrome*, and such recent nonfiction as *Lost in the Cosmos*. None of the essays has been published before.

Percy's prose essays are rarely just factual; they also contain fictional elements. Similarly, his philosophical considerations naturally spill over into his novels. It is therefore somewhat artificial to departmentalize his work as we have done in the structuring of this volume. In the analytical process it is helpful, however, to focus on certain prominent aspects of his work. The first group of essays looks at Percy, the novelist at work. In the second part the essays trace Percy's complex relations to his family, his region, and their traditions. Percy's roots in Søren Kierkegaard's existentialism and his creative relation to twentieth-century philosophers and novelists are investigated in the third part. Finally, in the fourth part, the contributors analyze Percy's standing as a moralist.

Recent manuscript studies have demonstrated that Percy is a dedicated and conscientious artist, who "writes and rewrites, over and over" (*Con.*, 8), an artist who never forgets his academic background in medicine, psychiatry, and linguistics. Nor can there be any doubt that Percy's work, like that of his admired fellow writer Flannery O'Connor, bears witness of his Catholic convictions. Lewis A. Lawson argues for a synopsis of all these elements in Percy in the opening essay of part One. Neither the Judeo-Christian explanation of fallen man under the cross nor an attempt to explain the human situation in a worded world through the advent of the delta factor is in itself a sufficient explanation of the present situation of the self. Only the two together lead to a true anthropology where "the individual delta also provides the capacity to conceive of omega (communion) both human and heavenly."

Two essays look into the artist's workshop: Gary M. Ciuba has had access to the manuscript of one of Percy's early and as yet unpublished novels, called "The Gramercy Winner." In the heavily autobiographical material Ciuba detects striking parallels to Thomas Mann's *The Magic Mountain*, yet with the significant difference that William Grey, Percy's protagonist, in the end "has won home thanks to God's grand mercy" (Gramercy), where Thomas Mann's protagonist Hans Castorp was satisfied with "knowledge, health, and life." Patrick Samway, Percy's official biographer, was allowed to study all of the manuscript and pre-publication material for *The Thanatos Syndrome*, Percy's last novel. Patrick Samway's careful scrutiny of the material reveals that the two conversations—constantly growing in the creative process—between Dr. More and Father Placide and between Dr. More and Father Smith (and their partly autobiographical genesis) are essential keys to an understanding of the novel.

Theme and character relations among several of Percy's works are the subject of the last two essays in this part. Walker Percy's characters are often haunted by the experience of *déjà vu*, and he invites his readers to cope with this phenomenon by presenting us with two sets of sequels: *The Last Gentleman* and *The Second Coming*, and *Love in the Ruins* and *The Thanatos Syndrome*. W. L. Godshalk analyzes *The Last Gentleman*, focusing on Will Barrett's development from his early New York days to the moment we see him chasing Sutter's old Edsel in Santa Fe. Unanswered questions in *The Last Gentleman* haunt the reader, who in *The Second Coming* meets a middle-aged Will Barrett. Yet in this novel more clearly than in *The Last Gentleman*, "suicide (seen as the ultimate rejection of immanence) is rejected in favor of engagement with life," according to Godshalk. In contrast, Joseph Schwartz sees *The Second Coming* as a sequel that "seriously diminishes the achievement of *The Last Gentleman*, Percy's finest novel." Schwartz contests Percy's own statement that his endings are "more or less inconclusive" (*Con.*, 190) by proving that they are all *un*ambiguous and that *The Second Coming* is therefore not a sequel written for the sake of clarification; it is yet another story about a wayfarer *en route* to discovery.

Walker Percy lived for many years in the small town of Covington, Louisiana, and from this vantage point on the bayou he learned and wrote about life in the American South. The essays in part Two argue that the presence of the South, southern settings, and southern themes in Walker Percy's fiction is of great significance. It may be a surprise to many readers—as indeed to Percy himself—that his family had strong nineteenth-century literary precursors. Bertram Wyatt-Brown has detected Catherine Ann Warfield, Eleanor Percy Lee, and Sarah A. Dorsey, all published but not well-known authors in their day. In the entire Percy family Wyatt-Brown finds a connection between depression and the artistic creation of a central antihero who is supported by a certain Catholic steadfastness and is set in Gothic surroundings. Susan V. Donaldson analyzes *Lancelot* as the Percy novel most pervasively imbued with southern stories and traditions, so much so that she calls it a southern metafiction: the stories have become reified and are no longer communicable. Lancelot therefore looks for a new order, yet he cannot finally put the old stories to rest. Percy's lifelong struggle with southern Stoicism is shown in Jan Nordby Gretlund's essay. He traces its roots through William Alexander Percy back to Marcus Aurelius, the Roman propagator of the Stoa. Though highly attracted to it, Percy recognizes that Stoicism is not enough: it needs Christian faith as its necessary complement. Percy has never been hesitant to comment on contemporary political issues. Peggy Whitman Prenshaw looks into the radically different ways in which Walker Percy and Eudora Welty, his fellow southerner, render their civil rights experiences of the early sixties in their fiction. In *The Last Gentleman* Percy lets his characters experience and discuss the events. Welty, on the other hand, does not want in her art, in, for example, "The Demonstrators," to be directly involved in the problems; instead, she prefers to indicate the enticing complexity of the situation.

For Percy life in his region never leads to provincialism; his philosophical mind always sees universal significance in the particular. In the first essay of part Three, Marion Montgomery investigates the roots of Percy's existentialism. Though he confesses that he is deeply influenced by Søren Kierkegaard, Walker Percy the writer finally comes down on the side of intuitive simplicity as opposed to the ratiocination of philosophy (hence Montgomery's subtitle, "By Word, *Away from the Philosophical*"). Even in his earliest writings Percy was engaged in discussions with Jean-Paul Sartre, Kierkegaard's twentieth-century successor in existentialism. Kathleen Scullin tracks reactions to Sartre's existentialism in Percy's early essay "Symbol as Hermeneutic in Existentialism" (1956) and in the much later *Lancelot*. Scullin points to similarities between the two existentialists, but she also underlines the essential difference between the ontologies of Sartre and Percy: Percy's answer to Sartre is implied in Percival's "Yes" at the end of *Lancelot*. Linda Whitney Hobson diagnoses *Lancelot* as a Christian comedy, with the final "Yes" as a comic reversal, comparable in its monologic form to Ivan Karamazov's "The Grand Inquisitor" in Dostoevsky's *The Brothers Karamazov*, which influenced Percy in the conception of *Lancelot*. Both authors fight darkness by paradoxically seeing light in darkness.

The shadows of death loom large in the lives and fictions of Walker Percy and William Faulkner. John F. Desmond demonstrates this essential brotherhood between them. He analyzes the similarities in their interest in language—and in suicide. Yet, once again, Percy proves to be fundamentally different: where Faulkner's fiction may end with a suicide, Percy's characters choose life. Few critics would deny that focus on human existence is at the core of Percy's work. John Edward Hardy focused on Percy's depiction of the essentially human in his monograph *The Fiction of Walker Percy*. In his present essay he counterbalances his earlier view by challenging Percy's emphasis on the uniqueness of man in favor of Percy's many positive depictions of animals. Walker Percy has repeatedly analyzed the triadic character of human existence. Robert H. Brinkmeyer, Jr., therefore reaches the logical conclusion that, according to Percy, all human communication is tetradic, since "all acts of consciousness are by their very nature intersubjective." And fiction is an important constituent in establishing an intersubjective community: the reader learns and grows through the narrative process. Brinkmeyer sees *Lancelot* as the most obvious example of such a "novelistic" therapy. Only interaction can function as a cure for existential isolation: this is the help the priest-therapist-novelist can offer.

Coupled with Walker Percy's choice of life is his trust that novelistic therapy can help, provided it is administered and accepted properly. This moralizing tendency, which seems to become more prominent in Percy's late works of fiction, is the overall theme of part Four. Ashley Brown points out in his essay on the novelist as moralist that already in 1962 Percy considered himself "a moralist or propagandist." Brown places Percy in the long tradition of literary moralists and praises him above all "for bringing so much intelligence to bear on the art of fiction." Utopian visions are closely connected with the moralist mission. François Pitavy throws light on Percy's presentation of a brave new world against the backdrop of earlier and contemporary utopian writers. According to William Rodney Allen, we find in *The Thanatos Syndrome* Percy's most outspoken attack on utopian dreams of a new society based on genetic and other kinds of manipulation. Like Patrick Samway, he scrutinizes "Father Smith's Confession" as the undeniable center of *The Thanatos Syndrome*. He sees the confession as yet another of Percy's *jeremiads* in which the moralizing intent is only too obvious. Allen seriously questions Percy's reliability in his presentation of the effects of recent scientific achievements upon modern American society. Elzbieta H. Oleksy parallels Percy's most complex novel, *Lancelot*, with Herman Melville's *Moby Dick*. Both Melville and Percy draw upon the Old Testament story of Ahab and Jezebel. In this context Oleksy propounds that Lancelot has demonic relations with women and that we find a considerable number of psychotic, helpless women in Percy's fiction. Percival's patient presence and the final "affirmation" suggest that the novel has a cathartic character.

The last two essays in the collection are companion pieces. Both Patricia Lewis Poteat and Sue Mitchell Crowley discuss Percy's presentation in *The Thanatos Syndrome* of the dangers of dissociating tenderness from its source. Purely immanent tenderness presents itself as acceptable, but it is only a cover for its practitioners' selfish will to power: the scientists' experiments for the good of mankind prove this, Poteat argues. Crowley attributes Percy's treatment of tenderness cut loose from its supernatural source directly to Flannery O'Connor's introduction to *A Memoir of Mary Ann*. In this work O'Connor stated: "When tenderness is detached from the source of tenderness, its logical outcome is terror. It ends in forced-labor camps and in the fumes of the gas chamber." Percy's warnings against this type of tenderness permeate his work. According to Crowley, it is not surprising that *The Thanatos Syndrome* ends on the feast of the Epiphany, "the feast of the revelation of Christ, the source of tenderness, to the Gentiles." Flannery O'Connor and Walker Percy, both newsbearers, "understand their fictions as works whose ultimate intention is just such revelation."

Sue Mitchell Crowley's final remark harks back to the beginning of this introduction: to Walker Percy's understanding of himself as novelist and philosopher. This may be taken as one sign of the remarkable unity of vision in Percy's work. In spite of Percy's learned diversity, which the essays in the four parts of this volume exemplify, we always sense behind it the unified vision and mission of the complex human existence of Walker Percy.

Karl-Heinz Westarp
Århus
March 1990

Abbreviations

Con. Walker Percy. *Conversations with Walker Percy.* Ed. Lewis A. Lawson and Victor A. Kramer. Jackson: University Press of Mississippi, 1985.

L Walker Percy. *Lancelot.* New York: Farrar, Straus, and Giroux, 1977.

LC Walker Percy. *Lost in the Cosmos: The Last Self-Help Book.* New York: Farrar, Straus, and Giroux, 1983.

LG Walker Percy. *The Last Gentleman.* New York: Farrar, Straus, and Giroux, 1966.

LR Walker Percy. *Love in the Ruins: The Adventures of a Bad Catholic at a Time Near the End of the World.* New York: Farrar, Straus, and Giroux, 1971.

M Walker Percy. *The Moviegoer.* New York: Alfred A. Knopf, 1961.

MB Walker Percy. *The Message in the Bottle: How Queer Man Is, How Queer Language Is, and What One Has to Do with the Other.* New York: Farrar, Straus, and Giroux, 1975.

SC Walker Percy. *The Second Coming.* New York: Farrar, Straus, and Giroux, 1980.

TS Walker Percy. *The Thanatos Syndrome.* New York: Farrar, Straus, and Giroux, 1987.

Part I
The Novelist

Lewis A. Lawson

The Cross and the Delta: Walker Percy's Anthropology

For some time now, the role of Catholicism in Walker Percy's fiction has been examined by the critics. More recently, his fiction has begun to be read in light of his theory of language. So far, though, there has been very little attention paid to the relationship that joins his Catholicism and his theory of language.

Walker Percy himself offers a précis of that relationship in the prologue to his collection of essays *The Message in the Bottle:* "In the beginning was Alpha and the end is Omega, but somewhere between occurred Delta, which was nothing less than the arrival of man himself and his breakthrough into the daylight of language and consciousness and knowing, of happiness and sadness, of being with and being alone, of being right and being wrong, of being himself and being not himself, and of being at home and being a stranger." This prologue offers a meaning on two levels—the transcendent and the immanent, the world of the cross and the world of the delta.

The Cross

With the segment "In the beginning was Alpha and the end is Omega," Percy is conflating three texts vital to Christian belief. The first, originally vital to Hebrew belief, of course, is Gen. 1:1: "In the beginning God created the heavens and the earth." The second is John 1:1: "In the beginning was the Word, and the Word was with God, and the Word was God." The third consists of two verses: The Apocalypse of John 1:8, in which God the Father is said to be speaking—"I am Alpha and Omega, the beginning and the ending, saith the Lord, which is, and which was, and which is to come, the Almighty"—and the Apocalypse of John 22:13, in which Jesus the Son of God is said to be speaking —"I am Alpha and Omega, the beginning and the end, the first and the last." The three texts must be considered in sequence: the first describes the establishment of the world; the second offers a radical redefinition of that establishment; and the third reveals the end. Percy's composite segment drawn from the three texts implies that the book that follows will be a revelation of the salvific nature of language. Buried in his prologue is a deep substratum of Christian theology of language, knowledge that he gained from the Bible and from Saint Augustine and Saint Thomas Aquinas.

The phrase "in the beginning" locates us immediately in our oldest cultural tradition, one rooted in Hebrew thought. Before time and space was God, who, the Hebrews imagined, spoke the world into being, who objectified his will by uttering sound, who allowed energy to become matter. Thus Hebrew thinking, as it developed, relied primarily upon sound as an avenue to knowledge, in contrast with Greek thinking, which emphasized sight. This contrast is fundamental in distinguishing the two epistemologies, a distinction that has become very useful in theology and in post-Cartesian science in the twentieth century. A clear presentation of the contrast between the two ways of experience may be drawn.[1] The Greek way stresses the static, space, the abstract, and dualism—ultimately, the Greek way contemplates. The Hebrew way stresses the dynamic, time, the concrete, and monism— ultimately, the Hebrew way acts. Walter Kaufmann draws a significant truth from this distinction: the Greek visualized his gods and eventually lost faith in them; but the Hebrew was forced to speak and listen to his God, who remains a mystery,[2] invisible yet present in his Word.[3]

When Christianity erupted in time, it did not reject the Hebrew belief in the primacy of uttered word, the belief that speech was first a divine possession and then a divine gift. On the contrary, it glorified even more the idea that speech was not merely another phenomenon among the phenomena of life, but that it was a special nature of the Godhead. In the New Testament, the treatment of speech as divinity reaches its full presentation in the prologue of the Book of John.[4]

The synoptic Gospels (Matthew, Mark, Luke) had laid the foundation for the concept of the Incarnated Word, the concept of Jesus as the presence of God in the flesh. But John boldly asserts another concept. His boldness is attested to by the fact that he dares to echo the first verse of Genesis, to realize more fully the role of sound in the Creation.

His new concept—which was not entirely original, being influenced by both the Hebrew personification of Wisdom and the Greek idealization of *Logos*—was that the Divine Word preexists its physical, historical incarnation. Fully developed, this doctrine asserts that "Jesus Christ is not only the subject-matter of the Christian *logos*, but . . . himself the Logos of God, his agent in the creation of the world as well as in the new creation."[5] This concept, the beginning of the Christian doctrine of language,[6] is fundamental to Percy's regard for language—when he retitles the central essay of *The Message in the Bottle*, from "The Act of Naming" to "The Mystery of Language," he is asserting that language may very well be a mystery in the plain sense of the word, but it is also a mystery in the Christian sense of the word, a sacrament, the channel through which the human meets the divine. Racially, the capacity for language may have developed a million years ago (*MB*, 42); individually, that capacity now appears in the period from twelve to twenty-four months; but these events do not strip language from the world of the cross to the world of the delta.

As Percy is referring in his prologue to Genesis, so is he certainly referring to the Apocalypse, for in it the Word speaks with a tone of absolute urgency, just before offering the invitation "Come" four times in the ultimate chapter. That word "Come" haunts Percy's thoughts. As he clearly acknowledges at the conclusion of the essay "The Message in the Bottle," it is a word that anyone can use: "In these times everyone is an apostle of sorts, ringing doorbells and bidding his neighbor to believe this and do that. In such times, when everyone is saying 'Come!' it may be that the best way to say 'Come!' is to remain silent. Sometimes silence itself is a 'Come!'" (*MB*, 148). Following his mentor Søren Kierkegaard, who wrote that he had not been able to speak directly, being without authority, Percy knows that he must use silence, speak indirectly. Thus he fashioned a fiction as an apocalypse in which to say "Come." In that fiction he acknowledges that the Fall was and is into language (the ground of consciousness and therefore of will); but then he offers language as the medium of salvation. When one comes to himself (a favorite Percy image), he speaks to himself, knows, as does the prodigal son, that all he has to do is to return to the father.

There is yet another tradition in language which informs the first segment of Percy's prologue. Members of this school of language are referred to as the speech-thinkers, the father of whom was Johann Georg Hamann (1730–88). Percy probably learned of Hamann through his study of Kierkegaard, for Hamann was the strongest influence on

Kierkegaard.[7] Two possible allusions to Hamann by Percy are relevant to this essay.

Recall the author's note to *The Message in the Bottle*, just before the prologue:

> This book was twenty years in the writing. All chapters except the last appeared as articles in journals. One chapter was published in 1954, another in 1975. Since my recurring interest over the years has been the nature of human communication and, in particular, the consequences of man's unique discovery of the symbol, a certain repetitiveness in the articles is inevitable. Some of the repetition has been preserved here, for example, the "Helen Keller phenomenon," if for no other reason as evidence at least of the longevity of my curiosity and my inability to get rid of it. This particular bone, I thought, needed worrying.

The "particular bone" that "needed worrying" must be the "Helen Keller phenomenon," Percy's name for the event-series during which a child ordinarily comes to understand speech as a symbolic act. What might be thought as Southernism in Percy's concluding sentence may instead be a suggestive allusion to a statement by Hamann: "If I were as eloquent as Demosthenes I would yet have to do nothing more than repeat a single word three times: reason is language, *logos*. I gnaw at this marrow-bone and will gnaw myself to death over it."[8] Percy's note appears perfectly immanent, depicting language as a natural event, yet the allusion to Hamann, who sees language as a supernatural event, suggests that the note, like the prologue that follows it, signifies on two levels.

The other possible allusion to Hamann is directly connected with the first segment of Percy's prologue. Here is Hamann's credo: "For me it is a question neither of physics nor theology, it is a question of language which is the mother of both reason and revelation—their Alpha and Omega."[9] Using the same image, alpha and omega, Percy, in *The Message in the Bottle*, wishes to position language between physics and theology, to reconcile the two forms of knowledge, reason and revelation, that were sundered by the Cartesians.

But such was the domination of Cartesian science that Hamann's ideas were virtually forgotten. During World War I, though, several writers in Germany, both Catholic and Protestant, formed what they called the Patmos Circle, taking their inspiration from the evangelist who, some hold, wrote both the Fourth Gospel and the Apocalypse, and therefore provided the seed for Hamann's thought. These writers were Eugen Rosenstock-Huessy, Leo Weismantel, Werner Picht, Hans

Ehrenberg, and Karl Barth. Their primary interest was to foster what Harold Stahmer calls a "dialogical philosophy."[10] They founded a journal, *The Creature*, which published works by, among others, Franz Rosenzweig, Nicholas Berdyaev, and Martin Buber before it was discontinued in 1930. There were other writers not formally allied with the Patmos Circle who nevertheless shared the same desire to reformulate the concept of the self and to reawaken a reverence for language—such men as Ferdinand Ebner, Gabriel Marcel, Max Scheler, and Martin Heidegger.

The Delta

While Percy has told a correspondent, Dale Johnson, that he does not know of the Patmos Circle, he nevertheless has felt its influence through Marcel, Heidegger, and Buber. Especially Marcel, with his "intersubjectivity," and Buber, with his "I-Thou" relationship, helped him move his concept of the origin of symbolism beyond the points advanced by Susanne Langer's *Philosophy in a New Key* (and, behind her, Ernst Cassirer's *Philosophy of Symbolic Forms*) and by Jacques Maritain's *Ransoming the Time*, each of which in a different way, described a speech-act model that was much more abstract than his own developing model, which was to be fixed by an ordeal, an existential situation familiar to readers of his essays and fiction.

In the midfifties raw existence contributed to Percy's formulation of the Helen Keller phenomenon. To Henry Kisor, Percy said, "I became interested in man's use of the symbols of language when I discovered that my daughter was deaf, . . . I'd been reading about Helen Keller's famous breakthrough in discovering that words stood for things: when Annie Sullivan poured water over her hand and spelled the word 'water' in her palm, and Helen made the connection" (*Con.*, 193). Perception, through a mysterious agency, becomes conception. Linda Hobson has described the pains that husband and wife took in trying to teach their daughter language: "One friend tells the story that when Walker and Bunt would take the child to New Orleans for her lessons, Walker would drive the car and Bunt, unwilling to waste a second, would sit in the back seat with Ann doing hearing exercises."[11] Surely that rearview mirror showed Percy that an adequate language-model required a tetrad, two symbol-mongers involved in triadic behavior. It is tempting to speculate that it was on one of those afternoons, after a trip to New Orleans, that Percy saw that what he had read in a book and what he had seen in the mirror were identical. This must have been when he discovered what Charles Peirce and Harry Stack Sullivan had already asserted: that consciousness—which depends upon symbolism—is not isolated but related.[12] It follows that the Cartesian model of the separate seer viewing the distant spectacle is invalid as the fundamental way of knowing. Our vision is guided by our hearing.

Helen Keller's experience is the classic paradigm of language acquisition. Langer, Cassirer, and Maritain had cited it. So had other writers with whom Percy is familiar. He speaks in two interviews of *Symbol Formation*, a study by Heinz Werner and Bernard Kaplan. He has read other books by Arthur Koestler, so he must have read *The Act of Creation*, in which Helen Keller personifies "the Eureka act—the sudden shaking together of two previously unconnected matrices."[13] Since Percy, David Bleich's *Subjective Criticism* has given an excellent analysis of Miss Keller's feat.

When Percy thought of locating the Helen Keller phenomenon on the continuum of human development, he cast about for another name for it: "What to call it? 'Triad'? 'Triangle'? 'Thirdness'? Perhaps 'Delta phenomenon,' the Greek letter Δ signifying irreducibility" (*MB*, 40). As Percy has noted, there is often a wisdom in etymology. Delta signifies irreducibility for Percy, but it derives ultimately from the Egyptian hieroglyph for *door*. The "Delta phenomenon" must also mean *door*, for symbolization is the connection between *outer* and *inner* and between *inner* and *inner*. While Percy independently discovered the phenomenon, he had learned, at least by 1972, that Charles Peirce had made the original discovery. Percy's mention of "Triad," "Triangle," and "Thirdness"—terms essential to Peirce's system of logic—acknowledges Peirce's priority.

Still, it may be anticipated, Percy has merely taken Peirce's triadic theory of signs, which enjoys some intellectual respectability, and introduced it into his presentation of orthodox Christianity, alpha to omega. That is not the case, however, for Peirce offers a precedent: "The starting-point of the universe, God the Creator, is the Absolute First; the terminus of the universe, God completely revealed, is the Absolute Second; every state of the universe at a measurable point of time is the third."[14] Since man alone measures, Peirce would have to accept Percy's continuum, alpha (Absolute First)–delta (measurable point)–omega (Absolute Second), for it conforms to his triadic logic. Indeed, Peirce says as much:

Here, therefore, we have divine trinity of the object, interpretant, and ground. Each fully constitutes the symbol, and yet all are essential to it. Nor are they the same thing under different points of view but three things which attain identity when the symbol attains infinite information. In many respects this trinity agrees with the Christian trinity: indeed I am not aware that there are any points of disagreement. The interpretant is evidently the Divine Logos or word; and if our former guess that reference to an interpretant is Paternity be right, this would also be the *Son of God*. The ground being that, partaking of which is requisite to any communication with the Symbol, corresponds in its function to the Holy Spirit.[15]

Since Peirce's logic is very much present in Percy's theory of symboliza-tion, the impact that Percy attributes to the delta phenomenon—"which was nothing less than the arrival of man himself and his breakthrough into the daylight of language and consciousness and knowing"—must be understood by reference to Peirce's thought.

Now the sequence "language and consciousness and knowing" must be discussed. By placing "language" first, Percy is asserting his funda-mental opposition to Descartes, who conceives of thought as originating in isolation. Percy speaks directly to this matter in "Symbol, Conscious-ness, and Intersubjectivity": "I am frank to confess a prejudice in favor of [George Herbert] Mead's approach to consciousness as a phenomenon arising from the social matrix through language" (*MB*, 266). In a homey passage Peirce particularizes the same view:

The child learns to understand the language; that is to say, an association between certain sounds and certain facts becomes established in his mind. He had previously noticed the connection between these sounds and the motions of the lips of bodies somewhat similar to the central one [that is, his own], and has tried the experiment of putting his hand on those lips and has found the sound in that case to be smothered. He thus connects that language with bodies somewhat similar to the central one. By efforts, so unenergetic that they should be called rather instinctive perhaps than tentative, he learns to produce those sounds. So he begins to converse.

About this time, I suppose, he begins to find that what these people about him say is the very best evidence of fact. So much so, that testimony is even a stronger mark of fact than appearances, themselves. I may remark, by the way, that this remains so through life; testimony will convince a man that he himself is mad. The dawning of the conception of testimony is the dawning of self-consciousness. Because testimony relates to a fact which does not appear. Thus, a distinction is established between fact and appearance. For example, suppose a child hears that a stove is hot; it does not seem so to him, but he touches it and finds it so. He, thus, becomes aware of ignorance and it is necessary to suppose an *ego* in whom this ignorance can inhere.

But, further, although appearances generally are either only confirmed or merely supplemented by testimony, yet there is a certain remarkable class of appearances which are constantly contradicted by testimony. These are those predicates which *we* know to be emotional but which *he* distinguishes by their connection with the movements of that central person, himself. These judgments are constantly denied by others. Moreover, he has reason to think that others also have these appearances which are quite denied by all the rest. Thus he adds to the conception of appearance as something other than fact, the conception of it as private, as connected with some one body. In short, *error* appears and it can be explained only by supposing a *self* which is fallible.[16]

Understandably, Peirce here treats consciousness and knowing as well as language—the phenomena are simply inextricable; hence his statement will also interpret Percy's use of "consciousness and knowing" in his prologue.

Percy does not mean by either word what many of his readers probably assume. By placing "consciousness" first he does not mean that he accepts the popular theory of the primacy of unintentional or pure awareness. In "Symbol, Consciousness, and Intersubjectivity," he writes: "There may be such a thing as an isolated ego-consciousness, but far from being the apodictic take-off point of a presuppositionless science, it would seem to correspond to Buber's term of deterioration, the decay of the I-Thou relation into the objectivization of the I-It" (*MB*, 275). Knowledge begins, in other words, in the symbolic transmission, which requires a social context. As he puts it: "The *I think* is only made possible by a prior mutuality: *we name*."

Yet Percy must have known that most of his readers would continue to conceive of consciousness as an isolated awareness. Thus he must have decided to add "knowing" to suggest the kind of mentation that transcends mere registering of sensory data. His inspiration surely must have been Genesis, which establishes knowing as the capacity to distinguish between good and evil, a capacity that God himself confessed was godlike, so that He sent Adam and Eve forth before they could eat the tree of life and become immortal (Gen. 3:22–24).

Alienation in the biblical account, then, results from knowing; alienation in a more recent account results from the acquisition of language and the corresponding loss of the original object. Cross and delta coincide, as Percy seems to acknowledge in a remark to Linda Hobson: "Sin is simply being born human. When you are born human, you are born to trouble as the sparks fly up. You have this capacity to symbolize the world. And everything is ordered for you in the form of symbols except oneself. The self is unformulable, you see, and that means you're in trouble."[17]

Walker Percy's Anthropology

Both the explanation provided by the Judeo-Christian story and that provided by modern language study, then, are necessary to situate the human in a worded world "of happiness and sadness, of being with and being alone, of being right and being wrong, of being himself and being not himself, and of being at home and being a stranger." The unification of the two has provided Walker Percy with what he calls "an anthropology, a theory of man—that man is a certain way, in traditional terms a fallen creature, or as both the Old Testament and Freud would say, he's born to trouble, as the sparks fly up. So there's something wrong with man. That's why Father Smith says the words are no good; the words have been deprived of meaning. . . . Words are like the original sin, the fall of man."[18] Such an anthropology colors every trait of the human being that Walker Percy creates in his fiction. That person comes into our view nursing an obscure wound, possessed of a dialogic consciousness and a capacity for knowing that is godlike but alienated by that very possession. The cost of the achievement of wordedness (the sparks flying up) has simply been so great that the person distrusts saying and hearing and instead falls prey to the temptation to rely entirely upon sight (especially as it is enhanced by instruments of visuality). Yet none of these instruments, not even the lapsometer, plumbs the psyche. The decisive turn occurs when the person comes to himself in ordeal, to realize that the road back (repetition) is by words. The self is unformulable, can be known only through communion with another human being and with God. The individual delta, occurring soon after the individual alpha, is both the greatest gain (individuality) and the greatest loss (individuality)—but the individual delta also provides the capacity to conceive of omega (communion) both human and heavenly. Once the individual wills to use this capacity, the world is no longer marked by silence and distance but becomes "incarnational, historical, and predicamental" (*MB*, 111).

How can this individual be helped by priest or physician (or Walker Percy)? In *The Thanatos Syndrome*, Tom More tells us: "We, . . . like our mentor Dr. Freud believe there is a psyche, that it is born to trouble as the sparks fly up, that one gets at it, the root of trouble, the soul's own secret, by venturing into the heart of darkness, which is to say, by talking and listening, mostly listening, to another troubled human for months, years" (*TS*, 13).

Gary M. Ciuba

Walker Percy's Enchanted Mountain

Walker Percy almost seems like a character in *The Magic Mountain* who has left the International Sanatorium Berghof only to write under its continued and creative enchantment. Thomas Mann's twentieth-century fairy tale recounts the adventure of Percy's life and of all his fictional seekers: the quest of an unaware but unsatisfied wanderer who comes to himself through catastrophe, who questions his education in scientific humanism and despairing romanticism, and who must finally make his own way in the world. In a 1978 letter Shelby Foote quipped to his longtime friend that Mann had really written Percy's own magnum opus in *The Magic Mountain*.[1] But if the three weeks during which Mann visited his wife at a Swiss sanatorium in 1912 gave him first claim on the story that Percy's three years at Saranac Lake and Gaylord Farms would make uniquely his own, Percy rewrote Mann's novel in his early and unpublished "The Gramercy Winner."[2]

Mann, who once described doctors as some of his best readers, provided the physician-novelist with a model that helped him to convert autobiographical fact into diagnostic fiction.[3] While never even trying to duplicate his mentor's exhaustive realism, elaborate motifs, or experiments in the relativity of narrative time, Percy, in his less expansive novel about the world of the sanatorium, focuses on the initiation of the young and rather passive William Grey through the same path that Mann charted for Hans Castorp in "The Making of *The Magic Mountain*": through "disease and death as a necessary route to knowledge, health, and life."[4] Yet Percy's apprentice-work defines itself as much through as against Mann's *Bildungsroman*. It views humanity not as Mann's ironic "lord of counter-positions" but as a lost searcher who must choose the single direction that leads home.[5]

Before the student-heroes of both novels discover by chance the tuberculosis that begins their coming to consciousness, Mann's affable naval architect from a dynasty of Hamburg merchants and Percy's equally prepossessing scion of a wealthy New York businessman were absorbed in prosperous, pragmatic, and pleasant lives. The book that each brings to the asylum defines the honorable mediocrity of his education to date. As Hans travels by rail to visit his consumptive cousin for three weeks, Mann's wayfarer, who only recently passed his last exam, reads *Ocean Steamships* in preparation for a not particularly distinguished or desired career in mechanical ingenuity. Since William views language and literature as "non-essentials" ("GW," 6), the Princeton sophomore takes *Subatomic Particles* with him to the Adirondacks rest home, where he hopes to discover some underlying cosmic order through nuclear physics. Modestly identifying himself as an engineer, Hans possesses scientific and technical knowledge, as do William Grey and Percy's later "engineer," Will Barrett. But all of these novices lack news about their own lives, the human quandary that Percy himself was forced to acknowledge by his own tuberculosis: "what it means to be a man living in the world who must die."[6]

Mann's version of the disheartened "man on the train" from *The Message in the Bottle* finds the end of the line signaled not by a coronary attack but by a case of tuberculosis. According to Mann's diagnosis, the frustrated seeker in "an age that affords no satisfying answer to the eternal question of 'Why?' 'To what end?'" may develop a spiritual disease that manifests physical symptoms (*MM*, 32). Yet this illness is potentially lifesaving, for it may force victims to explore original answers to these unresolved questions. Looking at his chest X-ray or listening to his pulse, Hans confronts "the pulsating human heart . . . alone with its question and its riddle" (*MM*, 478). In her critique of illness as metaphor, Susan Sontag explains that the mythology of sickness has made tuberculosis "a way of affirming the value of being more conscious, more complex psychologically." It is the "disease that individualizes, that sets a person in relief against the environment."[7] Tuberculosis reveals to Mann's engineer his distinct outline against the background of his unreflective life in the flatlands and of his possibly fatal prognosis in the Alpine asylum. He glimpses a macabre variation on Percy's favorite image of seeing one's hand for the first time when the magic window of the X-ray screen shows him a view of his own grave. As Hans gazes at the skeletal projection of such a familiar part of his own body, "for the first time in his life he understood that he would die" (*MM*, 219). The patient is compelled by illness to attend to his own unique predicament, the mortality at hand, the incongruity of living before the end as Hans Castorp. His *Lehrjahre* in the wonderland and underworld of the sanatorium is a prolonged course in such disorientation through death that may prepare him for a reorientation to life.

Mann's case history of a novel chronicles the phantasmagoria of Hans's seven years as a student: the multiple meals and carefully timed walks, frequent monitorings of temperature and periods of enforced indolence—all still practiced thirty years later during William Grey's cure at a hospice "as famous as any Swiss Kurhaus," where patients "got well and stayed on, bewitched by the spell of the old mountain village" ("GW," 9). Like Hans Castorp lulled by the repose of the Berghof, Percy's idle student, at the beginning of "The Gramercy Winner," lies motionless in bed, feeling that he has arrived at "the dead center of things from where he might look out" ("GW," 17). Although suffering from only a minor case of tuberculosis, William Grey discovers his identity from the perspective of possible disaster. Beforehand, the nondescript twenty-year-old lived as a nonentity. "If there was anything remarkable about his past life," Percy writes, "it was that absolutely nothing had happened to him" ("GW," 10). Having neither won nor lost at anything because it would be in bad taste, Percy's first gentleman was impeccable but ill-defined. William's tuberculosis, like Hans's strangely revealing syndrome, is not just a malady but a sign of the malaise, the sickness at the heart of these travelers without an ultimate purpose or direction. But the threat of fatal defeat makes the would-be winner from the elite enclave of Gramercy Park at last live as if now something has happened in his grayish life. William feels that he "had died to one life and meant to come alive in another. Already he was awakening to a strange new world" ("GW," 64).

William is initiated into this bewildering world through his conflicting loyalties to four characters, Percy's variations on the central quartet of *The Magic Mountain*. Like Mynheer Peeperkorn, Laverne Sutter can captivate William by the sheer charisma of his commanding and reckless personality. After arriving at Mrs. McLeod's rest home with six suitcases and golf clubs, the dashing aviator bursts into William's bare room and speaks as if he had known Grey for a long time. In *The Magic Mountain* Peeperkorn's fragmented and incoherent rhapsodies nearly overwhelm all the novel's earlier disquisitions by the intensity of their pure emotion. He appropriately delivers his last exhortation near a deafening waterfall whose might he would rival through his own terrible fury even if not through his enfeebled flesh. Percy's more voluble lieutenant regales William with stories about army bases and visits to doctors, yet the "torrent of words which broke over him like waves of the sea" fascinates as well as frustrates his listener ("GW," 32). William sees in the feverish Laverne Sutter the same dynamism and despair that enthrall Hans in Mynheer Peeperkorn. Dying and rendered impotent by their diseases, both live with such overpowering urgency and anguish before death that they reach out to the novels' initiates for instructive camaraderie. Peeperkorn proposes a "'brotherly alliance, such as one forms against a third party, against the world, against all and sundry'" (*MM*, 611), a typically heartfelt bond of consummate feeling that exposes the austere intellectualism of Hans's previous tutelage. Sutter's claims of friendship, celebrated in long talks, afternoons listening to baseball games, and even the silence that only years of conversations usually make acceptable, draw William further into the human dilemma that the daydreamer constantly seeks to avoid through scientific abstraction. Since William comes to feel that he has never known anyone as well as he knows Sutter, he also is inevitably entangled in an alliance against a third party, a woman who resembles Peeperkorn's mistress—Sutter's disconcertingly cordial wife.

William regards Allison Sutter with the honor owed to his friend's spouse, a South Carolina lady whose kindnesses make the exile see her as the incarnation of Dostoevsky's Sonia. The northerner considers it "the surest sign of her noble southern origins" that late at night she can bring him a stack of mysteries with naked women on their covers and yet never seem indecent ("GW," 52). William's good manners accord her such respect precisely because she seems free from the moral taint that keeps the equally proper Hans Castorp so outraged and yet so entranced by Madame Chauchat's bad manners. The respectable burgher detects the very symptoms of her perversity in her habit of slamming the door as she comes late to dinner every evening. Yet if the deluded romantic, according to Binx Bolling, sets "just beyond his reach the very thing he prizes" (*M*, 215), William's courtesy and Hans's censure create the emotional distance that only intensifies their desires.

Both lovesick students consummate their hermetic education by pursuing potentially sickly loves that cultivate only one extreme of humanity. Settembrini admonishes Hans that "'a human being who is first of all an invalid is *all* body; therein lies his inhumanity and his debasement. In most cases he is little better than a carcass'" (*MM*, 100). Castorp's love for the ill-bred Clavdia introduces him to a world of irrational passion that he simply cannot engineer, but it also nearly turns him into a corpse. From his early sight of Madame Chauchat, when his heart starts palpitating without any accountable emotion,

Hans's involuntary tremor makes him feel like a dead body that is not really dead because it keeps growing hair and nails on its own in the grave. Charmed by Clavdia's flesh, he contemplates her arm from afar, praises the clinical verisimilitude of her portrait by Dr. Behrens, and, after the climactic carnival scene, finally enjoys carnal knowledge. As a love token, Hans gets Clavdia's X-ray, the grim outline of his morbid eroticism. In a cosmos that Hans regards as a downfall and disease of the Spirit, his obsession with this lovely mistress of the material world keeps him spellbound to reverie rather than reason, stasis rather than progress, the power of death rather than the power over death.

Percy converts this necromancy into William Grey's more ambiguous romance with a fellow exile, yet he never makes completely credible all of her contradictions. Allison Sutter seems like a febrile and feline Clavdia Chauchat who is already becoming in Percy's imagination the lost, pretty Kitty Vaught of *The Last Gentleman.* Just as Clavdia proposes "'a league—not against but for'" the ailing Peeperkorn (*MM*, 598), Sutter's illness brings William and Allison together as if they were "the loving parents of an attractive but retarded son" ("GW," 88). In this complex triangle, William becomes not only Sutter's foster father but also Allison's surrogate spouse, before whom she often acts as subtly provocative as the vamps from her detective fiction. Her embittered husband reveals that Allison's own taste in mysteries favors not puzzling whodunits but the more hardboiled crime stories in which in "'every other chapter some beautiful babe either gets beat up or laid'" ("GW," 81). Even such a courtesy as telling William to dismiss his taxi and accept her ride to the hospital may conceal a proposition. Shortly before he leaves Mrs. McLeod's for another rest home, William overhears an argument between the Sutters in which the jealous army officer charges that his wife is known for picking up in her convertible any second lieutenant standing on a corner. Yet if she anticipates Percy's later temptresses, Allison at times seems William's soul mate, a possible companion to the Percyan searcher, much like the young Will Barrett's southern lady. When the two share an island picnic, the castaway from South Carolina tells William of a homesickness that yet is not for home. Allison grieves because William does not recognize that he exists complete in her love; instead, he imagined "that he was legion and showed her whichever mysterious self he pleased—the Billy of the cave, of desire, of pilgrimage" ("GW," 250). At this moment the bedeviled scientist plays the Billy of desire, arguing that nothing is as important as his sexual discoveries. Like her husband, Allison becomes an object lesson in William's search for knowledge. Together, the Sutters initiate a baffled student into the world of desire and death, the dual complexities of living in the flesh.

When William moves to Mrs. Zabel's, a second way station for a Percyan wanderer, he confronts again the same imperatives of Eros and Thanatos. Having seemingly left behind the Sutters, he finds new tutors in Van Norden and Scanlon, two doctors whose disagreements echo the central dialectic between Settembrini and Naphta in *The Magic Mountain*. But whereas Mann's Alpinist grows wiser than either of his pedagogues, the Gramercy winner discovers complete loss as the student of Van Norden and finally lives up to his name only as the islander who listens to Scanlon's news. As Settembrini tirelessly and sometimes tediously proselytizes for classicism, humanism, rationalism, liberalism, and individualism, he speaks for what Percy has called "the old modern age" (*MB*, 23). Since Mann's intellectual places his faith in *scientia*, he tends to glorify the mind and to discredit the flesh as the principle of disease, sensuality, and death. Hence, he challenges Naphta, who claims that Galileo erred in philosophy if not in astronomy: "'Do you believe in truth, in objective, scientific truth, to strive after the attainment of which is the highest law of all morality, and whose triumphs over authority form the most glorious page in the history of the human spirit?'" (*MM*, 397–98).

Van Norden believes religiously in such a scientific humanism, for he does not know that the old modern age has ended. In all of Percy's writings, its terminus is the same catastrophe that exposes the folly of Settembrini's blithe faith in civilized progress—the Great War, which explodes in the last pages of *The Magic Mountain*. Yet although living amid the century's second great war, Van Norden still espouses a more extreme version of an already exhausted creed. He turns Settembrini's quest for *scientia* into pure scientism. Since Van Norden only wants to know, the pathologist views the living as if they were the dead: corpses to be entered for the pursuit of carnal or scientific knowledge. Scanlon appropriately accuses his libertine rival of necrophilia. Settembrini only ogled and chirruped at women, but his more abstracted descendant commits graver indignities, driven by what Scanlon denounces as "'the lust and fornication of Science'" ("GW," 161). Van Norden discourses on the immense variety of females, all needing cultivation by his sex, and provides details about his affair with a former patient, which embarrasses William. The pathologist is just as ruthlessly objective in performing the autopsy that his protégé watches near the end of the novel. Warned by the mortician not to disfigure the body's face, Van Norden is determined to remove the medulla and finally succeeds through a transpharyngeal approach. Only after Van Norden has confirmed his theory about the cause of death does William push back the flap of skin hiding the corpse's face and reveal the body to be Sutter's. Under Van Norden's analytic gaze women and men lose their identities. Every person becomes a body, and every body becomes just an object for his probing flesh and inquiring mind.

Although William Grey attends the autopsy because he has become the doctor's unquestioning disciple, the more critical Hans Castorp practices Settembrini's teaching *"placet experiri"* so wholeheartedly that he tests the pleasures of intellectual independence. Mann's student turns from a silent listener to his mentor's lectures into the best of all pupils who questions, evaluates, and argues with his instructor. Hans comes to recognize the extremism and contradictions of his prolix schoolmaster, an activist debilitated by disease, a pacifist eager to destroy Vienna, a rationalist foolish enough to fight a duel. Hans learns that Settembrini, who loathes paradoxes, is part of that lordly paradox, humanity, but William is less pleased to experiment. Although he is chagrined by Van Norden's tales of his liaisons and sometimes feels rather anonymous as his patient, he never follows what Settembrini recommends as youth's "'inclination to play with all possible points of view'" (*MM*, 201). Instead, William pursues the very limits of the pathologist's scientific transcendence. From this single and self-defeating viewpoint he sees again Laverne and Allison Sutter at the end of the novel. His friends become impersonal experiments in the facts of death and life that they first made him contemplate, mortality and carnality.

During the climactic autopsy Van Norden instructs William to describe precisely what he sees. However, William is drawn to the mystery that the triumphant pathologist ignores: the face of the body obscured by the skin curled from the incision. William sees that Van Norden's aloofness eviscerates humanity, turning the self into a scientific sample while completely overlooking the very essence of Sutter, despite all of the doctor's prying. The corpse is only "a hopeless enigma, almost a blank space in the room," as if "the dead man had taken his secrets with him when he died" ("GW," 262). The devitalizing objectivity of the postmortem cannot reveal what William discovered through the living interchange on so many afternoons when the confidants talked away death. Although William begins to face the impenetrable mystery of existence, in despair and frustration he continues to seek a fatal abstraction. Just as Van Norden's zeal for medical knowledge emptied the person of Sutter, his pupil's search for carnal knowledge reduces love to sex with Sutter's wife. Convinced that some secret still eludes him, William demands that he wants Allison on her back after she has been tracing the channel down his own spine. Allison wonders whether he ever thinks of her as human, but when Grey finally admits that he loves her, she abruptly orders, "'Get up and lock the door'" ("GW," 296). After spending several days with William, Allison virtually disappears from the end of the novel, as do Kitty in *The Last Gentleman* and Lucy in *The Thanatos Syndrome*—or the equally transitory Clavdia Chauchat. William's femme fatale exacerbates his spiritual decline just as Hans's consuming passion intensifies his consumption. If "'all disease is only love transformed,'" as Dr. Krokowski theorizes in *The Magic Mountain* (128), William feels in his own flesh how the perversion of sex breeds death.

None of the doctors can understand the sudden worsening of William's illness, for their angelism prevents them from realizing that the victim is dying of the same professional detachment. Only Scanlon, who speaks not to a patient but to William Grey as a homeless and homesick wanderer, recognizes both the physical and metaphysical origins of his virulence. Indeed, like the monkish Dr. Krokowski, he once proposed an erotic etiology of tuberculosis in which the disease impregnates the body of the welcoming beloved with the sperm of bacilli. Van Norden mocked his adversary for such a typically mystical theory, and Scanlon laughed at his own unconventional explanation. Van Norden's disputes with Scanlon are animated by the same increasingly acrimonious spirit as Settembrini's debates with Naphta, his Jesuit rival, who defends conservatism, medievalism, communism, and terrorism. When Settembrini exalts scientific truth, Naphta objects, "'Faith is the vehicle of knowledge, intellect secondary. Your pure science is a myth'" (*MM*, 397) and sounds to the modern son of the Enlightenment like an ignorant child of the Dark Ages. Percy reduces all of the arguments between Settembrini and Naphta—clashes over art, education, politics, and philosophy—to this central conflict between Van Norden and Scanlon: the limits of reason and the possibility of revelation. Whereas Scanlon criticizes the pathologist for "organolatry" ("GW," 193), Van Norden caricatures his opponent as a medieval doctor of physic whose attendance at a Catholic medical school has taught him to believe in humors and demons. Yet even Van Norden concedes that his antagonist is quite skilled in his profession. Scanlon's *religio medici* does not so much obscure his scientific insight as allow the sometimes disenchanted doctor to see beyond its limited purview.

Although Scanlon looks back to the fideist Naphta, he heralds even more clearly all the later messengers in Percy's fiction. The physician does not just provide the necessary counterpoint in a novel's dialectic; he brings the unequivocally good news that gives William a new orientation. Appearing in the second half of *The Magic Mountain*, Naphta voices a salutary antithesis to Settembrini's rationalism. If Mann's humanist sounds like the precursor of so many of Percy's utopian planners as he envisions a world free from suffering and disease, Naphta views illness as a purifying rite that disciplines the body and liberates the soul. His explanation of the initiation ceremonies once practiced by Masons enables Hans to understand his own descent into this moribund realm. Yet Hans sees the contradiction between Naphta's asceticism and his luxurious apartment, senses the dangerous spell of the Jesuit's quietism, and is repelled by the savagery with which he defends torture and terror. The true descendant of Naphta is not Scanlon but every suicidal romantic, violent zealot, and crazed apocalyptist in Percy's subsequent novels. Lacking their common love of Thanatos, Scanlon shows the love in the ruins that may alone prevent death from winning William Grey.

As William lies dying, he reaches a state of terminal despair caused by the collapse of his belief in Van Norden's old modern world. Having sought some revelation beyond even the secrets of sex, he discovers that "'the secret is that there is nothing'" ("GW," 328). However, William even seems discontent with this reductive nihilism, for he keeps asking Scanlon what his visitor knows but is not telling him. Although Scanlon has given William his bed in the doctor's lodge and tended to him as if he were his patient, the Hospitaler keeps denying that he conceals any private gnosis. He does not know a sublime version of Van Norden's scientific truth; rather, he bears the gospel that must be heard as personally spoken to a listener otherwise in jeopardy of losing self and soul. William's sufferings enable him to heed the message at first hand. He gains the education that Lewis A. Lawson describes as the origin of Percy's own novels about physicians and patients: "Rather than penetrating the world to know it spatially," at the sanatorium Dr. Percy was "penetrated by the world and . . . taught by pain to know himself temporally."[8] Living at this same critical hour, William can receive Scanlon's guidance that brings the exile from Gramercy Park to his first and final home.

In making this journey William again comes into the company of George Boetjeman, a friend recently killed in the war whom he has recalled throughout the novel. William once laughed explosively with George even though his schoolmate jumped several of his kings while playing checkers. The Gramercy winner rejoiced at the heart of loss because the apparent defeat was dissolved in a more victorious communion. During his illness William dreams especially of the day when he and George returned to Penn Station from Christmas vacation in Aiken. He wakes with "an agreeable sense of profit," as if to win is to recover from being sidetracked ("GW," 310). William cries to Scanlon, who has always seemed to come from afar, that he is homesick and has been so all his life. Before he dies, he remembers the rest of that day in New York when he set out to ride the train with his friend before eventually going home to Gramercy Park. William suggested that they walk down to the Battery and take the elevated back uptown. George did not really want to go, "but he went anyway because he was very fond of William and because he didn't want to be left alone" ("GW," 331). After the fifteen-year-olds walked through the vaulted waiting room of the train station, George passed first through the concourse and into the city. William has attempted to rediscover this cordiality in all of his friendships—with Sutter, with Van Norden, even with Allison, whose boyish appearance may remind him of George Boetjeman, just as Clavdia makes Pribislav Hippe once again present to Hans Castorp. But in his quest for transcendence William has continually strayed from this primal bond. As with the death of Sutter or his sex with Allison, he found the news that George had been killed by a sniper strangely devoid of all significance. Now, after a lifetime of looking and being lost, William finds his way by following a fellow traveler.

As William sets out for his eternal destination, Scanlon helps the Gramercy winner to return to this holiday adventure, the communion amongst all wayfarers, living and dead. In these last days the doctor speaks with William in a low voice, "as if he were imparting information, data, of great value and usefulness, William interrupting once in a while to put a short sharp question. It was as if one were going somewhere and the other were giving him instructions for the journey" ("GW," 336). Scanlon's whispered confidences to a friend in transit enable William to join George in a sacramental progress through death. No one can understand the laughter that punctuates their secret conversations, the mirth that the defeated William once shared with George Boetjeman. And the night supervisor is scandalized when she sees Scanlon sneaking into the patient's room with a glass of water to baptize William shortly before he lapses into a coma and dies. Yet if the words of grace must sound disgraceful when judged by the manners of Van Norden's scientific world, Scanlon has brought to William the glad tidings that give final direction to a spiritual seeker.

Although in "The Making of *The Magic Mountain*" Mann can envision Hans Castorp as seeking the Grail, his knight-errant intimates a salvific humanism rather than the pilgrim faith of Percy's quester. Hans understands that the passage through sickness and death may lead to sanity and health, just as "a knowledge of sin" may be necessary "to find redemption." Yet Mann's redemption never goes beyond a "reverence before the mystery that is man" to Percy's consummate homecoming, the end to human estrangement from the divine mystery.[9] Hans Castorp learns during his odyssey that both of his guides are too excessive and exclusive, for "man is the lord of counterpositions, they can be only through him" (*MM*, 496). He comes to accept and reject all absolutes, believing that love is more powerful and creative than Settembrini's reason or Naphta's death. Even if Hans forgets this revelation amid the beguiling diversions of the sanatorium, he continues to hope that "between two intolerable positions, between bombastic humanism and analphabetic barbarism, must lie something which one might personally call the human"(*MM*, 523).

Percy's questers become truly sovereign wayfarers, lords of these counterpositions, only when they recognize a bond with the Lord, who is the native ground of their being. Suffering from the novelist's earliest version of the Thanatos syndrome, William Grey languishes in the sickness unto death precisely because he lacks such an ultimate connection. In *The Message in the Bottle* Percy defines religion by its etymology as "a radical *bond* . . . which connects man with reality . . . and so confers meaning to his life" (102–3). It is the primal ligament in his diagnostic fiction. Although Hans Castorp's education initiates him into the contradictory realities of life and of death as a part of life, William Grey's reception of baptism, the sacrament of initiation, signifies not just that the lost wanderer has at last traveled away from the gramary of the enchanted mountain and back to Gramercy Park but also that he has journeyed beyond death. He has won home thanks to God's grand mercy.

Patrick Samway, S.J.

Two Conversations in Walker Percy's *The Thanatos Syndrome*: Text and Context

On 12 July 1985, Walker Percy finished the manuscript of *The Thanatos Syndrome* and, less than a year later, on 19 May 1986, he sent his editor, Robert Giroux, what Percy called "the corrected ribbon typescript" of the novel. One month later, on both 18 June and 26 June, Percy, profiting from the advice of some friends who had read the novel, sent Giroux short inserts for the purposes of coherence and clarification. On 27 August 1986, Bryan Makishi of the contract and copyright department of Farrar, Straus, and Giroux (FS&G) in New York City sent Eugene Winick, Percy's agent, likewise of New York City, two fully executed copies of the agreement for *The Thanatos Syndrome*. With this formality finished, Giroux could officially edit the novel with a view toward publishing it by April 1987, as indicated on the bound, unrevised, uncorrected proofs, with an estimated first run of 75,000 copies. (The novel's actual publication date was March 1987, with a first run of 59,000 copies.)

On 30 December 1988, Dr. Percy gave me a box containing what he said was all the manuscript and typescript material for *The Thanatos Syndrome* that he had kept in his house in Covington, Louisiana; I photocopied this material in the exact order (rectos and versos) as I found it.[1] About this time, FS&G also allowed me access to the "dead matter" of this novel in their possession before it was sent to Covington. Thus, as far as I can tell at this point, there is one holograph manuscript for *The Thanatos Syndrome* in addition to four important recensions.[2]

In composing this novel, Percy wrote steadily, stopping periodically to list characters, to make notes concerning plot development, and to revise, for the most part on the page opposite the one he was working on, scenes that needed elaboration. In particular, two related episodes —the initial conversation between Dr. More and Father Placide and the more important, subsequent initial conversation between Dr. More and Father Smith—go a long way toward unlocking the genetic history of this text, for some of the material in these two conversations casts new light on our knowledge of the history of the novel as revealed partially in the several interviews and conversations Percy has had about this work.[3] It is interesting to note that neither "Father Smith's Confession" nor "Father Smith's Footnote"—two important sections in this novel—can be found in the holograph manuscript or in the first typescript. While the first edition is the final product and deserves our closest scrutiny, a study of the manuscript and typescripts of *The Thanatos Syndrome*, like looking at the delicate springs and gears behind the face of a clock, can show us hidden subtexts that serve, as Mikhail Bakhtin put it in his discussion of language and significance, as an "apperceptive background of understanding."[4]

Before writing the scene in which Father Placide asks Dr. More to help him intercede with Father Smith, Percy made two pages of random notes to prime his literary pump (hm/439–40).[5] In all, Percy took eleven pages to dramatize the encounter between Dr. More and Father Placide (hm/449–59), which leads directly in the manuscript, as it does in the first edition, into the encounter between Dr. More and Father Smith. Many of the ideas and much of the dialogue were incorporated for the most part into the first edition (only Father Placide and Dr. More, however, are in the rectory in the manuscript version). Though one might suspect that World War II would figure as a dominant motif in the initial encounters between Dr. More and the two priests, particularly Father Smith, it does so only occasionally, yet always with telling effect. There are hints that the war will play a role in this novel; for example, Old Saint Mary's Hospice (later changed to a hospice in Abita Springs [hm/659], then to Saint Francis's Hospice, and finally to Saint Margaret's Hospice [t1/200]) is linked with a convent, nuns, and World War II.

Significantly, this brief section reveals four oblique familial references, which make the novel more autobiographical than one might initially suspect. First, the scene opens with a description of a statue of Saint Michael brandishing a sword. Though this sword had been instrumental in saving Dr. More in *Love in the Ruins*, Percy returns to it again and here seems to emphasize how easily the sword can be removed. This is an allusion, I believe, to the statue erected by William

Alexander Percy in honor of his deceased father, LeRoy Percy (9 November 1860–24 December 1929). Entitled *The Patriot*, this statue in the Percy family cemetery plot in Greenville, Mississippi, depicts a medieval soldier in mail standing almost erect with one hand crossing the other. The soldier leans on a sword, which, much to the chagrin of the Percy family, has a history of being stolen by local vandals.[6] One could speculate that "Uncle Will" serves as a type of spiritual (and Freudian) guardian in this section of the novel. Secondly, once Father Placide has made his request for help, he mentions that the local bishop (a person whom Percy later dropped from the text) wants ten laymen to assist with an ecumenical gathering—originally mentioned were Presbyterians, Lutherans, Episcopalians, and Methodists—in order to deal with both a local ashram and young people taking up with radio preachers. It should be noted that Percy was active in a similar ecumenical gathering in his own local parish, a connection that tentatively identifies Percy with Dr. More. Thirdly, in thinking about Malcolm, Father Smith's friend, Percy gives him the last name of Jones, then of Jenkins (hm/457), and, finally in the setting copy, of Guidry, the real last name of a woman who worked for the Percys and who had also worked for the local rectory, a fact that undercuts my previous observation. Lastly, before concluding this encounter, Percy drew a map of a river, of Fedville, and of a fictional (as far as I can determine) Belle Isle (see *Lancelot*, too) and Grand Mer, which somehow are linked with epidemiology and the discovery of a "water source" (hm/459). This rough map has bends in the river resembling those in the Mississippi River near Saint Francisville, where Lucy Percy Madox (Mrs. Lynch Madox) still lives in the Carter Percy plantation called Ellerslie. She is not, however, the only woman named Lucy who owns a plantation in this area. It should also be recalled that the name of a real ancestor of Percy, Alice Pratt, is the name of a character in this novel. In addition, these and other autobiographical allusions are supported by the fact that real place-names mentioned in the novel are in this area—Tunica, Angola, Raccourci [Island], and Saint Francisville itself (see hm/484, 485, 487, for three more maps that Percy drew of this area). Likewise, Pantherburn, mentioned in the novel, is an actual plantation, but it is located farther north of Saint Francisville, just south of Hollandale, Mississippi.

In the first typescript version of this scene (t1/187–96), Percy, in reworking this encounter between Father Placide and Dr. More, added three characters in his own hand—Sarah Saia, Ernestine Kelly, and Jan Greene, who discuss the possible reasons for Father Smith's being up in the firetower (t1/188v, 190v, 191–94). The projected ecumenical group has been transposed here into a meeting of the Blue Army or Legion of Mary, representatives of the conservative element—in contrast to Father Smith—of the ordinary laity of this parish. Jan Greene says that Father Smith is doing vicarious penance, as the Carmelites and Trappists did for centuries; this was changed to Carmelites and Desert Fathers (tl/194), more clearly designating Father *Simon* Smith as a *Simeon*-the-Stylite character, thus downplaying any possible hint that Father Smith might be based on Thomas Merton, O.C.S.O., a Trappist monk-hermit admired by Percy.

Though Percy had written about priests in the past (briefly about Father Smith in *Love in the Ruins*, Father Boomer in *The Last Gentleman*, Father Weatherbee in *The Second Coming*, and, at more length, Father John in *Lancelot*), the only other Smith in his fiction who shares the mystical bent characteristic of Father Smith is Lonnie Smith in *The Moviegoer*; it could well be argued that Father Smith is a Lonnie *redivivus*. In a later three-page holographic insert into the first typescript (tl/221–23), Father Smith resembles a priest-teacher at Spring Hill College or Spring Hill Prep (a nonexistent school); since Spring Hill College is a Jesuit college in Mobile, Alabama, it may be argued that this character shares some characteristics with one or other Jesuit known to Percy from this college. During the Father Placide–Dr. More conversation in the first typescript, Percy began to think about the character of Father Smith, and he jotted down some preliminary notes, some of which anticipate material found in "Father Smith's Confession" and "Father Smith's Footnote":

Fr. S. Rinaldo Smith—
  (1) Recounts symptoms. Cannot perform duties.
  (2) "Perhaps you are depressed."
  (3) No, I feel fine.
  (4) Have you lost your faith.
  (5) No, I have scientific proof. The Jews. It is there for all to see. It is like landing on the moon and seeing a footprint.
  Jews are the sign of God. The other proofs didn't work="proofs of Satan."
  I became a priest because of Jews. Holocaust. Do you know that most will say the Holocaust did not occur? I was a clerk typist at the Nuremburg Trials.
  This great end. My becoming a priest. (tl/197)

Percy further modified these ideas as he probed Father Smith's inner core: "No, I am not Jewish. Secret. I was pro-German" (tl/198). In revising this material a second time, Dr. More recounts how he and

Father Smith were in a rest home in Florida, facing Perdido, when a strong wind came from the gulf and Father Smith thought of the time he had spent in Germany: "'I spent some time there.' He told me without raising his eyes. He told me about visiting his cousins in Germany when he was a boy, and again fell silent" (t2/156–64). While the full implications of this conversation have yet to be realized in Percy's imagination, the planning for it occurred fairly late in the composition of this novel. (Dr. Percy told me that he thought the theme of the novel was not explicit enough and that he progressively drew his inspiration for Father Smith's confession from Dostoevsky's *The Brothers Karamazov* ["I decided that since Father Smith was important to me I was going to develop his personality more clearly"].)[7]

When Percy came to structure the initial conversation between Dr. More and Father Smith in the manuscript (hm/461–79), he followed the pattern of a Socratic dialogue, but with a twist: he kept the nature of the conversation mostly religious, though he does avert to a fire in the area. Perhaps the most startling revelation is that when Dr. More first sees Father Smith in the tower (they had seen each other at Fort Deposit in Alabama, not Fort Pelham, as in the first edition), he remembers that Father Smith is a veteran of Vietnam and had recuperated in a VA hospital (hm/461v). Such a detail shows the drastic development that took place in Percy's imagination as he fleshed out such an important character. There is little subtlety in Father Smith's thinking as his polar mind grapples with the existence or nonexistence of God. He notes, for example, that we are all going to die in ten or twenty years: "Everybody knows this. Nobody talks about it, because deep down no one believes he can do anything about it. Nobody really believes that the 2 solutions offered will work." The solutions are either to arm or disarm, and both are useless. In an afterthought, to break the polar thinking, Percy spells out a *tertium quid*. Up in the tower, Father Smith feels free, but down below he suffers "ground stress." Therefore, he will use his weakness and stay in the tower: "'Pray. That is the tertium quid!' He opens his hands waiting for me to see the breakthrough." In pursuing the notion of weakness, Father Smith asks Dr. More, "Do you think that a person can act from his own weaknesses and still serve God?" (hm/468). Dr. More is not sure. Father Smith explains: "Well, you see I am a failure as a priest. I just can't cut it in a parish." The question seems to boil down to whether one can use one's weakness and cop out and still accept God's will. Saints and martyrs endured great suffering and were put to death. "Don't think I'm carried away by the Apocalypse like so many nuts. . . . But, on the other hand, I am not sure but what a fellow like St. Francis didn't finally fail in the world, in the family business, then drop out, cop out, then put his weakness to good use" (hm/467v, 468v). At this point Father Smith thinks he may have received a sign from God (468v), and as he tries to articulate the logic of his spirituality, he explains that he is up in the tower so that the land and the children will not be hurt; adults, not children, have created the folly that exists. This mention of children anticipates the horror happening at Belle Ame. To find possible sources for this unexpected dimension of the novel, one has only to read, in addition to Frederic Wertheim's *A Sign for Cain*, the local papers about the pedophilic activity happening in the region of Lafayette, Louisiana, in the mid-1980s, as discussed with me by Mrs. Percy.[8] It is possible, too, that Percy, according to a note he made in the manuscript (hm/898v), was probing an area not really treated by his friend Robert Coles, who interviewed southern children under stress, a number of whom lived in New Orleans, for his work on the award-winning five-volume *Children of Crisis*.

As Dr. More and Father Smith continue to discuss the Qualitative Center, government standards, doing what one can in this world, and the impact of Father Smith's beliefs, Dr. More sardonically says he is not sure what Father Smith does. The response is simple: he watches fires and prays to God. Thus, at this point in the development of the character of Father Smith, Percy has not really found what energizes Father Smith; the lackluster dialogue between Dr. More and Father Smith is without punch or coherence. As they rehearse again the logic of Father Smith's spirituality, Dr. More breaks the flow and tells about the case histories he has witnessed (hm/472). Father Smith replies, "You seem to be saying, Tom, that these people, your patients, have lost their souls." When Dr. More says he would not use the word "soul," but prefers "pre-frontal deficit" (hm/473), they seem to have reached an impasse. Their closing words suggest that another character might be introduced to solve Father Placide's problem: "'Tell Fr. Placide, help is on the way. The bishop told me.' 'The bishop doesn't mind you being here?' 'No'" (476). Genuine communication has not really taken place, and clearly what is needed is some indication that Father Smith has an insight into man's relationship with God that comes from the depths of his reflective self.

When Percy reworked the first encounter between Dr. More and Father Smith in the first typescript, he changed it considerably; the clearer relationship between religion and semiotics represents in this text a second level of imaginative composition. Percy followed his manuscript version with its several revisions, though he did not feel obliged merely to recopy his text. The first typescript would be discernibly different from the first. As he moved along, there are trial passages never incorporated into the final text, some of which would have played off well against the pedophilic activity at Belle Ame: "Tom, as a psychiatrist, what would you think of a man who thinks that all of his fellow men are helplessly trapped and that the only happiness is to be found in children?" (t1/204v). As Percy makes the fire on Bootlegger Road more graphic (t1/205) and links this with belief in God, he added to the typescript a large holographic insert that concerns how Father Smith feels both lazy and depressed (t1/206v–17). Here, Percy begins to explore the mystical aspect of Father Smith's personality, such as his preoccupation with Jews, who are "a chosen people of God—and they *are still here*" (t1/213). Father Smith realizes that there is something abroad, an agent, that is the source of his depression. It is "the devil, Satan, an evil one, the Prince of Liars, our eternal enemy"(t1/211).

By introducing the devil as a possible intelligent being who has possible power over men and women, Percy located the source of negativity and destruction in Father Smith's world. Any discussion of the immensity of the universe or the big bang theory of creation means, in comparison, "nothing" (t1/214), for the simple reason that some power is depriving humanity of the very meaning of what we scientifically know: "Even words have been deprived of their meaning. The very name of God himself is no more than a word. How else can you explain this except through the agency of a power?" (t1/215). Percy found in the notion of the devil as the depriver the connective to his formula that the "Holocaust was a consequence of the sign which could not be evacuated" (126, first edition). "Who else but the devil," Father Smith asks, "could have devised the fiendish trick of removing meaning from everything we know? Don't we think of the devil as a blasphemer, a demon who possesses souls and curses God?" (t1/215).

As Father Smith revs up his engines about the devil, Dr. More senses it is time to leave, and he is pleased to hear Malcolm come up through the trapdoor. Dr. More awaits the arrival of Malcolm, but Father Smith continues to comment on how the Jews are different from other groups: "Because the Jews are in fact the chosen people of God and nothing any power can do can change that and they are here—a visible sign of God which not even the devil can reverse. Do you think that anyone can explain the Holocaust?" (t1/217). In an insert to this insert, Father Smith rages about the madness of Hitler (t1/216v) and mentions that he was in Germany in the 1930s: "I was in Germany before the war with my family who were Schmidts from Koblenz." And once the war had started, Father Smith as a young man joined the Third Army. Percy never developed Father Smith's German background; there was enough here to warrant a fuller treatment later in "Father Smith's Confession."

In another long holographic insert (t1/226–52), which indicates clearly that most of this chapter is a second level of composition, Dr. More assumes the initiative and talks about the syndrome he has discovered in Feliciana. Dr. More believes, too, that Father Smith is in the tower to wage a protest; his presence there has something to do with the prochoice movement (t1/229–30), which is connected with a legal case that defines a person as one who acquires language at eighteen months (*Doe v. Dade*). Father Smith replies: "'Well, [what] I am saying, Fr., is that I tend to agree with you. It worries me, that the state has presumed to decide such matters. It seems to me we are on a slippery slope indeed, an Orwellian world, when a committee decides in a room of so-called humanity and so-called quality of life. That's not what I call true humanism. . . . There is no longer any use in those old arguments about abortion, euthanasia, infanticide. Their reasons sound sufficient to them'" (t1/230, 232). At this, Dr. More becomes irritated: "'Fr., I think that you're putting me on. Bob Comeaux said that you said that most American Dr.s were going to fry in hell.'" To this Father Smith replies: "'I said I hoped they would not. Actually, they're mostly very good fellows and generally mean well.'" The argument then shifts to the more fruitful discussion of the relationship between Satan, the Germans, the French, and signs. "Signs no longer point. Do you remember when the Germans invaded France, the French changed all the signs at even the country crossroads and that the Germans learned to ignore the signs. The signs meant nothing" (t1/234). The only exception is the Jewish race: the depriver could not point this sign around any which way. Thus, in Father Smith's mind, Christians cannot be deprived of their Jewish roots, nor can anyone deprive the Jews of their singularity. Father Smith raises the problem of the Catholic Ukrainians, fifteen million of whom were killed by Stalin. But the death of six million Jews is in his mind more than a tragedy, it is a mystery. In talking about the Holocaust as a myth, Father Smith says that he was "in Germany visiting his relatives in Bonn" (t1/240), a city Percy visited in the summer of 1934. "We were Schmidts and came here 200 years ago and lived in the Bayou des Allemands." His father was a musician who taught music at Loyola University; when his father went back to Germany on a kind of pilgrimage, he took his son. Father Smith is quick to assert that the Holocaust did occur and that six million Jews were killed. Yet he asks, "Do you think that you can blame the Holocaust on some fatal flaw in the Germany psyche, on a unique villainy or madness in the German soul?" (t1/241). The two reach another impasse as Father Smith tries to claim that the Nazis were by and large like smalltime burghers, similar to local cops or shopkeepers, to which More says he cannot agree. The time for parting has come.

Not yet satisfied with what he had written, Percy went back and rewrote what had become by now familiar material, with Father Smith having the final say:

> "I merely mentioned a curious . . . fact. That in the years of history of the Western world, beginning with Abraham coming up out of the Ur and Hippocrates and the pagan Greeks, and in 7,000 years of medicine from Israel and Greece to all of Europe and the farthest reaches of much of South America, it never occurred to a Dr. to violate his oath and kill people—until the American Dr.s. In one generation, American Dr.s have revolutionized medicine and killed 10 million unborn humans, 2 million infant humans and 3 million aged humans and not one Dr. has so much as blinked an eye. Not one Dr. has protested. The august JAMA and New England Journal are silent, not one single article of protest. (t1/251–52)

Before Dr. More leaves, Father Smith makes a startling revelation: he, too, studied medicine as a specialist fourth-class medical technologist and clerk typist in Germany after the war, when he was assigned to Judge Jackson's staff at Nuremberg, though not at the Nuremberg trials (t1/259). What the young Smith discovered at Nuremberg was that it was the best of the Germans, the scientists, who began practicing euthanasia on useless people (t1/260).

Once finished with this information about Father Smith's background, Percy had sketched out this chapter (with its cryptic autobiographical references) and would keep a good bit of what he had written. If one can argue that Father Smith embodies within himself the crucial insights and judgments that sustain this novel, then it is clear from the manuscript and typescript evidence that Percy allowed this character to grow slowly and develop as the novel itself evolved. Percy had to discern and struggle to locate what he intuitively suspected about this character, and what he ultimately discovered was a character who perceived a haunting, radically disturbing mystery of such cosmic proportions about the Jews, the Holocaust, the devil, semiotics, and pedophilia that Percy himself could only be awed by it.

W. L. Godshalk

The Engineer, Then and Now; or, Barrett's Choice

In *The Last Gentleman*, in what he later thinks of as "the early days," Will Barrett, of the many names and the precarious identity, calls himself "the engineer," "trying to 'engineer' his own life" (*SC*, 180). As a young man, the engineer assumes a series of roles in his attempt to define himself—the Princeton man, the midwesterner, the bird-watcher, the companion, and he looks to others for the answer to who he is and where he fits in his "world." A young man short on redeeming qualities, strangely disengaged, disoriented, dislocated, and in erratic orbit, he watches life through his telescope, an emblem of his distance from the immediate scene.

When we first meet him in Central Park, "he [has] lived in a state of pure possibility, not knowing what sort of a man he [is] or what he must do, and supposing therefore that he must be all men and do everything" (*LG*, 4). *The Last Gentleman* shows how this young man of pure potential becomes realized, how "his life took a turn in a particular direction" and how "he came to see that he was not destined to do everything but only one or two things" (*LG*, 4). That "particular direction" is toward the Southwest, where the engineer travels in quest of himself and where he must witness the death of his new companion.[1]

The narrator comments, "Lucky is the man who does not secretly believe that every possibility is open to him" (*LG*, 4). To make choices is to close doors as well as open them. When the engineer accepts the invitation to become Jamie's companion, he becomes enmeshed with a family that forces him to confront the psychological issues surrounding both sex and death. Limited in his experience with sex, he has, we learn, known death intimately: his father has committed suicide

(*LG*, 331). But, given the inevitability of sex and death, what choices can the engineer legitimately make?

The Vaught family suggests a fairly narrow, but representative, range. Kitty offers the engineer sex, wealth, and a conventional life—a job at her father's agency, a home, and a large check with "a little army of red Gothic noughts" marching "clean to Oklahoma" (*LG*, 286). The engineer wonders why he can not happily accept Kitty's version of his future.

Strangely, Sutter, not Kitty, brings the engineer to an understanding of the uses of sexuality. Sutter philosophically focuses the connection between sex and our mundane attachment to ordinary life.[2] In his discarded casebook, a casebook avidly read by the engineer, Sutter expounds his ideas:

> Man who falls victim to transcendence as the spirit of abstraction, i.e., elevates [the] self to posture over and against [the] world which is *pari passu* demoted to immanence and seen as exemplar and specimen and coordinate, and who is not at [the] same time compensated by [the] beauty of [?the] motion of [the] method of science, has no choice but to seek reentry into immanent world *qua* immanence. But since no avenue of reentry remains save genital and since reentry [is] coterminus c̄ [with] orgasm, post-orgasmic despair [is] without remedy. . . . *There is no reentry from the orbit of transcendence.* (*LG*, 345)

Suicide is the consequence of this "spirit of abstraction" (*LG*, 345).[3]

In his quest for answers, the engineer leaves Kitty to follow Sutter. The engineer wants Sutter to give him answers, but Sutter resolutely refuses.[4] If Kitty quite willingly plans how the engineer should spend his life, Sutter emphasizes freedom of choice. The engineer has to decide for himself.

Val represents the "religious dimension of life" (*LG*, 383), and we learn most about her choice from Sutter's casebook, a good deal of which is a running argument with Val. If Sutter presents her position correctly, she believes that humans are neither transcendent nor immanent but wayfarers who stand "in the way of hearing a piece of news which is of the utmost importance"—their salvation—and which had better be attended to (*LG*, 353). We would do "well to be afraid" and "to forget everything which does not pertain to . . . salvation" (*LG*, 354).[5]

The engineer is presented with these three visions of life: the "conventional," the "existential," and the "religious." A twentieth-century

Candide traveling in search of meaning, Barrett is given a range of choices, and, like Candide, he decides to accept the conventional life, to, as it were, cultivate his own garden (*LG*, 384). He tells Sutter, "I am going to take a good position with your father, settle down on the South Ridge, and, I hope, raise a family" (*LG*, 383), judging that he will make "a pretty fair member of the community," and, as he says, "It is better to do something than do nothing" (*LG*, 384). "For the first time I think I really might live like other men—rejoin the human race" (*LG*, 386). He apparently stands by this decision, though he protests a bit too much and his gaze is gloomy (*LG*, 385).

The engineer is convinced that Sutter finds "something wrong" with this choice (*LG*, 384), and although Sutter denies that he does, the reader may feel otherwise. Kitty's view of the world seems superficial and thoughtless; she is a woman with a dancer's body, but not an intellectual's head. That the engineer's quest should end here is disturbing.

But, at the same time, Sutter's existential vision, though thoughtful, is hardly life affirming. Torn as he is between angelism and bestialism, with no tool to mediate between the two, Sutter sees the inevitability of suicide. He is the isolate, the doctor who can no longer minister to anyone, least of all himself. The engineer turns to him for help, and Sutter refuses. Although this refusal bears a kind of fruit, Sutter's worldview seems self-destructive. If Kitty has a beautiful body, Sutter is too thin—a physical wreck.

Val forces the engineer to act by commissioning him to have the dying Jamie baptized. Jamie's baptism, an elaborate comedy, is a biting commentary on the inadequacy of Val's Catholicism. The reluctant priest, Father Boomer, is urged on by the insistent engineer (*LG*, 397). Jamie himself greets with irony the priest's assurances of the truths of religion, and before the priest can ask his final questions, Jamie's "irony" is "shot through with the first glint of delirium" (*LG*, 404). While Jamie mumbles and has diarrhea, the priest apparently baptizes him. After Jamie's death, Sutter curtly dismisses the priest. It is a scene that reminds us of our mortality, but it hardly glorifies the sacraments or gives us any hope of eternal life in Jesus Christ our Lord.

At the end of *The Last Gentleman*, the engineer has three fairly clear options. He can choose the common life—to live as other men live—and accept Kitty's offer. Or he can choose Sutter's vision of life as a conflict between transcendence and immanence, with suicide as a distinct possibility. If Kitty's offer is oriented toward the body and life, Sutter's vision is oriented toward the intellect and death. Or the engineer can choose a spiritual orientation that opts for life and accepts death. But, as we have seen, the narrator offers none of these as the clearly best or only choice; each is flawed or undercut.

The narrative ends inconclusively. Val and Kitty have not yet arrived. Sutter—to all appearances—is driving away to commit suicide. But a final question occurs to the engineer; he runs after Sutter's Edsel, and Sutter stops to wait for him

But what happens next?

With the appearance of *The Second Coming*—the return of the engineer in his incarnation as the retired, middle-aged Will Barrett—the reader learns that Sutter has not committed suicide and that the engineer has not married Kitty, though he has led a rather conventional life as a New York lawyer. At the same time, the reader is confronted with a series of further questions. Is the same narrator responsible for this new narrative? And what is this narrator's purpose in returning to Will Barrett? Does the second narrative imply questions that make *The Last Gentleman* even more problematic? Or does this narrative clarify the implications of the first?

These are only a few of the questions raised by *The Second Coming*. I am not sure that I can answer any of them completely or satisfactorily. But let me begin with the narrator, whom I suppose to be male because of his obvious interest in topics that are generally considered of "masculine" interest in American culture. I also propose that the narrator is the same for both narratives and that the narrator himself suggests that identification by beginning *The Second Coming* as he had begun *The Last Gentleman*. In each, the central character is presented as a man with a problem, and only after the problem is introduced do we learn the character's name (*LG*, 17; *SC*, 14): Will Barrett. He also ends each narrative with Barrett's comic confrontation with a priest concerning one of the sacraments, a sacrament that the priest is reluctant to perform.

The narrator selects these two narratives because they, in a certain way, bracket Will Barrett's life. As the engineer, all of his options are open, while, as Will Barrett in *The Second Coming*, his options have apparently run out. The man with so much possibility has come to the end of his road, or so it seems, and, as it did with Sutter in the earlier narrative, suicide appears to be the only path left. We may say that the narrator's interest in both stories is his interest in choice and the problems of choice. Choice implies that we have control of our lives, while fortuitous events indicate that control is limited or nonexistent. How much control does Will Barrett have?

Will's difficulties on the golf course initially focus the problem. The golf course for Will appears to be an emblem for his disengaged life, life as a game rather than life as a serious, meaningful pursuit. First, he repeatedly falls with no more choice than the ball itself.[6] Second, he repeatedly slices out-of-bounds; he can no longer control his ball.[7] Third, he "finds himself overtaken by unaccountable memories, memories of extraordinary power and poignancy" (SC, 12), vivid memories that are beyond his control.

Although he remains in North Carolina, Will's memory returns to Georgia again and again in the narrative, each time adding details to what initially appears to be a hunting accident, until Will realizes that his father had tried to murder him and then commit suicide and that this murder-suicide is botched. But Will also realizes that his father missed intentionally. "Was it love or failure of love?" (SC, 148), he asks himself. Can he ever be sure?

After this revelation, Will decides to enter Lost Cove cave. Later, when Allison says, "Let's go in the cave!" Will responds, "No. We don't have to go in the cave. The cave is over and done with. We can live up here" (SC, 330–31). This response suggests that the cave is more than a plot necessity. In the narrative, the cave comes to symbolize chthonic energy, the past, isolation, madness, and death. Into this cave, Will descends "looking for proof of the existence of God and a sign of the apocalypse like some crackpot preacher in California" (SC, 198). The descent is Will's escape, a search for death, and a descent into madness. He believes that he will die in the cave "only if God [does] not manifest himself, [does] not give a sign clearly and unambiguously, once and for all" (SC, 192). Although the narrator ironically confirms Will's vision of an insane world in its latter days, the narrator equally confirms Will's own madness (SC, 197–98). He is a madman in a mad world.

But Will's descent into the cave is also his attempt at taking charge of his life and coming up with some viable answers. To help control his appetite (he will take no food into the cave), he takes two handfuls of Placidyl capsules in his pants pockets. The capsules will enable him to control his body, thus enabling his mind to wait for a message from God. "There is no way I cannot find out" (SC, 211), Will thinks to himself.

At this point, the narrator openly and significantly addresses the reader: "Unfortunately things can go wrong with an experiment most carefully designed by a sane scientist. A clear yes or no answer may not be forthcoming, after all. The answer may be a muddy maybe. In the case of Will Barrett, what went wrong could hardly be traced to God or man, . . . but rather to a cause at once humiliating and comical:

a toothache" (*SC*, 213). The pain is so bad that Will is nauseated. The narrator comments, "There is one sure cure for cosmic explorations, grandiose ideas about God, man, death, suicide and such—and that is nausea. I defy a man afflicted with nausea to give a single thought to these vast subjects" (*SC*, 213). The narrator thus emphasizes the foolish spiritual pride that stands behind Will's attempt to fathom the secrets of God.

"Let me out of here, he [says] with no thought of God, Jews, suicide, tigers, or the Last Days" (*SC*, 223). And in a series of falls, he struggles out of the cave (*SC*, 223–26). His final fall is most spectacular—"a fall through air not vines or bushes, through air and color, brilliant greens and violet and vermilion and a blue unlike any sky, a free-fall headfirst with time enough to wonder if he might not be dead after all" (*SC*, 226). Is this a symbol of Will's reentry into the immanent world of light? Or is it, like the fall of Satan, a fall of pride? Does he fall because, like Adam, he is seeking forbidden knowledge?

He lands squarely in Allison's greenhouse.

Although I have been concentrating on Will Barrett, the narrator divides his interest between Will and Allison, implicitly comparing them. Both are problem solvers. If Will wants to solve the problem of God's existence, Allie wants to solve the problems of the physical world and everyday life. Although both are mentally unstable, Allison escapes from the hospital where she is being given shock treatments, while Will seems to be moving in the opposite direction—toward diagnosed problems and confinement in an old folks' home. While Allie is striking out, Will is caving in, and yet both feel that this October is a significant time in their lives (*SC*, 43, 78). If Will is torn by personal problems centering on God, death, and suicide, Allison is troubled by practical and social problems that center on language. His problems are metaphysical, hers are physical and semiotic. Barrett is in orbit; Allie is immanent. "She remembered nothing" (*SC*, 80); "he remembered everything" (*SC*, 79).

For Will, memory is a curse. Incapacitated by history, by his attachment to the past, he recurrently thinks of Roman history. But, of course, it is his own history that proves most inhibiting. Although Marion's recent death appears to affect him less than does the suicide of his father years before, both deaths lay claims on him. Marion's wishes are recurrently used to manipulate him, while the memory of the attempted murder-suicide in Georgia haunts him. Will Barret cannot move into the future until he resolves the past.

Allie's inability to remember the past allows her to begin anew, to create and to recreate both her environment and her world through the use of tools. "Man," she decides, "is pitiful without a tool" (*SC*, 235); she is a "hoister, a mistress of mechanical advantage" (*SC*, 199). "Perhaps," she thinks to herself, "she ought to be an engineer or a nurse of comatose patients" (*SC*, 234). If Will carries with him the seeds of death from the past (*SC*, 171), Allison embodies the life force and looks to a creative future.

Symbolic of that life force is Allie's greenhouse—a place of growth, healing, and sexual union. A good deal is made of the fact that Allie's greenhouse is heated in the winter and cooled in the summer by air from Lost Cove cave; energy from the depths of the earth as well as from the sun helps to keep the greenhouse viable. This double energy source is indicative of the greenhouse's symbolic nature; it unites, in an Edenic dream, the chthonic and the Apollonian, the man-made and the natural, the dark/passionate and the light/reasonable. Although man falls again, he is redeemed by human love and human action.

But Will's return to the world of ordinary mortals from the darkness of the cave is fraught with its own difficulties. Diagnosed as having Hausmann's syndrome, a disease characterized by religious delusions, among other things (*SC*, 302), Will is cured by hydrogen, "the simplest atom" (*SC*, 304), which controls his blood pH. Unfortunately, the cure leaves him without passion. "His life was out of his hands" (*SC*, 305). Placed in an old folks' home, Will has no choice in the matter, and choice, as we know, is the fundamental human privilege. Only after he rejects the old folks' home and his medication does he regain himself and his ability to make choices (*SC*, 326). To be able to choose is to be able to make the wrong as well as the right choice. True life is a mixed bag, and the only way to get the good is to deal with the bad.

In Will's case, the bad is his father's insistence on suicide. In the Holiday Inn, Will experiences the pull between love and life, and love and death, between Allison and his dead father. In the remarkable dialogue between living son and dead father, the father commands: "Go like a man, for Christ's sake, a Roman, here's your sword" (*SC*, 337). The tension is high as Will walks to his Mercedes to get both shotgun and pistol, the Greener and the Luger, his father's weapons. As he walks toward the place designated by his father as the place of suicide, Will throws, in rejection, both guns into the gorge next to the inn.

But what can Will substitute for his father's dreadful vision of senility —"the drools and the shakes" (*SC*, 337)? In his stay at the old folks' home, Will sees the reality of institutionalized aging and dying. Here he will die "with good Christian folk to look after every need" and ease him out of life. Surely this is "a better way than swallowing gun barrels" (*SC*, 325). It may well be a better way, but Will decides that this passive acceptance of aging, senility, and dying must also be rejected. From the old folks' home Will returns to the world of action and decision, to the world of relative madness and love, to the quotidian, immanent world of life as a married lawyer in Linwood, North Carolina.

Will Barrett's return includes his plan to marry Allison, and the final pages of the narrative describe his comic attempt to get Father Weatherbee to marry them.[8] I find myself laughing aloud as the relatively mad lawyer tries to persuade the partially senile priest to perform a suspect marriage that he wants no part of. Metaphysics are replaced by the realities of the common life, apocalypse replaced by comedy.

Though Will tells Father Weatherbee that he is "not a believer" (*SC*, 357), we may wonder what he means precisely by that disclaimer. He seems still to believe that the Jews are a sign—a religious delusion that the skeptical narrator traces to Hausmann's syndrome (*SC*, 357). And as the scene ends—Father Weatherbee watching Will with a "new odd expression"—Will thinks of "Allie in her greenhouse." His heart leaps with a "secret joy," and he asks himself, "What is it I want from her and [the priest], . . . not only want but must have? Is she a gift and therefore a sign of a giver? Could it be that the Lord is here, masquerading behind this simple silly holy face? Am I crazy to want both, her and Him? No, not want, must have. And will have" (*SC*, 360).

Given the fact that the narrator has told the reader that Will's pH is rising and that this rise is associated with religious delusions, the reader may well be inclined to suspect the religious and/or intellectual quality of these final questions. Nothing in the narrative clearly points to divine intervention, and Will's religiosity is more clearly linked to hydrogen than to the descent of the Spirit. In the grip of Hausmann's syndrome, does Will have free choice? Or, paradoxically, is choice always linked to madness?

But no matter how the reader answers Will's final questions, Will is still torn between "her and Him"—the immanent Allison and the transcendent God—and still feels that he wants, must have and will have both. He desires both to transcend and to engage. Of course, his dichotomous desires focus both the existential dilemma and the major contrast in the narrative between Will and Allison, the orbiter and the inhabiter.

As I read him, the narrator prefers reentry to transcendence. In both narratives, *The Last Gentleman* and *The Second Coming*, suicide (seen as the ultimate rejection of immanence) is rejected in favor of engagement with life. Relative madness in a completely mad world is better than bland sanity in an asylum, which is little more than a ghetto for the disenfranchised. Delusions and terrors notwithstanding, life is better than either death or death in life.

Why, then, does our narrator tell us this second story? First, to reaffirm and to clarify the values implicit in his first narrative. Second, to emphasize that the problems of transcendence and immanence are recurrent, not simply a young man's dilemma, but equally attendant on both youth and age. Third, to show how Will Barrett's quest for selfhood becomes his misguided quest for God. Needless to say, that quest remains incomplete at the end of *The Second Coming*. Although Will Barrett has come again, Christ has not, and Will is driven to look for him in strange places and, as the narrator ends his story, to remain unsatisfied.

In the cosmos, absolute answers are hard to come by.

Joseph Schwartz

Will Barrett Redux?

The Second Coming, a successful novel in its own right, presents a vexing problem for me because it is a sequel to *The Last Gentleman*. I offer this argument because of a statement that Walker Percy made about *The Moviegoer* but that applies to the theme and structure of all his novels: "I begin with a *man* who finds himself in a *world*, a very concrete man who is located in a very concrete place and time. Such a man might be represented as *coming to himself* in somewhat the same sense as Robinson Crusoe came to himself on his island after his shipwreck, with the same wonder and curiosity."[1] An artistic narrative that ends with the kind of discovery that interests Percy has, I submit, an ending; that is to say, it does not merely stop, it ends. What began is concluded. The train may go on with its cast of characters, but the writer gets off the train and the characters are no longer subject to history, as they would be in a nonfictive narrative. I appeal to Henry James, who wrote, in his preface to *Roderick Hudson*, "Really, universally, relations stop nowhere, and the exquisite problem of the artist is eternally but to draw, by a geometry of his own, the circle in which they shall happily *appear* to do so."[2] Not even the author may alter the way in which the circle that ends the novel has been drawn. Will I with all his baggage challenges the veracity of *The Second Coming*. There is a completeness about *The Last Gentleman* that argues against the kind of sequel Percy wrote. The work is successfully enclosed within its form, each element in harmony with every other.

While *The Second Coming* is a great success in its own right, where it succeeds it succeeds on its own terms. But in those it seriously diminishes the achievement of *The Last Gentleman*, Percy's finest novel, because of the brilliant way in which Will's crucial discovery is presented. Barrett is the perfect example of the bewildered, dislocated, postmodern person. His fugue states are a metaphor for his alienation from the only sources of value he knows. It is his state of mind and heart which makes the novel's ending one of the most thrilling episodes Percy has ever written. "I," he says, pointing to himself so that there can be no mistake, "I, Will Barrett," naming himself and celebrating the discovery of true identity by baring it. The phrase also says, "I will bear it," the point of greatest significance in the novel. He chooses life (that is to say, reality) and will bear the slings and arrows of outrageous fortune (our Hamlet), rejecting suicide because he has discovered, inadvertently from Sutter, the "prime importance of the religious dimension of life" (*LG*, 383). He will not only bear but rejoice in the ordinariness that is the only way of reentry into reality, the single means of reaching the transcendent. "For the first time I think I really might live like other men—rejoin the human race" (*LG*, 386). In preventing Sutter from committing suicide, Will makes the most decisive life-affirming gesture it is possible for him to make.

What happened to Will Barrett between his twenties and his forties? His discovery in *The Last Gentleman* of the meaning of existence was so carefully crafted, so joyous, so exuberant that it is unimaginable for him to have wasted the intervening years. Yet the same situation that opens *The Last Gentleman* opens *The Second Coming*, and he must go through the same process of discovery again. What are we to make of the seminal sentence of *The Second Coming*? "Only one event had ever happened to him in his life. Everything else that had happened to him afterwards was a non-event" (*SC*, 52). The event referred to his father's attempt to murder him and then, later, his father's suicide. The sentence would cause no problem for me if it were spoken, say, by Tom Applegate or Phinizy Hunnicutt anyone except Will Barrett. In *The Last Gentleman* Will has a history fixed in artistic cement. Percy has already imagined the significance of beginning and end for a character who acts out a remedy for our own inability, because we must die, to experience completeness, wholeness. While Will and the other characters necessarily appear to act in time, their fictive being is out of time. Will is at his fullness in his Will-ness, a kind of inviolable perpetuity —in amber laid, so to speak. If thirty years later Will knows no more than he knew as a boy in Dalhart, Texas, he seems to have forgotten (impossible!) heavyweight events and their significance—notably, meeting the Vaughts. It is no wonder that critics had difficulty describing the relationship between the two novels. Gene Lyons called *The Second Coming* "a kind of sequel." Whitney Balliet said it was "a left handed

. . . continuation of *The Last Gentleman*." Richard Gilman wrote, some-what in surprise, "Percy has in fact given him the same name as the protagonist of his earlier novel." Thomas Williams wondered if "the earlier novel somehow doesn't quite apply to" the later one.[3]

Following is a central passage from *The Second Coming*: "Is it possible for people to miss their lives in the same way one misses a plane? And how is it that death, the nearness of death, can restore a missed life?" (*SC*, 124). Two points are made: one, that Will II has missed his life, and, two, that death or the nearness of death is the condition for restor-ing his life. But the latter has already happened to Will I—death in the persons of his father and of Jamie and nearness to death in the person of Sutter. He does not know who he is until he meets the Vaught children. When he becomes aware of Sutter's resolve to commit suicide for instance, "for the first time in his life he was astonished." It is this moment of astonishment that "marked the beginning for the engineer of what is called a normal life. From that time forward it was possible to meet him and after a few minutes form a clear notion of what sort of fellow he was and how he would spend the rest of his life" (*LG*, 389). We are to read this passage in the light of Sutter's notebook entry, again inadvertently true: "The certain availability of death is the very condition of recovering oneself" (*LG*, 372).

What these passages confirm is that Will I's history is not a nonevent, that, in fact, his history is full of weighty events that draw from Percy the most potent comparisons and allusions. The Bible, for one, is used generously to help us understand a character so important that only the Bible will do: he is compared to Adam and to the apostle Philip. His name suggests Hamlet, and he is Ferdinand freshly renewed from *The Tempest*. Homer is called upon to define his journey, and Huck Finn scrambles around every edge of the story. The most continuously used implied comparisons are to Dostoevsky's Prince Myshkin in *The Idiot* and Tolstoy's Levin in *Anna Karenina*. His destination is Holy Faith (Santa Fe), where he is a neophyte/participant, interpreter, and observer in the miracle of saving water. Two extraordinary ministers guide him —Val, knowingly, and Sutter, unknowingly. An Eve/Miranda (Kitty) is created for this Adam/Ferdinand. Events and experiences of such im-portance cannot be ignored in measuring a creation set in the timeless world of a successful work of art. Are Val, Sutter, Jamie, and Kitty nonpersons in a wasted life of nonevents? Both the craft and the theme of *The Last Gentleman* suggest the importance and value of Will I's his-tory. I believe the tale, not the teller, a choice necessary to make because in this case the teller has told me something different from what the tale tells. Here is Walker Percy's comment:

> I would point out that at the end of *The Last Gentleman*, Will did not really know what was going on with Jamie's baptism and death. He has to ask Sutter: "What was going on back there?" Thus, while it was clear that Jamie asked for baptism, Will gives no indication of an overt understanding of what Father Boomer was talking about, let alone accepting it. It was my intention to leave him somewhat up in the air, capable of returning to Kitty and going to work for Confederate Chevrolet. The only positive element in his experience is his fastening on Sutter as knowing something he, Will does not know. But even if Will's "conversion" in *The Last Gentleman* had been bonafide, who is to say it "takes" and "takes" for good—except a born-again Baptist who believes one is saved once and for all. I'm sure Dr. Schwartz has heard of Gabriel Marcel's "second conversion," a kind of belated coming to oneself—anyhow that is what I had in mind.[4]

To James Atlas, Percy said, "[*The Second Coming*] is about his belated crisis in coming to a decision for the first time in his life. He's facing death. It's only the prospect of death that enables him to act at last" (*Con.*, 183). But in *The Last Gentleman*, does not Will come to a most significant decision (rejoining the human race), and is not this caused by his facing death?

To explain my puzzlement concerning the second coming of Will Barrett and Percy's response to my objection, I would like to focus on only one of many instances—the ending of *The Last Gentleman*. It is the most telling evidence of the tale differing from the teller's remembrance of the tale. Percy's endings are always special in the affirmation (and sometimes celebration) they give to the reader. I think he is indebted principally to Dostoevsky and Tolstoy for this. The ending of *The Brothers Karamazov* is in particular a rich model for him. In *The Moviegoer* Binx, surrounded by his brothers and sisters, is surely an echo of Alyosha surrounded by the children. The question they put to each protagonist is similar: "When our Lord raises us up on the last day, will Lonnie be in a wheelchair or will he be like us?" (*M*, 240). Both heroes answer yes to the question. Again, when in *The Brothers Karamazov* the children cry, "Hurrah for Karamazov! . . . Hurrah for Karamazov!" they are the model for the children in *Love in the Ruins* who cry, "Hurrah for Jesus Christ! . . . Hurrah for the United States!" (*LR*, 400). The Mass of Resurrection in the Dostoevsky novel resonates quite nicely with Christmas mass in *Love in the Ruins*, for both celebrate birth. And when Alyosha tells the children they must go to the funeral dinner because "it's a very old custom and there's something nice in that," we recognize the similarity to Tom and Ellen preparing the Christmas dinner, also a very old, nice custom.

The likenesses between *Crime and Punishment* and *Lancelot* are numerous. We have the same prison window through which Lance and Raskolnikov view the outside world, the similarity of Sonya and Anna, the sacramental and eucharistic images that haunt both heroes in spite of the terrible "dream" of reality both have. "Love had raised them from the dead," both having discovered "nothing at the heart of evil" (*L,* 253). The yes of *The Brothers Karamazov* is echoed in Percival's eloquent yes. This yes is repeated at the end of *The Thanatos Syndrome,* just before the "well well well" variation of Julian of Norwich ends the novel. And "yes yes yes" prepares us for the beautiful, unequivocal ending of *The Second Coming* (*SC,* 349).

What I wish to suggest by this very brief examination of endings is that Percy's novels do not end ambiguously, inconclusively, or equivocally, despite his own statements to the contrary.

> Most of my novels end up more or less inconclusively . . . with the hero not having his problems resolved and being in a situation not greatly different from the beginning. This [*The Second Coming*] may be the first time where the ending is not ambiguous. Maybe for the first time I saw the possibility of a clear resolution, a classical, novelistic resolution, a victory of eros over thanatos and life over death. (*Con.,* 190)

His endings are so *un*ambiguous that he is the only major novelist now writing who uses regularly a variation of the *deus ex machina* to make his thematic statements clear: Father Boomer, Father Smith, Father Percival, and Father Weatherbee. To be fair, I think what he means when he uses terms such as "inconclusive" and "ambiguous" is that he has not provided a sermonic ending such as the final paragraphs of *Crime and Punishment.* He does not want to be "edifying."

> Seven years, *only* seven years! At the dawn of their happiness both had been ready, for some few moments, to think of those years as if they were no more than seven days. He did not even know that the new life would not be his for nothing, that it must be dearly bought, and paid for with great and heroic struggles yet to come. . . . But that is the beginning of a new story, the story of the gradual renewal of a man, of his gradual regeneration, of his slow progress from one world to another, of how he learned to know a hitherto undreamed-of reality. All that might be the subject of a new tale, but our present one is ended.[5]

Although this is the *implied* ending of every Percy novel, it is not the kind of ending he writes. What Henry James said of himself is also true of Percy—that he wrote the same novel over and over, playing variations on his central perception, conversion. This is a major reason why second comings are finally impossible for Percy without the problems that *The Second Coming* and *The Thanatos Syndrome* create.

What appears to be a sequel is actually another variation of his only subject—discovery. His strength is in his fixation on the discovery of or the possibility of the discovery of something that makes life worth living—that being is better than nonbeing. But what follows the discovery is a new tale, not one that he writes. It is left to the reader to interpret this new tale using the signs and signals Percy gives. His heroes, like Raskolnikov, do not open the New Testament, upon which their future lives depend. Lazarus is raised or can be raised; the Nicodemus question is asked with full expectation of getting an answer. However, the sequel to the Lazarus story is not told, and we must make guesses about the future of Nicodemus, but the guesses are educated. The "great and heroic struggles yet to come" in Will I's life are never presented, certainly not in *The Second Coming*. Hence, Will II must begin again to make the discovery upon which the great and heroic events never depicted depend. While deeply indebted to Dostoevsky for his endings, Percy does not use the tidy reflection that Dostoevsky appends to *Crime and Punishment*, for instance, because of his sense of his audience and the times. It is a rhetorical problem. The Catholic novelist must be sly. "Does goodness come tricked out so as fakery and fondness and carrying on and is God himself as sly?" (*SC*, 349). Following is Percy's latest comment on the problem of deliberate obfuscation.

> The Catholic novelist has to be very careful. He has to be under-handed, deceitful, and damn careful how he uses the words of religion which have all fallen into disuse and almost become obscenities, thanks to people like Jimmy Swaggert. . . . On the other hand, if the subject of religion comes up in a novel, or any hint of any kind of conversion or revelation, it's disapproved of. The secular reviewers say: the author did a good job, his characters are well drawn, and the plot moves along, but his religion shows. It's a game you can't win. What you do is, you tell the story. As Flannery O'Connor said, the worst thing the novelist can do is be edifying. She kept most specific references to the Church out of her work, yet God knows she was as powerful a Catholic as I ever knew.[6]

In short, what Percy means by inconclusive and ambiguous is sly and indirect. It is up to the reader, given the clues, to figure out what is meant by one eye not quite meeting another eye and not quite winking. Ah, says the reader, yes, yes, yes, like one of Percy's characters. I would like to look at the various elements of the ending of *The Last Gentleman* that demonstrate without doubt that the events in the life of Will I were hardly nonevents and that Will I and Will II are, at best, only tenuously related.

"Strength flowed like oil into his muscles and he ran with great joyous ten-foot antelope bounds" (*LG*, 409). This sentence is the narrator's final comment on the significance of Will I's experience. If his experience is short of extraordinary, the sentence is a silly overstatement. If, on the other hand, it is a pithy response to his experience, it is exhiliratingly appropriate because Will I is at the apex of his discovery, even though, like Raskolnikov, he has not learned completely about that "undreamed reality" toward which his experience aims him.[7] Next, the play on "wait" is a powerful affirmation that revises the earlier refusal of his father to "wait" when he suicides. That Sutter's Edsel "waits" for Will is one of the loveliest and wittiest conceits in the novel. The Edsel waits for him because he has "in God's name" affirmed the triumph of being over nonbeing. I do not know what happens to Sutter's ever-ready pistol, but he will not use it on himself. Maybe he throws it away, as Will II does. How does this affirmation come to Will I? It comes through Kitty, whose role as Eve/Miranda has not been given by some the significance it deserves. She is worthy of Will I's repeated assertions that he will marry her. She is his anchor to the real world; it is through her that his inclination toward utter transcendentalism is modified by the quotidian. "I think I'll call Kitty," he says at the critical juncture when he destroys Sutter's notebook: "Perhaps if he could talk to a certain someone he would stop hankering for anyone and everyone, and tender feelings of love would take the place of this great butting billygoat surge which was coming over him again. He clung to the pole buffeted by an abstract, lustful molecular wind, and might even have uttered a sound, brayed into the phone, for the Hoosier looked astounded again and rushed into his deluxe Sun-Liner" (*LG*, 375).

This desperate cry for help is sent to Kitty because she is responsible for his identity. When, earlier, it came over him suddenly that he did not live anywhere and had no address, he remembered Kitty, and by calling her number, he started to recover his identity (*LG*, 313). It is after talking to Kitty on the telephone for two hours that "he remembered everything, knew what he knew and what he didn't know and what he wished to know. He even remembered every sentence in Sutter's notebook" (*LG*, 379). In that conversation they "settled a great many things" (*LG*, 380). He sees Sutter "for the first time as the dismalest failure, a man who had thrown himself away" (*LG*, 381). He is surely indebted to Sutter, but in paying Sutter back, he does not leave a notebook for him to read but tells him what plans he and Kitty have made and what matters they have agreed upon. Will feels fairly certain of what he wants to do, and he has decided he will take a job as personnel manager with Confederate Chevrolet. He and Kitty will accept the same religion, Will having learned from Sutter's notebook of the "prime importance of the religious dimension of life" (*LG*, 383). They will marry, settle down, and raise a family. It is better to do something than do nothing; it is good to have a family; it is better to love and be loved. It is good to cultivate whatever talents one has, to make a contribution, however small. One must do one's best to promote tolerance and understanding between the races. Violence is bad. It is better to make love to one's wife than to monkey around with a number of women. "I think I see for the first time the possibility of a happy, useful life" (*LG*, 385). Suicide is "a lot of damn foolishness." Laughing with relief, Will summarizes, "For the first time I think I really might live like other men—rejoin the human race" (*LG*, 386).

I submit this is a powerful litany of affirmations, a stunning discovery for Will to have made. He has embraced being and rejected Sutter's gnosticism. We can see better the significance of Kitty's role in this if we compare this ending with the picture we get of Kitty and Levin at the end of *Anna Karenina*, the model, I think, for the relationship of Kitty and Will. The likenesses appear to indicate a conscious memory of Tolstoy's novel—but their significance, not their origin, concerns me. To see Percy's novel as a mirror for Tolstoy's is to see it illuminated in a most significant way. As is the case with the Vaughts (and the Barretts), "everything was in confusion in the Oblonsky household," the second sentence of the novel, which ends in the household of Kitty and Levin, where "everyone was in the best of spirits."[8] Levin is called to the nursery by Kitty, and he walks to it with his mind filled with thoughts about the abstract meaning of the transcendent. When he reaches the nursery, Kitty informs him that the baby now recognizes them as persons. When he leaves the nursery, he realizes that some kind of knowledge unattainable by reasoning has now been revealed to him personally, to his heart. The truth of the nursery takes hold of him, entering imperceptibly into his soul and lodging firmly there.

I shall get angry with my coachman Ivan, I shall still argue and express my thoughts inopportunely; there will still be a wall between the holy of holies of my soul and other people, even my wife, and I shall still blame her for my own fears and shall regret it; I shall still be unable to understand with my reason why I am praying, and I shall continue to pray—but my life, independently of anything that may happen to me, every moment of it, is no longer meaningless as it was before, but has an incontestable meaning of goodness, with which I have the power to invest it.[9]

What Will and Levin have learned from their Kittys has fixed an ending onto their experience which cannot be unfixed without doing violence to their artistic life. This is not to say that Will and Levin are not capable of changing, but any change must be consistent with these endings. And if the change is to be radical, then imaginatively that must be in its specific details the subject of a sequel. Nor can one solve the problem by appealing to the real, that is to say, the nonfictive world for justification, saying, well, it can happen—Percy's appeal to Gabriel Marcel's "second conversion." "Unconvincing possibility" has no place in artistic narrative.[10]

Having moved away from his full dependence on Sutter, Will needs one more thing from him: the news that Jamie got from Val—the meaning of Treasure Island. Hence, there is one more element to the ending of the novel which must be discussed. Sutter knew the meaning of Jamie's baptism, and, indeed, for a while he agreed with Val "in every respect. About what has happened to the world, about what God should be and what man is, and even what the Church should be. . . . (And I agree! Absolutely!)." When Sutter first came to the desert, he was waiting for a sign (*LG*, 378). But there was no sign in response to his arrogant request (as with Tom in *The Thanatos Syndrome*). Val remained hopeful; Sutter did not. But Sutter knew what Val knew, and it is this news that Will wants of him, the answer to his "final question." Earlier he had said that Jamie had Val. In light of this we can make sense of the scene—Sutter's joke—that takes place in the desert surrounding Santa Fe (Holy Faith).

> "Sir," said the courteous engineer, trotting along and leaning down to see the driver.
> "What?" But the Edsel kept moving.
> "Wait, sir."
> "Are you Philip?" asked the driver.
> "Eh?" said the engineer, cupping his good ear, and for a moment was not certain he was not.

"Are you Philip and is this the Gaza Desert?" The Edsel stopped. "Do you have something to tell me?"

"Sir? No, sir. I am Williston Barrett," said the engineer somewhat formally. "I knew that, Williston," said Sutter. "I was making a joke. Get in." (*LG*, 359)

This scene is continued at the very end of the novel: "'Wait,' he shouted in a dead run. The Edsel paused, sighed, and stopped" (*LG*, 409). The allusion is to Acts 8:26–40, with Will, Jamie, and Sutter fluidly playing the roles of Philip and the Ethiopian eunuch. "What happened back there?" asks Will. "Do you understand what you are reading?" asks Philip. "How can I," says the Ethiopian, "unless I have someone to guide me." The passage that he does not understand is about the suffering servant (Isaiah 53)—Jamie. Starting with the mystery of death/life, Philip explains the good news to him. The allusion is powerful and conclusive; it is difficult to miss its meaning unless the imagination sleeps and words are emptied of their meaning. "There's also a rather conscious parallel between Binx going to Gentilly and Philip going to the Gaza Desert. A man goes to the desert to seek something. Gentilly is a desert if ever there was one. The same thing happened in *The Last Gentleman*. They end up in the Western desert" (Con., 65).

Earlier, Will had wanted to know what Jamie expected. He had also referred to Jamie's upper berth as his monk's pad; when Jamie is hospitalized, Will uses it as his own bed. The signs and signals are abundant. By the testimony of the characters in the novel and Percy's nonfictional comment, we know Will is highly intelligent, perceptive, and intuitive —"a real searcher" existing in Kierkegaard's religious mode who is after something that Sutter knows. Sutter "understood the good news, the Gospel, he knew exactly what was going on in that baptism" (Con., 204). That Will did not know what was going on in the baptism does not mean that he could not come to know and did not find out. On the contrary, the signs and signals given by the ending indicate that he could and probably would. The ending is neither inconclusive nor ambiguous. The ending is fully what it should be. The consequence of the discovery is left open, more in the manner of James than of Dostoevsky, but the circle is closed. The desperate, suicidal lady who called Percy late one night, saying, "You don't know who I am, but I've just read your book . . . and you know the answer," was, despite Percy's demur, dead right (Con., 191). One cannot say of such a journey as that of Will I, so eloquently depicted, that it was a nonevent without demeaning the artistic circle in which it is enclosed. It must appear to have changed Will forever, and it did.

Part II
Novelist and Regionalist

Bertram Wyatt-Brown

Percy Forerunners, Family History, and the Gothic Tradition

Until recently told so in an interview, Walker Percy was unaware that some of his literary concerns and approaches could be found in the work of three of his collateral ancestors. Nor, in fact, had he ever heard of the southern mid-nineteenth-century female gothic fiction writers and poets in question. Indeed, who has? Although unmentioned in nearly all modern studies of American literature, they were Catherine Ann Warfield, Eleanor Percy Lee, her poetic sister, and Sarah A. Dorsey, their niece—none of them famous even in their own day.[1] Insofar as the literary canon is concerned, these writers were merely the "scribbling women" whom Nathaniel Hawthorne denied his respect. Yet all are fascinating for the psychological issues their productivity brings to light.

Catherine and Eleanor were Walker Percy's great-great-aunts and Sarah his cousin many times removed. This paper will concern only the first of the trio, with particular attention to just one of Warfield's nine novels, *The Household of Bouverie; or, The Elixir of Gold*, published on the eve of the Civil War. A comparison of this work and *Lancelot*, the most gothic of Walker Percy's fiction, helps to explain that psychologically explicit mode. Moreover, it illuminates the relationship between the creative process and the familial experiences of authors in general. Despite obvious differences in style, conceptualization, execution, and philosophical purpose, the link between the Victorian predecessor and the modern novelist was a common family heritage: a genetic predisposition to chronic depression.

For nearly two centuries, each generation of the southern Percy clan included a suicide or a severe case of insanity or both. For the creative members of the lineage, art not only served literary ends but also provided a means of coping with an unmanageable phenomenon. Depression and mania struck with perverse unpredictability. As a result, a full sense of identity, a confidence of self-control, a hopefulness about the future were hard for some members of the Percy clan to achieve. The arbitrariness of fate meant that the individual sufferer could not be sure when the malady would materialize and, when it did, whether disease would overwhelm the rational self. The victim must have often felt as if an alien spirit had entered the body. Walker Percy personified the disorder in *The Last Gentleman* as "the sweet beast of catastrophe." Others who have known the complaint, including Winston Churchill, have sometimes adopted names allusive of similarly bestial, accursed forces.[2] The insupportability of depression lies not only in the emptiness, vacancy, and despair of a "dehydrated" personality, as it should be called, but also in the dread of its return. Even when the individual recovers, the illness remains a family legacy to curse the next generation. Under these trying circumstances, the Percy writers mastered their feelings of grief or loss and found the means to express those feelings in a medium detached from direct human contact—the printed page.

The connection between depression and creativity among philosophers, scientists, poets, and writers is so evident that psychoanalysts have begun to study the matter with considerable acuteness. The depressive is one who has known love early in childhood but later has reason to doubt its permanence—the loss or sometimes the emotional withdrawal of parents being a common factor. The young depressive feels that he or she cannot openly express frustration and despair, for fear of further betrayals. But such "aggressive feelings," argues Anthony Storr, can be translated into imaginative form. "The practice of an art," the psychoanalyst argues, "gives a man an opportunity to express himself without any immediate need to fit in with the opinions of others. In fact, the work may be a much more valid piece of self-expression than what is revealed in action or conversation in 'real' life."[3]

The gothic genre is particularly well adapted to express feelings of hostility, especially with regard to ties between the artist and his or her father. Such conflict involves a struggle for self-identification and independence from parental control on the one hand and a sense of dependency and loyalty to the parent on the other. Indeed, one of the major themes running through Percy family history from the American beginnings to the career of Walker Percy himself has been the quest for paternal approval and affection against heavy psychological odds, especially in the realm of father-child connections. No critic would deny that Percy's interest in existentialism and his fictional themes are related to the suicides of his father and grandfather, the tragic madness of his Aunt Ellen (his father's sister), and the accidental death of his mother when he was almost sixteen. No wonder the strain of melancholy and gothic violence is evident in his novels. With a stress upon the cruelty of fatherlike figures, the gothic formula expresses not just the fears arising from living in a dangerously untrustworthy and unpredictable world but also the resentment of the emotionally abandoned victim and the dread of powerlessness that a desertion arouses. The gothic form explores, says literary critic Elizabeth McAndrew, "the misty realm of the subconscious," the fragility of mankind's hold on sanity.[4]

In comparing the works, three areas of common ground are evident: first, the preoccupation with a central antihero who represents an idealized father and husband gone mad; second, the creation of gothic surroundings that are meant to symbolize the actions and moods of the principal characters, an almost Jungian construction; and third, a theme of Catholic steadfastness and hope by which some degree of order, love, and serenity can emerge.

In Erastus Bouverie, Catherine Warfield created a figure typical of the gothic genre: a dark, ostensibly aristocratic, wealthy squire of a lordly estate. In Walker Percy's *Lancelot*, Lance Lamar is similarly placed both socially and financially. Both antiheroes are victims of mania and depression. They swing between complete nullity and passivity of an androgynous character to violent, compulsive actions as a means not only of proving their own existence but of reasserting their power over those near them. Upholding the ancient ideal of vengeance for infidelity, Percy's Lance Lamar kills both his wife, Margot, and her lover. Percy makes clear that Lance, in his sense of alienation, commits these hideous crimes with a degree of numbness, as if another hand were set to the task. His detachment of feeling acutely reveals an inability to love, to reach out. Similarly, Warfield has Bouverie murder his wife's first suitor and later her husband, whom she married when Bouverie was thought to have died on a diplomatic mission to Russia. The reasons that the novelists offer in both cases are very much the same: depression-driven, honor-conscious feelings of jealousy. The passion serves as their unstable source of self-identification, one that requires a possessive domination of others. Both authors make clear that these antiheroes are subject to impulsive rages and paranoid suspicions which they cannot control, even though, as the writers emphasize, they are morally responsible for their actions.

Yet no less important are similarities between the characters' familial prototypes. Insofar as biographical factors are concerned, Percy's Lance Lamar represents the psychotic aspect of the family's depressive inclination rather than any particular individual, though one easily finds in Lance's words unmistakable allusions to William Alexander Percy's notions of honor, as earlier exemplified in Aunt Emily in *The Moviegoer*. Yet the author may also have had in mind an earlier, even more mysterious Percy. The concept of a southern plantation owner who is morose, cheerless in character, and without an active conscience owes something to family memories of Charles Percy. As the founder of the family in America, he was Catherine's grandfather and Walker Percy's thrice-great-grandfather. Just as Charles ("Don Carlos") Percy, Tory nabob of English, then Spanish, Natchez, laid spurious claims to noble lineage, so too does Lance Lamar take pride in his ancestry. Lance's mistrust of others—his furious outbursts against his father, his wife, her lovers, his disappointing children, his mockery, at times, of his confessor Father John—resembles the ultraconservative suspicions of Charles Percy and his hallucinations of phantom enemies, which tortured his mind not long before his suicide in 1794. There are even references to an eighteenth-century killing over an issue of honor: Lance Lamar slays his wife's lover, Jacoby, with the same kind of weapon and in the same manner that his Spanish forefather had used in defense of family and self-reputation. Warfield's Bouverie shares similar characteristics with the charismatic but hopelessly mad progenitor. As the first of the Percy "wayfarers," so to speak, Charles was not only a depressive with classically psychotic delusions but also a rogue and bigamist with three marriages. Although founder of the family's Mississippi slaveholding fortune, this Thomas Sutpen–like figure has ever since haunted the "illegitimate" branch of the Percy family, to which Walker Percy belonged (*TS*, 136).

In Catherine Warfield's imagination, Erastus Bouverie is also fashioned after the character of her own father, whom she both loved and passionately hated. In 1813 Major Nathaniel Ware, coldly intellectual financier of Natchez, Mississippi, had married widow Sarah Percy Ellis, Charles Percy's eldest daughter. No doubt she was attracted to the formidable, haughty planter and politician because he reminded her of her father, who had died when she was an impressionable thirteen-year-old. Upon the birth of their second child, Eleanor Percy Ware, in 1819, Sarah completely lost her reason. Her soon-embittered husband consigned her to Philadelphia's Pennsylvania Hospital and made that city his residence.[5] For the daughters, whom Sarah was never again to recognize, Sarah seemed a gothic personification of the living dead.

In choosing her second mate, Sarah Percy Ellis had apparently picked a man as reticent, cold, and Voltairean as her father. Unlike Charles and his treatment of his first wife, however, Ware did not desert his family altogether (although he seldom visited his wife either at the Philadelphia hospital or at her later home with her son in Natchez). Rather, as an explorer and gifted land speculator, he left the little girls alone much of the time. Catherine never forgave him for the long absences, despite the unusually attentive and sophisticated education that she and her sister received. In a sense the portrayal of Bouverie was her revenge against him.

From a modern clinical perspective, Bouverie's mental state is remarkably well described, particularly with regard to the underlying feminine nature which he cannot recognize any more than Percy's Lance Lamar can. In fact, the portrayal of both figures brings to mind Carl Jung's concept of anima, the notion that a vital inner part of man involves a feminine component.[6] Their fury against rival men and their misogyny suggest that their self-proclaimed masculinity is suspect. As a cruelly sarcastic recluse—not unlike Major Ware—Bouverie hides in the mansion's upper rooms. He is the madman rather than madwoman in the Brontëan attic. In this respect the analogy with Lance Lamar, confined to a cell in a New Orleans Center for Aberrant Behavior, reflects the lethargy and the restrictive, rigid interiority that afflict both these antiheroes. Later, after blowing up his portion of the house during a scientific experiment, Bouverie flees to a cave. As in Walker Percy's *The Second Coming*, the cave represents the primordial, maternal womb that man has loved, resented, and half-hated to leave. The tomb, as it were, is safe but cold, dreary, meaningless, a point noted in both novels.

Like Lance Lamar, Bouverie represses his feminine passivity and inability to act except in sudden Hamlet-like bursts of violence during crises. As a result he cannot endure any spirit of independence exhibited by the women who surround and, in a sense, imprison him. Such freedom threatens his fragile sense of himself as a man. Like Lance Lamar, Bouverie is portrayed as at least in part a victim of parental violation. Lance's father was a weak cuckold whom his son discovered to be a taker of bribes. Ursus, Bouverie's uncle and brutal guardian, rich from the African slave trade, had so demeaned his young charge that the child lost all self-confidence.

To restore his uncertain manliness, Bouverie adopted the manner of indifference, hauteur, and secretiveness that also characterizes Percy's sometimes sexually impotent Lancelot. After Lilian discovers her grandfather in the mansion's upper gallery, Bouverie quickly establishes dominion over her, much to the distress of Camilla, his long-suffering wife. In the climax of the first volume, he induces Lilian to give him a cup of her blood. Warfield chooses the common gothic symbol of seduction and provides the necessary language of lust, but with a religious overtone: "Welcome, my love, to this solitary life of mine, art thou, as morning to the sleepless, or showers to the sere grass. *Henceforth thy being shall be blended with my own*, and the shadow that envelops me fall over thee also, even as from thy young existence, some light and joy shall gild the clouds of mine. For of this nature is the mighty and inscrutable bond of blood."[7]

Some discerning critics argue that in his fiction Walker Percy at times perceives women in a sacramental light. Certainly Warfield made a similar point in depicting this encounter. The nineteenth-century ideal required of women the honor of self-sacrifice. Thus, the granddaughter Lilian's offering of her blood was meant to recapitulate Camilla's daily sacrifice in the service of her master and husband, suggesting, however indirectly, that womanly self-abnegation could reach the grotesque. Bouverie, the author stresses, comprehends the implications: he delights in the prospect of a new relationship over which he has such full control. Lilian's surrender to his charm provides a second coming, if you will: the advent of a new, younger woman to help him surmount his depression and the barrenness of his existential imprisonment, both physical and spiritual. Like Percy's epiphanic novel, *The Second Coming*, *The Household of Bouverie* provides hints of father-daughter incest. In *The Second Coming*, Percy has the spiritually wayfaring Will Barrett leave the cave and fall—literally fall—into the arms of Allie, possibly his own daughter by his former love Kitty. So too does Warfield imply a sexual connection between a rapidly aging man and the budding young granddaughter. He seeks her blood to mix in his gold-laced elixir, a restorative of youth, as he delusively thinks it is. The fantasy of renewal for the middle-aged or elderly male through the reassurances and love of a beautiful virgin is given much darker, more insidious tones by Warfield, as a female observer, than it receives at the aging Walker Percy's hands.

The second point of commonality in the fiction of Warfield and Percy is the explicit tradition of the gothic form itself. In this respect, both authors are partially indebted to Edgar Allan Poe, who, like them, had special ties to European literature rather than to more localized southern letters. Like the two Percy novelists, Poe dwelt intensely on the obsessional, depressive, overly rationalistic mind and fatalistically denied the reformability of man. Poe, too, often placed his characters in frighteningly confined spaces—cages, maelstroms, tombs for the living. That horror of lost self-mastery was no doubt related to his wretchedness as an orphan reared by a loveless, tightfisted Richmond family whose father constantly reminded him of his marginal status. Certainly Lance Lamar and Erastus Bouverie share characteristics with Poe's Montresor, the first-person narrator who, for revenge, walls up Fortunato in "The Cask of Amontillado." With its incestuous implications and blasted mansion and family, Poe's tale of the Ushers may well have influenced both Warfield and Percy in their applications of the gothic mode.

Indeed, like so many of Poe's semisuicidal characters who live a cell-like existence, both Lance Lamar and Erastus Bouverie inhabit a private world. All three chose the gothic approach because it has always blended the realm of science with subjectivities of the mind. That combination would naturally draw the interest of writers concerned with the uses of rationality, the dangers of nothingness and insanity. The scientific experiments that their characters conduct are a means to cut human ties, ostensibly for some loftier, abstract goal. Fame and a gift of universal health to mankind are Bouverie's aims. For Lance, the goal is a nostalgic return to a richer, less vulgar ideality, the resurgence of old-fashioned honor. Lance ruminates in his pigeonnier, an outcropping at Belle Isle, his plantation home. Erastus occupies the second-floor chambers and cupola of Bouverie. These are solitary retreats where they seethe over violations to their honor. Amateurs with dilettantish whimsies, they use the pursuit of science as self-justification for an impotence and deep self-loathing that they vainly try to conceal.

Walker Percy's Lancelot utilizes the new technology of a blood test to prove his daughter's illegitimacy and infrared video equipment to detect the shadowy signs of his wife Margot's lovemaking. Bouverie employs devices appropriate to nineteenth-century science, including a galvanic battery by which he surreptitiously delivers a kind of shock treatment to his previously drugged wife, Camilla, to subject her totally to his will. One is reminded of Tom More's lapsometer, also an instrument to alter consciousness. Like George Orwell, Aldous Huxley, and others, Percy, of course, was satirizing the hubris of modern mental tinkering. Warfield had neither her descendant's light touch nor his philosophical inclination.

Like all gothics, both novels look backward more often than forward

—toward legends of patriarchy and chivalric deed. *Lancelot* does so with regard to Malory's and Tennyson's versions of the Arthurian romance. There are similar allusions in *The Household of Bouverie*: Bouverie uses the blood obtained from the compliant Lilian to mingle with his alchemical potion of melted gold sovereigns, medieval emblem of lust for worldly power and wealth. Despite its Christian overlay, the Arthurian legend has always been associated with the earthbound, pagan religion of ancient alchemy (Jung). Warfield knows well the symbols of the cult (they appear in the furnishings and octagonal design of Camilla's quarters, for instance), but Warfield offers no explanation of what alchemical worship might mean. Quite ingeniously, however, Percy turns medieval myth upside down. Lance informs Father John, his silent analyst and father confessor, that he seeks not a Holy Grail but rather an "unholy" one: the source of evil instead of salvation. But like other gothic writers, Warfield does perceive the blasphemy of man's assumption of godly powers and at some level identifies that repudiation with her agnostic father, with the arrogant, irreligious Charles Percy, and with the half-pagan portion of southern patriarchy itself.

With respect to the third issue, the religious underpinnings of the novels are also curiously similar. Throughout Percy family history, the Catholic faith has offered for the literary Percys an ecclesiastical structure, a welcome place for the rationalistic seeker of an elusive mystical faith, a religion that merged the traditional functions of nurture and authority through the alchemy, it could be said, of ritual. Moreover, the church condemned suicide as a violation of God's law—the denial of his mercy in granting life, the crime of utter despair against the Holy Spirit. But its appeal to the depressive is scarcely limited to that. In Charlotte Brontë's brilliant novel, *Villette*, Lucy Snow suffers from unremitting depression as a result of the early loss of her mother and abandonment by her father, an echoing of Brontë's personal woes. At one point, Brontë has Lucy Snow attend confession in hope of some emotional relief. A shrewd Catholic priest declares, "You were made for our faith: depend upon it; our faith alone could heal and help you—Protestantism is altogether too dry, cold, prosaic for you."[8] Brontë's words bear much truth for understanding the appeal of Catholicism to the depressive. Walker Percy's well known and often explained conversion to and literary use of Catholic spirituality as antidote, however complex and profoundly felt and revealed, cannot be discussed here, but a relationship between depression and Catholic conversion is evident.

Like Brontë's Lucy Snow, Catherine Warfield ultimately rejected the faith out of pride and prejudice. Yet she was attracted to the possibility, partly because her beloved, poetic sister, Eleanor Percy Lee of Natchez, Mississippi, had converted to Catholicism.[9] In *The Household of Bouverie*, she creates a Bishop Clare based on her sister's father confessor, Bishop Chanche of Natchez. Parenthetically, Sarah Dorsey, the Ware sisters' niece and the third female Percy writer, became a High Anglican and extolled the virtues of that semi-Catholic sect in her novels.[10]

In *The Household of Bouverie*, the highlighting of the Catholic impulse was not only part of the gothic paraphernalia but a reflection of the personal sources connected with the family's attempts to deal with the problems of genetic depression. Still more, Catholicism was a faith that seemed to recognize man's duality of nature in the Jungian sense. Though patriarchal, the church personified the feminine in the worship of Mary, something missing from the Protestant tradition. That vision of ideal womanhood was deeply conservative, but as a part of the southern cultural heritage the image of the gently subordinate helpmate has always governed the male Percys' notion of woman's fit place. In Catholic terms, the spirit of the anima, as it were, came in the form of the mother of mankind, the mother, in a sense, Charlotte Brontë had lost as a child, the mother that Catherine and Eleanor had known and yet not known at all.

In *The Cardinal's Daughter*, a later romance from Warfield's hand, the author again associates Catholicism and misshapen fatherhood. The young heroine discovers that her long-absent father had deserted her mother (as Charles Percy and Nathaniel Ware had) and entered holy orders. She pursues him to the Vatican itself, since by then the dour intellectual had become a chief advisor to the ultramontanist pope, Pio Nono. Her fascination with Catholicism is evident even if the novel itself is too conventional in plot and characterization to be of permanent interest.

The critic is by no means obliged to declare Catherine Ann Warfield as significant a novelist as her latter-day descendant. She artistically falls short partly because, as a woman, she found herself in a situation that was more crippled and circumscribed than that of her twentieth-century kinsman. A comparison of the endings reveals it. Both authors permit the antihero to escape justice for the atrocities they committed. After all, neither Lancelot nor Bouverie deserves a moment's sympathy for their jealous acts of murder, even if Lance's pagan code of honor, as opposed to Christian precept, so permitted. But the author allows Lancelot's reprieve, so to speak, in order to make clear that only when the sinner in this "cautionary tale" learns to *feel* does he regain contact with life and human affection and awaken to the enormity of his offense, a state of mind preparatory to salvation (*Con.*, 169). That is the meaning of Father John's emphatic *"Yes"* as the final statement. He means, in effect, that Lance is at last ready to receive the *bad* news. Percy provides a profound conclusion to his angriest novel.

In contrast, Warfield was unable to find a satisfactory close. In the sentimental style then popular, the writer simply has a much diminished, aged Bouverie beg forgiveness, which, dutiful as always, Lilian readily supplies. In defiance of all verisimilitude or philosophical meaning, the granddaughter even obtains a governor's pardon for the old sinner. Moreover, Warfield was unable to properly dispose of her heroine. She has her die in a convenient train and carriage accident at the end of the novel's 783 pages. Warfield's artistic limitations are self-evident, yet her fiction contributes to an appreciation of the creative process and its relationship to a grim but ultimately triumphant family history.

Susan V. Donaldson

Tradition in Amber: Walker Percy's *Lancelot* as Southern Metafiction

Walker Percy has periodically insisted that his literary and linguistic interests have, in his own words, "very little to do" with one another, but his 1977 novel *Lancelot* suggests that these two concerns overlap to a striking degree.[1] *Lancelot*'s preoccupation with language, communication, movies, storytelling, and listening has in fact led a number of critics, such as Robert Siegle, J. P. Telotte, and William Rodney Allen, to describe the novel as metafiction that brings attention to and ponders the making of fiction and consequently the codes by which we live and communicate. Indeed, so large does fiction-making loom in *Lancelot* that Lancelot Andrewes Lamar, Percy's mad and voluble narrator, observes with disgust that everyone around him has "been in the movies too long" (*L*, 205). From Elgin Buell, MIT student and Lamar house servant, to Robert Merlin, a Hemingwayesque film director, people surrounding Lance ape the well-worn gestures, postures, and dialogue of Hollywood films and by doing so remind us of the way narrative in general dominates the smallest details in our lives.

Nevertheless, it is not so much Hollywood as old southern tales and the regional tradition of storytelling that attract *Lancelot*'s metafictional musings. As Percy himself notes, the novel is "a kind of cautionary tale," one, I might add, that both repudiates old southern stories as calcified and commodified *and* acknowledges their lingering and compelling power (*Con.*, 154). For if Lancelot Lamar does his best, as does Percy, for that matter, to break away from the southern past and to establish a new language, order, and story, the tale Lance tells Percival, the priest and friend serving as silent listener, underscores what Percy himself once called the "seductiveness of narrative" (*Con.*, 244). The more Lance strains to start anew, the more tightly bound his story is to past southern tales. His plight is, in a sense, Percy's plight as well, along with Percy's generation of southern writers, a generation, Percy says, that "has spent most of its time getting out from under Faulkner" (*Con.*, 99).

It is with William Faulkner, after all, that Percy associates "the Southern tradition of folklore, yarns, storytelling, family histories, and such."[2] From Percy's perspective, Faulkner is the end of a long line of regional storytellers defined by an oral tradition of yarn swapping in the courtroom, on the back porch, and around the campfire. The tradition's earliest antecedents, as students of the region ranging from Allen Tate to Waldo W. Braden have argued, can be traced back to the nineteenth-century South's preoccupation with political oratory and to the southwestern humorists of the 1840s, 1850s, and 1860s.

More to the point, perhaps, the framed narratives and oral storytelling of the southwestern humorists—and the southern writers that followed —tended to portray storytelling as one of the principal means by which regional communities defined themselves. Looking back on frontier life in central Georgia, Richard Malcolm Johnston observed in the late nineteenth century that country lawyers "spent the long evenings in story-telling about their neighbors, friends, one another, and even themselves, to be followed by shouts that when on the long piazza, and even sometimes when in the tavern hall, would be heard throughout the village, driving pious elderly ladies to wonder aghast."[3] Such evenings, Johnston suggested, retraced the communal bonds linking storytellers to listeners and drew the lines of the inner circle (no pious ladies admitted).

But even in the heyday of the southwestern humorists—the 1840s, 1850s, and 1860s—those lines had a decidedly blurred look to them. In an age when frontier was rapidly giving way to settled country, backcountry tales told by Thomas Bangs Thorpe, Joseph Glover Baldwin, and George Washington Harris already had a strongly nostalgic air about them. Such stories served, in a sense, as acts of preservation, records of endangered life, and chief among the artifacts to be preserved was the spoken word—the accents, broken grammar, and pungent immediacy of speech in the backcountry.[4] For the spoken word, from the perspectives of Jacques Derrida and Walter Benjamin, suggests direct contact between storyteller and listener and conjures up the immediate and reassuring presence of community, "a community of speech," Derrida says, "where all the members are within earshot."[5] In contrast, the written word implicitly acknowledges the dispersal of community, the problematic nature of audience, and the limits of memory transmitted orally. Such an acknowledgment, though, is resisted by the stories of the southwestern humorists—and, one could argue, by a good deal of the southern literature to follow in which the vaunted oral tradition of the region figures large. It is a tradition, after all, that strains to preserve the tenuous boundaries of community and region in the midst of rapid socioeconomic change.

For Percy, those boundaries have become increasingly problematic and the tradition itself untenable for the writer working in late-twentieth-century America. "Whatever impetus I had towards writing," he once told an interviewer, "owes nothing to sitting on a porch listening to anybody tell stories about the South, believe me." And with a good deal of conviction, he added, "I think the day of regional Southern writing is all gone. I think that people who try to write in that style are usually repeating a phased-out genre or doing Faulkner badly" (*Con.*, 69).

Lancelot, I would argue, suggests just how untenable that storytelling tradition is by Percy's lights, for the first-person narration of Lancelot Andrewes Lamar offers precious little opportunity to celebrate the bonds between storytelling and community. On the very first page of the novel, disconcertingly enough, we learn that Lance is an inmate of the Center for Aberrant Behavior, a madman confined to a solitary cell. The setting is, in many respects, all too appropriate for the story that follows. What emerges from Lance's cagey and sometimes infuriating narration is a portrait of corrosive solitude and alienation. Nearly every detail that Lance adds to the story—from the cold prickling of interest he feels upon discovering his wife's infidelity to his murder of Janos Jacoby—serves only to underscore the distance lying between him and Percival, his silent, appalled listener, a listener, not incidentally, with whom the reader is implicitly allied through the use of second-person address. The longer Lance tells his story, the less likely appears the possibility of communication or communion.

Much of the blame for this difficulty in communication, the novel implies, lies not just with Lance himself but with the deterioration of southern tradition, in particular the calcification and commodification of southern stories and tradition in an age in which everything seems to be up for sale. Lance lives in a world, after all, that appears "safely embalmed in memory and movie film"—Percy's own apt phrase from *The Message in the Bottle* (*MB*, 52). Whatever tradition remains in that world has been remade and neatly packaged for the consumption of tourists and for the interests of historic preservation. Lance's family has long made ends meet by opening up their River Road house, Belle Isle, to tourists eager to pay for glimpses of antiques and for yarns about Bowie knives, master-slave relations, and hiding places during the Civil War. Now, through the energetic efforts of his wife, Margot, Belle Isle has been restored "to a splendor it had never known" (*L*, 117). A wing destroyed by fire a hundred years ago has been reconstructed, a pigeon-nier has been transformed into a splendid study for Lance, and Lance himself has been recreated "according to some Texas-conceived image of the River Road gentry, a kind of gentleman planter without planta-tion"—a combination, oddly enough, of Ashley Wilkes, Leslie Howard, Jeff Davis, Gregory Peck, and Clark Gable as Rhett Butler (*L*, 120).

Even fragments of southern stories have been transformed into effi-ciently packaged commodities. The story that Lance tells Percival is, appropriately enough, set against another story—the making of a pre-posterous film at Belle Isle about a collection of various regional stereo-types, from a Cajun trapper to a decadent aristocratic planter, all taking shelter in a southern manor from a hurricane. As told to Lance by Robert Merlin, the producer and the director, the movie is a pastiche of regional tales worn by time—sharecroppers battling landowners, a community trapped by bigotry, a plantation that "goes to pot" (*L*, 147). All in all, the movie's story seems even more unreal and ossified than Belle Isle itself, which, in its restored state and populated by Hollywood film folk, more nearly resembles a movie set than a viable representation of regional tradition.

It is hardly surprising, then, that Lance, sober, cannot "bear to look at Belle Isle and the great oaks" (*L*, 95). Surrounded by refineries, the house and the trees "seemed so sad and used up and self-canceling" (*L*, 95). For Lance, dreaming away his life in mystery novels and alco-hol, tradition and its narratives have undergone something very like reification. Belle Isle and all that it represents no longer exist as a viable and organic part of everyday life but as objects rendered alien and au-tonomous by the pressures of a market economy. Tradition and the stories that define it now appear as mere commodities to be viewed and consumed, artifacts trapped in amber. In an early philosophical essay Percy labeled such an artifact a "hardened symbol," something that emerges "when the world comes to be conceived as Alice's museum of name-things: shoes and ships and sealing wax."[6]

To a certain extent, this sort of "hardening" process seems to be an inevitable part of what Percy, in *Lost in the Cosmos*, calls a "devolution" of signs in general, and here he resorts to the vocabulary of semiotics and the relationship between signifier, the mark or sound of representation, and signified, the concept being represented. In the first stage, Percy suggests, the signifier "serves as the discovery vehicle through which the signified is known." Then, he adds, "the signifier becomes transformed by the signified." For instance, a signifier such as the word "balloon" seems to take on the qualities of the "stretched-rubber, light, up-tending, squinch-sound-against fingers signified." But through familiarity and overuse this relationship between signifier and signified eventually fails. "Next," Percy argues, "there is a hardening and closure of the signifier, so that in the end the signified becomes encased in a simulacrum like a mummy in a mummy case." For all intents and purposes the signified disappears "into the sarcophagus of its sign" (*LC*, 104). At this stage the referent or original of the sign no longer seems to exist. All that remains is what Percy calls "the ossified signifier" (*LC*, 105).

It is this stage that seems to characterize the "preservation" of tradition and southern stories in *Lancelot*. More specifically, the world that Lance Lamar lives in resembles to a startling degree the contemporary situation that Frederic Jameson, following the lead of Jean Baudrillard, calls the simulacrum, by which he means "the reproduction of 'copies' which have no original." In this situation, Jameson argues, signs seem to have a "free-floating" existence because they are no longer tied to a "referent," that is, "the place hitherto taken by nature, by raw materials and primary production, or by the 'originals' of artisanal production or handicraft."[7] Signs become copies of other copies, not of originals.

A similar wilderness of signs without referents, copies of copies, seems to greet Lance at every turn. Indeed, one is never really sure where one particular variety of copies—the movies—begins and ends. Everyone from Margot to Lance's daughter, Lucy, parrots the language and gestures of film fragments. Even Lance seems to be a copy of Lipscomb, the decadent southern planter in the film, who secretly welcomes the prospect of apocalypse brought about by the film's hurricane, just as the hurricane in the novel's climax seems to be a copy of the film's hurricane. Ultimately, "reality" seems to be imitating the movies, not the other way around—or so the townfolk, mesmerized by the film company, would have us think. As Lance himself muses, "What was nutty was that the movie folk were trafficking in illusions in a real world but the real world thought that its reality could only be found in the illusions. Two sets of maniacs" (*L*, 152).

That real world, in fact, with all its carefully preserved bits and pieces of tradition, may be as fictional as the movie that Merlin and his company are making. In this respect, *Lancelot*, like other metafictional novels, brings attention to the making of fiction and the fictional nature of the world supposedly lying outside narrative texts. What concerns Percy in particular, though, is the refusal of people to recognize old and clichéd southern fictions as fiction and their determination to hold on to tradition and its narratives long past the period of their usefulness. However much Margot Lamar tries to make her restoration of Belle Isle as "authentic" as possible—Lance tells us that "the only important thing for her was that everything had to be exactly as it was"—what remains in the end are merely fragments of tradition carefully preserved under glass, bits and pieces of the past trapped in amber (*L*, 120). They no longer "signify," just as Lance Lamar himself, transformed by Margot into "Jeff Davis at Beauvoir, ready to write my memoirs," had nothing really to say or write. "There was nothing to remember," he tells Percival (*L*, 18).

Within the confines of *Lancelot*, in fact, language itself no longer seems to "signify" for either storyteller or listener. Indeed, the fragment of a sign that Lance sees outside his narrow window—"Free & Ma B"—suggests that the most basic building blocks of communication no longer offer any sort of viable link between one person and the next (*L*, 4). As if to confirm this possibility, Lance's narration nearly overflows with episode after episode of remarks, conversations, and incidents replete with questions, hesitations, multiple meanings, and misunderstandings. Just what, for instance, are Margot and the film people discussing after Lance leaves the room and tries to eavesdrop? What do their intimate gestures mean? Is Margot really having an affair with Robert Merlin, the director? Or is she having an affair with the codirector, Janos Jacoby? What lies behind Jacoby's huffing and puffing about "cinematographic language"? Is the codirector trying to impress Margot or intimidate Merlin? And what, finally, are Margot and Merlin actually saying on the videotape made by Elgin Buell? Is Lance correct in his "interpretation"? Little wonder, then, that Lance is excited by the possibility of communicating with the inmate next door simply by knocking. As he observes to Percival, "To *make conversation* in the old tongue, the old worn-out language. It can't be done" (*L*, 85).

Accordingly, Lancelot understandably yearns to make a clean break with the past and its reified symbols and to start anew. As he tells Percival, "the past, any past, is intolerable, not because it is violent or terrible or doomstruck or any such thing, but just because it is so goddamn banal and feckless and useless" (*L*, 105). In its place Lance yearns for a new time and age, a new language and a new set of stories

—signs, in short, that can signify and establish the possibility of "true communication" (L, 12). To bring about that end, he takes swift and merciless action: Belle Isle is blown up; Margot and her friends are killed; and Lance himself is determined to strike out for Virginia and a new life with Anna, the inmate next door, at his side. For the past and all it represents, he tells Percival, he has no regrets at all. "Belle Isle is gone," he says shortly, "and I couldn't care less. If it were intact it would be the last place on earth I'd choose to live. I'd rather live in Brooklyn. As gone with the wind as Tara and as good riddance" (L, 106).

The curious thing about Lance Lamar's search for the new, though, is that his "reading" and narrative of the events at Belle Isle are based on the very stories and fragments of the past that he rejects.[8] Even though Lance talks volubly of starting anew not once but twice—first when he discovers Margot's infidelity and then in the Center for Aberrant Behavior while he tells his story to Percival—he ends up inadvertently repeating in his own life a good many aspects of the worn-out past and all the calcified tales that he has repudiated. He insists, for instance, that Anna, the Georgia-born inmate next door, is the "new woman" with whom he intends to start a new life in Virginia, but the more he talks about her the more it becomes clear that he identifies her with another Georgia girl—his first wife, Lucy, who seems nearly interchangeable with Lance's own youth and early hopes. Moreover, when Lance finally decides to take revenge for Margot's infidelity, he does so in time-honored fashion—armed with a bowie knife in the grand tradition of his great-great-grandfather, who once fought a duel on a sandbar in the Mississippi River.

Above all, Lance's vision of a new age to be created in Virginia bears a suspiciously strong resemblance to the old, mythic southern past, as a good many commentators on the novel, such as Richard Gray, Robert Brinkmeyer, and William Rodney Allen, have already pointed out. Lance himself, of course, resists the possibility that he may be copying tradition. "Don't confuse [the new order] with anything you've heard of before," he warns Percival; but it is precisely this sort of confusion that distinguishes his notion of a reborn world (L, 156). In his call for a new world of chivalrous, violent men quick to defend honor and women, safely and conveniently categorized as either ladies or whores, we hear the muted echoes of the regional tradition Percy himself labeled long ago as southern Stoicism—that profoundly pessimistic code of tight-lipped honor ironically pondering its own demise in an increasingly hostile world.[9]

Lance is, in fact, more nearly a blurred reflection of his own father than a prophet of the new order. He may despise his father for withdrawing from the world, for succumbing to graft, for "permitting" his wife's infidelity, but these are qualities, after all, that Lance shares with his father to a great extent. Ultimately, Lance's condemnation of his father and his dreamy brooding over the past and poetry offers an all too apt indictment of Lance himself. Both father and son have sat idly on their gallery, "dreaming not so much of a real past as what ought to have been and should be now and might be yet: a lovely golden sunlit Louisiana of bayous and live oaks and misty green savannahs" (*L*, 215). In Lance's case, only the geography is different. He ponders the Shenandoah Valley and its possibilities, not the Louisiana landscape.

To the end, though, Lance refuses to recognize or acknowledge the parallels that link his life and dreams to those of his father. This refusal suggests that his reenactment of the past is of a different order than the Kierkegaardian repetition attracting Binx Bolling in *The Moviegoer* and Will Barrett in *The Last Gentleman*. From Binx's perspective, "A repetition is the re-enactment of past experience toward the end of isolating the time segment which has lapsed in order that it, the lapsed time, can be savored of itself and without the usual adulteration of events that clog time like peanuts in brittle" (*M*, 79–80). Lance's experience of repetition, though, seems to be more nearly akin to Freud's repetition compulsion. Freud, after all, has argued that a patient in analysis unable to remember experiences or material is often forced to repeat the repressed experience or material in the present "instead of remembering it as something belonging to the past." Such repetitive experiences, Freud adds, "are invariably acted out in the sphere of the transference, of the patient's relation to the physician."[10]

Percy has made no secret of his occasional exasperation with Freud, not to mention Freudian interpretations of his novels. I would suggest, though, that Lance Lamar and his curious reenactment of past southern stories do bear strange witness to the transferential nature of reading in general and in particular the way readers and interpreters often end up repeating, wittingly or not, the structures they have set out to analyze. However skeptical and iconoclastic Lance sees himself to be, he is, after all, a reader and interpreter of family and regional stories, and he tells bits and pieces of them to Percival, his silent listener, in a scenario that resembles nothing so much as a series of exchanges between patient and analyst.

Emerging from those exchanges is a fragmented narrative that inadvertently retraces the patterns of the past—cuckoldry, obsession with honor, vengeance seeking, and heroic posturing. Even the language Lance uses to describe his new order draws from the vocabulary of the past. The members of his reborn age, he tells Percival, will know each other "the same way General Lee and General Forrest would know each other at a convention of used-car dealers on Bourbon Street: Lee a gentleman in the old sense. Forrest not, but in this generation of vipers they would recognize each other instantly" (*L*, 157).

The result is a narrative that testifies to the lingering power of past southern stories even as Lance Lamar seeks to repudiate them. Clichéd and reified they may often appear, but they nonetheless are still forceful enough to require that repudiation, one, I might add, that Walker Percy himself seems to feel compelled to rehearse over and over again in his fiction. Repeatedly, his "southern sons," from puzzled Binx Bolling in *The Moviegoer* to Will Barrett in *The Second Coming*, reject the world of their fathers, but more often than not they find themselves inadvertently following in the footsteps of those that preceded them.

Lancelot, then, may be a story about the end of southern stories, but it is also a story about the difficulty of finally putting those stories to rest. Like Aunt Emily in *The Moviegoer*, they still possess the power to collect "all the stray bits and pieces of the past" and "transfigure" those who listen, read, and write about old regional tales—even those who tell stories about the demise of the old storytelling traditions (*M*, 49). If tradition from the perspective of *Lancelot* now seems to be trapped in amber, so too is a figure such as Lancelot Andrewes Lamar, who feels the need to tell stories about that end. Getting out from under William Faulkner, for readers and for storytellers, is apparently a good deal more difficult than it initially looks.

Jan Nordby Gretlund

On the Porch with Marcus Aurelius: Walker Percy's Stoicism

Walker Percy's Stoicism is one circumstance of his mental makeup that needs critical attention. In his existential search Percy has not separated his imagination from the southern community. He was born of a region that endows him with character and purpose, and he seems to know that he can only deny its parenthood to his own hurt. He confronts the world from his region, he tries to comprehend its past, he considers the values and limitations of his heritage, and in his search he also takes into consideration the continued presence in the South of the Stoic tradition. So far, Walker Percy's critics have only talked of his Stoicism in general terms. The use of the word is often biased, and it is treated as if it were simply a synonym for all non-Christian ideas, but it should not be dismissed so lightly. We need a critical discussion of what is meant by Stoicism in connection with Walker Percy's fiction.

The theology of the Christian church owes much to the ethical doctrines of Stoicism. Emperor Marcus Aurelius Antoninus advised the readers of his *Meditations* to keep their temper with the foolish and ungrateful and "even care for them" (8.8) because "men exist for each other" (8.59). In view of the reputation of Roman Stoics, it is perhaps surprising for some Christians that Marcus Aurelius considered the idea of "man's brotherhood with his kind" inherent in the constitution of every human being (12.26); but the existence of a brotherhood of man is one of the ideas that Christian theology shares with Stoicism. Epictetus, whose handbook *The Enchiridion* was the moral guide for generations of southerners, anticipated Marcus Aurelius by pointing out that a brother's injustice can be borne when we keep in mind that he is our brother (43). In this way brotherly love was accepted as a principle by Roman Stoics, if not as an emotion. The emperor's meditations on the lantern of eternal "truth, wisdom and justice" (12.15) became a guide for distinguished southerners such as William Byrd, Thomas Jefferson, and Robert E. Lee.[1] Stoicism offered them a gospel of endurance rather than hope, enabled them to reconcile social dependency with personal independence, allowed the idea that God is not separate from this world, and confirmed their suspicion that what is happening now will happen over and over, whatever our passions. Stoicism did for them the most that religion can do for any man, to paraphrase Henry James on Epictetus: it enabled them to live hopefully in a miserable world.[2] There are, of course, essential differences between Christian belief and Stoicism. Whether there is a God or not, the moral issues remain unaffected for the Stoic. Marcus Aurelius wanted to adopt "strict principles for the regulation of impulse" (8.1) simply for "the happiness of real integrity and dignity" (10.9). And for Epictetus the goal was the preservation of his own honor and fidelity and self-respect (24). The Stoics did not offer the promise of an afterlife. The emperor wrote, "One thing only is of precious worth: to live out one's days in truthfulness and fair dealing" (6.47). In this way the Stoic philosopher looks to himself for all help or harm (48) (compare the egoism of Aunt Emily in *The Moviegoer*). And he does good in order to be virtuous, that is, in order to be able to live with himself. It is a small but truly decisive step from the Stoic maxims to the ethical precepts of the gospel.

During Walker Percy's childhood his foster father was an explainer of the region to outsiders. William Alexander Percy felt a strong commitment to the preservation of the human values of the southern community, but he rejected its fundamentalist religion. The dominant evangelical protestantism emphasizes the individual's own role in saving his soul. Each individual is supposed to maintain his personal relation with God and is expected to work out his salvation without the help of any man-made institution. William Alexander Percy would have thought it natural that ultimately all responsibility is individual. What made him a skeptic about the dominant religiousness of his native region was its intense emotionalism in defense of revealed knowledge and mystery. Southern fundamentalism holds that temporal ends are not ultimate ends and that there is knowledge to which all "facts" are either subordinate or irrelevant. Most southerners live in a world peculiarly balanced between such Christian otherworldliness and the Greco-

Roman ethics of individual responsibility, but in William Alexander Percy's home there were only the philosophers of antiquity. It was to the Roman Stoics that he turned when faced with the task of educating his cousin's sons, LeRoy, Walker, and Phinizy. Throughout his autobiography, *Lanterns on the Levee*, it is obvious that William Alexander Percy admired the Stoic sense of duty (*kathékon*), which is the duty to do the most rational thing possible under the circumstances. And he considered the virtues of reason, courage, justice, and self-discipline ends in themselves. In writing on the education of the boys, he revealed his gloomy view of his time: "Should I . . . teach deceit, dishonor, ruthlessness, bestial force to the children in order that they survive? Better that they perish. It is sophistry to speak of two sets of virtues, there is but one: virtue is an end in itself. . . . Honor and honesty, compassion and truth are good even if they kill you, for they alone give life its dignity and worth."[3] He was here writing of "the unassailable kingdom" of Marcus Aurelius, which is simply a moral state where absolute virtue reigns supreme. It is "unassailable" as it remains with us whatever happens. It was not to Christian humility but to this "remaining fastness" that he hoped to guide his adopted sons. As their first books the "young Enzios" received the gospels and the *Meditations* of Marcus Aurelius. In this choice their educator had drawn the lines for an intellectual conflict between Christianity and Stoicism that in Walker Percy's fiction remained unresolved.

William Alexander Percy rejected truths that are considered fundamental by most Christians. He wrote, "We trouble our hearts with foolish doubts and unwise questionings—the fear of death, the hope of survival, forgiveness, heaven, hell. Rewards and punishments hereafter? What bribes we ask for our perfunctory righteousness! . . . There should be no question of reward: to function is the task assigned" (*LOL*, 320–21). He found that the prodigal son could have stayed in a more sanitary place than the hog-wallow, that he did not deserve a party but a whipping, and that the hardworking son, who did not go and get himself "hog-smelly," was quite right in being upset about the party for his brother (*LOL*, 28). This was a natural reaction for a man who believed in character, talent, and performance. He realized that the instruction offered his wards by the churches was not what he wanted for them; their teachings seemed but a burden. In his poem "Enzio's Kingdom" he wrote:

> When I have made my tablet of the laws
> To guide the flight of my young Enzios,

'Thou shalt not' shall be missing from its rubric.
Perhaps two words will make its decalogue:
'Courage: Unselfishness.' These two suffice.[4]

He knew that the standards he offered had already been defeated; and he knew that if they were to accept his standards, they would appear as boys left over from the age of chivalry. But, as he asked himself, "What could I teach them other than what I myself had learned?" He shared the concerns of the southern aristocrat, who thought churches more palatable when they were behind rows of Greek columns. And he hoped people would return to the old standards, but he was not optimistic about it.

William Alexander Percy's concern with ethical standards became Walker Percy's concern. In his novelized philosophy there is always a tension between the inherited Stoicism and the adopted Catholic faith. For Uncle Will the main torment in life was what seems to be "eternal isolation" (*LOL*, 321). Loneliness was seen by him as the saddest fact of our existence; and Seneca, Epictetus, and Marcus Aurelius do not suggest ways to overcome this problem. This existential concern is also a part of Walker Percy's heritage. And the inadequacy of Stoic philosophy and evangelical Protestantism in the face of isolation and loneliness gave rise to Walker Percy's search for other values. But William Alexander Percy's Stoic ideas remain essential for an understanding of Walker Percy's fiction. From the start the novelist defined his fiction in relation to his uncle's ideas, as if he were having a crucial argument with him. In 1973 *Lanterns on the Levee* appeared in a new edition with an introduction by Walker Percy. There he states, "Even when I did not follow him, it was usually in *relation* to him, whether with him or against him, that I defined myself and my own direction" (*LOL*, xi). There is no reason this statement should be in the past tense, for Walker Percy was still defining himself and his characters in relation to what Uncle Will taught him. There are several passages in his early work that attest to William Alexander Percy's presence in his mind. In the early 1930s the influence made itself felt in the poems and reviews he wrote while he attended Greenville High School. In *The Pica*, the high school paper, the young Walker Percy published an interesting poem, "If I Were King." One of the more notable lines asserts, "No sloth I'd be if I were King."[5]

Under the influence of the social issues of the 1950s, Walker Percy became increasingly aware of the gap between his uncle's Stoicism and his own thinking. He had an intuition of man's radical dependence in this world which did not justify his uncle's stress on individualism. Walker Percy's 1956 essay "Stoicism in the South" reflects the conflict in his mind. He maintains that through the centuries the South has managed to have the stoa beside the church, "one for living in, the other for dying in."[6] The Old South, Percy claims, always had a stronger Greek flavor than it ever had a Christian. He argues that the South is still on the porch with Marcus Aurelius and suggests that it is time to leave the stoa behind: "The Southern gentleman did live in a Christian edifice, but he lived there in the strange fashion . . . of a man who will neither go inside nor put it entirely behind him but stands forever grumbling on the porch. From this vantage point he caught sight of Pericles and Hector and the Emperor, and recognized them as his heart's elect. Where was to be found their like? In Abraham? In Paul? He thought not. When he named a city Corinth, he did not mean Paul's community. How like him to go into Chancellorsville or the Argonne with Epictetus in his pocket; how unlike him to have had the Psalms."[7]

In his essays from the 1950s and 1960s, Percy again and again referred to the Stoicism in the southern mind. In "The Failure and the Hope" (1965) Percy repeated his praise for the old Stoic tradition, but he allowed that it possessed "fatal weaknesses" (primarily that it was based on personal relationships and did not possess resources for renewal) and that it could not offer a viable alternative to racism. He recalled "the gentle tradition" with "affection and admiration" but found that its code had little relevance in the social and political order of the day. And again he implored the old-style, quasi-Christian gentleman of the South to get off the porch and into the church. Percy's polemical essays from this period no doubt amount to a rejection of Stoicism, but it is a peculiarly loving rejection. In January 1985, I asked him about his view of southern Stoicism. He replied: "Stoicism is the main southern ethos, which is not ordinarily recognized. . . . Everybody took Greek and Latin. And they called their cities Corinth, Ithaca, and Demopolis. All well-educated southern gentlemen knew their Cicero and their Horace, their Virgil and their Seneca, as well as their Marcus Aurelius. People don't usually know how strong the Greco-Roman tradition was among the educated classes."[8]

The reassessing of ethical heritage that Percy has accomplished is characteristic of the present mode of southern fiction. The existential search is not the only search; Percy is also struggling to comprehend the nature of memory and history. This possibly with the idea that it will ultimately prove to be one search, whether we seek answers in the past or in our present existence. *The Moviegoer* is an engaged analysis of man's situation in the twentieth century. Brainard Cheney reviewed this first Percy novel in the *Sewanee Review*, and his piece was praised by Percy.[9] Cheney claimed that Binx and Kate are left at the end of the novel in "Christian swaddling clothes" and that the moviegoer discovers "a candle-lit footpath" to faith. Whereas it is clear that at the end of the novel "grace has somehow *rubbed off*" on Binx, it is difficult to find an overt acceptance of faith. Binx is Percy's John Falstaff, a man of the little way, a man who finally turns out to be determined by the heritage of Aunt Emily, who is a true Stoic and who thinks that the world makes perfect sense without God. Binx may not understand or accept Aunt Emily's Stoic values, but as he matures, he acts in accordance with them. The facts of the ending of *The Moviegoer* are that we leave Binx at the ethical stage of existence, fighting physical and mental illnesses. In the final scenes Binx does behave like a responsible citizen, and everything he does, Marcus Aurelius would have applauded. But he is still dislocated, still caught between the Stoicism of his father's family and the Catholicism of his mother's family, and he is still exiled from both traditions. Like Percy himself, Binx is forever trying to combine individual ethical responsibility with faith in revealed knowledge. It may only be a short way from belief in the revealed knowledge of fundamentalism to the mysteries of the Catholic faith, but as Percy's fiction reveals, the journey from the sanctity of the inner self of Stoicism to the sanctity of the "we" of the Catholic community is arduous.

Williston Bibb Barrett of *The Last Gentleman* loves to hear his father's stories of their ancestors. He admires his father, who gave speeches on topics such as *noblesse oblige* and the importance of character, which are also important subjects in *Lanterns on the Levee*. Will Barrett reads Douglas Freeman's *R.E. Lee*; and in his mind he is constantly correcting Confederate foul-ups before they happen. At Princeton he blows up a small Union monument because it offends him (*LG*, 267). And when he is accused of being absentminded, Will admits that he was "thinking of the summer of 1864." He occasionally finds that the southern Stoic in him surfaces when he is most in need of it. At one point, when he is being ignored but needs the quick help of a nurse, Will finds the voice of his ancestors: "'Nurse,' he said sternly, four feet away. He actually raised a forefinger. She answered the telephone. All at once time fell in. . . . He seemed to be listening. 'You hear me, goddamn it,' thundered a voice terrible and strange. It was for the two of them to listen as the voice went on,'—or else I'm going to kick yo' ass down there.' An oddly Southern voice, then not his surely. Yet her glossy eyes were on *him*" (*LG*, 394). The voice may not be Will's, but it is surely a part of his voice. The southern stoa may have been "discredited as a viable way of life in the twentieth century," as Ellen Douglas phrases it,[10] but in the critical situation where Will Barrett is faced with his duty toward another, the force of the stoic thought exerted upon him reveals itself. But Will is also a representative modern man; he is insecure and concerned with what the world is coming to, and he is lonely. The battle formations of the lingering Stoicism that is Will's heritage and the Christianity that he hopes will help him are clearly visible.

When we meet Will Barrett again in *The Second Coming*, he is uncured of his malaise, and he is still preoccupied with the past. He distinguishes between two versions of the old Stoicism—one, represented by a Greener and *Ivanhoe*, which he inherited from his grandfather; the other, which is from his father, is represented by a Luger and *Lord Jim*. They both had enemies; the grandfather, like Ivanhoe, hated his enemies. Like Jim, Ed Barrett, Will's father, felt guilty and had only one hated enemy: himself. He hated his death-in-life existence so much that he decided to kill himself and planned to kill Will, too. Years later Will imagines that he hears his father urging him to kill himself: "Go like a man, for Christ's sake, a Roman, here's your sword" (*SC*, 337). Will tries to get away from this "secret love of death" by doing the exact opposite of his father. Because his father did not, he tries to believe in the Christian God, but does not succeed. His father's brand of Stoicism is summed up for him by Ewell McBee, who heard Ed Barrett tell "a preacher" how to define "a soul": "A soul is a man like you and me and Ewell here. You want to know what a man is? I'll tell you. A man is born between an asshole and a peehole. He eats, sleeps, shits, fucks, works, gets old and dies. And that's all he does. That's what a man is" (*SC*, 176). This is not Stoicism according to Epictetus or Marcus Aurelius. The primitive summing up of our existence is realistic enough, but it ignores the noble principles and codes that Ed Barrett also believed in. But in his irritation with this "savior of souls" he reveals his defiant despair. To the *Los Angeles Times* Percy explained that in this novel Will "actually sees a possibility of achieving love, work that he likes, a sense of identity, . . . freedom to choose for himself, and he demands the presence of God on top of that."[11] And Percy thinks it is clear that he gets it. That Will's achievement is topped by the bonus of the presence of God is about as clear as Binx Bolling's footpath to faith at the end of Percy's first novel. Throughout *The Second*

Coming the reader has been waiting for Will to act in order to set things right, and he finally does. In a Stoic effort to make life tolerable for the people about him, he decides to put to work all the old, bored, maimed, and generally miserable people in a project of building log cabins. Will finally accepts that he has to create his own answers and sets about ordering life for himself and others. What Will actually does would have been praised by the emperor.

Lancelot is a moralist concerned with the lapse of decorum and values, and he is disgusted with the cynicism and corruption of the present. He finds it difficult to live with dignity in a pornographic age. His story is an unpleasant statement of man's moral, psychic, and spiritual impotence. Behind Lancelot's perpetual jeremiad we can hear the voice of William Alexander Percy, and it is echoed by Walker Percy in a *Paris Review* interview, where he explains that his anger is caused by "the widespread and ongoing devaluation of human life in the western world." Lancelot's disgust with the modern world makes him plan a new society based on Stoic precepts, and this time Percy lines up his battle formations so that they are impossible to overlook. In another interview Percy explained: "instead of dealing overtly with Christianity, I deal with the old Roman ethic: what's wrong with him taking revenge in the way he did? Would Aunt Emily object to that? What he is doing is carrying Aunt Emily's ethic to its logical conclusion. If he has been cuckolded by somebody, a Hollywood producer, then what he does is *kill* him. That's what Ulysses did, and we look on Ulysses as one of the great heroes of Western culture. Ulysses and Telemachus kill everybody! Lancelot only kills three people. . . . And we applaud Ulysses" (*Con.*, 209). Percy brings it down to an either/or. The choice is between Lancelot and Percival, his Christian counterpart. The choice is also between the tradition of the stoa and that of the church, which may well be the reason why the book never became popular in the South. Percy tries to force his reader off the porch and into the church, but he has a hard time ridding himself of the Stoic stand in *Lancelot*. And it is no wonder, for he realizes the values that will be sacrificed if Lancelot's ideas are rejected. It is painful for a southerner to bracket Robert E. Lee with Adolf Hitler and Idi Amin because they all ordered killings, but a good Christian does not kill under any circumstances.

Lancelot represents the madness of our Judeo-Christian Western culture, but is he more insane than he has to be to survive in the society in which he lives? He makes some frightening statements about life in the Western world, but it is much too convenient to write him off as a madman. If Lancelot were indeed mad and therefore *not* responsible for his life, the moral questions raised through his actions would be uninteresting. If Lancelot were mad, his opinions would not have caused Father John's rediscovery of his faith, for he would probably not have attempted a dialogue with a mad person. Like Hamlet, Lancelot is "but mad north-north-west; when the wind is southerly [he knows] a hawk from a handsaw." Lancelot chooses the Stoic tradition as an instrument to tackle the problems of the modern world, and his reasoning cannot be written off as madness just because it is a secular revolution that he plans. "No, Lancelot is not beyond the reach of Percival and accordingly Lancelot is not beyond hope," as Percy has stated.[12] But Lancelot Andrewes Lamar is so deeply rooted in the Stoicism of the Old South that it would be impossible for him to start a new order from scratch—the Stoic past will be too much with him. It is because of his heritage that he feels the necessity to plan a new life in Virginia; and if he had lived in the twentieth century, the emperor would probably accept the need for a new order and perhaps even sanction Lancelot's plans.

The alluring tale of how Lancelot in the tradition of Western culture defended his family heritage by revengeful murders has awaited Percy's further rejection. But in *The Second Coming* Will Barrett combined Stoic and Christian thinking in an effort to help the elderly. In *The Thanatos Syndrome* it becomes clear that Percy now polarizes abstract scientism and Christianity as the extreme opposites. Percy has said, "My purpose is . . . to challenge science, as it is presently practiced by some scientists, in the name of science."[13] The idea is already clearly present in *Lost in the Cosmos*, where Dr. Aristarchus Jones plans to leave the genetically defective children behind on the dying planet Earth, as these children do not fit into his plans for a new society on another planet. His new society is to be based on reason and science; it will be a society "freed from the superstitions and repressions of religion" (*LC*, 246). Colonel John Pelham, CSA, known as "the Gallant Pelham," artillery officer under General J. E. B. Stuart, personifies old Stoic values in this book. On a *Donahue* show he lectures the audience on a gentleman's obligations. With Epictetus he believes that man achieves freedom through self-discipline; and even though he respects religious convictions, he believes that right behavior has little to do with religion (*LC*, 53). Because he reminds them of a character from *Gone with the Wind*, Colonel Pelham is well received by the *Donahue* audience.

In *Love in the Ruins* Percy gives us a frightening portrait of the demise of Western culture. As always in Percy's fiction, hope lies in putting into practice the Christian ethic, which in this novel is personified by the rather stoic Father Rinaldo Smith. The priest tells Tom More that he should think about doing his job, be a better doctor, and worry about people and the state of his unhappy country, and he advises him to stop daydreaming (*LR*, 399). When we meet Tom More again in *The Thanatos Syndrome*, he has just been released from Fort Pelham, after two years at this minimum security facility. Significantly, he was detained for trafficking in drugs; it was a minor offense that nevertheless anticipated Van Dorn and Comeaux's use of science in their gnostic attempts to improve on man. The time in Fort Pelham has restored Tom More's humanity, if not his faith (*TS*, 81). He returns to become an ally for Father Smith's Christian forces against an enemy that worships human intelligence. The nature of the enemy is revealed in "Father Smith's Confession." What Tom More should do to stop the scientists from experimenting on the people of Feliciana is implied in Father Smith's account of what he did not do or understand in Germany in the 1930s. This is why Father Smith talks of "the Louisiana Weimar psychiatrists" (*TS*, 252). Helped by the stoical Vergil Bon and Uncle Hugh Bob, Tom More does stop the "Blue Boy" heavy sodium experiment. By forcing Comeaux to transfer them to Father Smith's hospice, Tom More saves the infants who are considered undesirable specimens and therefore candidates for a swift "mercy killing." All in all, this is not a bad achievement for a man living in the Age of Not Knowing What to Do. Marcus Aurelius would be pleased with Tom More.

It is not Walker Percy's theological insight that makes him an important artist but his accomplishment in the art of fiction. Percy wants to testify to the consequences of God's becoming incarnate, and he has chosen to do so not through theology but in his fiction and through a discussion with his heritage. It is obviously impossible for the Catholic Percy to rid himself of the Stoic Percy or to extricate one from the other; instead, he can use his heritage to define his faith. Stoicism and Christianity are not necessarily antithetical, although it has taken Percy some time (and his critics somewhat longer) to realize this. What Percy shows us about his ethical Stoic heritage is *not* that there is something wrong with it but that Stoicism is not enough. He does not reject his inherited Stoicism, but he warns of its limits: for the Christian it is not enough to do the right thing for the preservation of "the unassailable kingdom."

Peggy Whitman Prenshaw

Elegies for Gentlemen: Walker Percy's *The Last Gentleman* and Eudora Welty's "The Demonstrators"

In a special supplement to the April 1965 issue of *Harper's* magazine, "The South Today," edited by Mississippian Willie Morris exactly one hundred years after the surrender of Robert E. Lee to General Grant, Walker Percy wrote one of his most direct responses to the 1960s civil rights movement in the United States. Entitled "Mississippi: The Fallen Paradise," the essay expressed Percy's analysis of southern history and his response to the contemporaneous violence and social upheaval that characterized the region in the early sixties. "During the past ten years," he wrote, "Mississippi as a society reached a condition which can only be described, in an analogous but exact sense of the word, as insane. The rift in its characters between a genuine kindliness and a highly developed individual moral consciousness on the one hand, and on the other a purely political and amoral view of 'states' rights' at the expense of human rights led at last to a sundering of its very soul" (168).

In Percy's view, the sorry, insane state of affairs represented a desecration of the honor and courage demonstrated by the brave youths of the Confederacy, notably the Mississippi regiment made up of university students who died, to a man, in a charge at Gettysburg. Nowhere is the desecration more visible, he said, than in the uses to which the Confederate flag had been put: "Once the battle ensign of brave men, it has come to stand for raw racism and hoodlum defiance of the law."

Nonetheless, for all his stinging indictment of racism, terrorism, and moral cowardice, he does not wholly remove himself to the high road. "No ex-Mississippian is entitled to write of the tragedy which has overtaken his former state with any sense of moral superiority. For he cannot be certain in the first place that if he had stayed he would not have kept silent—or worse. And he strongly suspects that he would not have been counted among the handful, an editor here, a professor there, a clergyman yonder, who not only did not keep silent but fought hard" (166).

As Mississippians and the rest of the world have been reminded in 1989, the twenty-fifth anniversary not only of the Voting Rights Act but of the murder of three civil rights workers in Philadelphia, Mississippi, and of countless other acts of terrorism, Mississippi in the mid-1960s was a frightening, violent state that tested the ethics, religion, and common decency of its people. In many ways it was a war zone, in which white moderates were forced to stand either with the white racists or, denouncing them, with the black civil rights activists and their northern supporters. These were days I myself lived through, difficult days that I remember with pain and guilt and, still now, with much of the confusion I felt at the time. It seemed then that one's choices were few: to acquiesce to the racism, that is, to keep the peace with one's neighbors and friends and family, or to join the opposing crusade—or leave. I left Mississippi in 1963, certainly for the reason I gave myself and others—to return to graduate school—but more certainly because I could not face the choice before me.

One Mississippian who did not leave, who shared Percy's revulsion against the hate-filled mobs, the demagogic governor, the murders, assaults, and church burnings—and one who brought at the time more maturity and understanding to the society than I did—was Eudora Welty. Several months after Percy's essay appeared in *Harper's*, she wrote a short piece in the *Atlantic*, entitled "Must the Novelist Crusade?" which directly took up the question of what response should be expected of Mississippi's writers in the face of the civil rights violence. Incited to write by a flip comment, "in some respectable press," calling for a reassessment of Faulkner because he was, "after all, only a white Mississippian," she delivered a sharp, if not quite angry, statement of her view of the moral responsibility of the artist in a society, imperfect or otherwise. Decidedly, it is not to crusade, which nearly always yields bad art, but to take life "as it already exists, not to report it but to make an object, toward the end that the finished work might contain this life inside it, and offer it to the reader. . . . Inherent in the novel is the possibility of a shared act of the imagination between its writer and its reader."[1]

Three years after the publication of these two essays, Carlton Cremeens opened an interview with Percy by asking him his view of Welty's position. Percy was tactful ("I can't say whether I think Eudora Welty is wrong and that I know what the right answer is"), but he did go on unequivocally to press a different position. "I don't quite agree with her. . . . I still think a writer, . . . particularly a prominent writer like Eudora Welty, who is influential, highly respected, can do a great deal of good, can have a great deal of influence without compromising her creative endeavors. My own feeling is: I don't mind saying or writing what I think on the social issues or the race issue in the South" (*Con.*, 17).

The differences between Welty's and Percy's readiness to take on a public role, to speak with the authority of the "influential writer," may be attributed to temperament, gender roles, or many other influences, but not, I think, to courage or a lack of it. To Welty, the domain of the writer is literary; as she sees it, she has no call on the public other than as readers of her fiction, and only then to the extent that her art warrants their attention because of its power and excellence. In her view, this is a field quite large enough for any writer to display his or her colors. "Morality as shown through human relationships," she writes, "is the whole heart of fiction, and the serious writer has never lived who dealt with anything else" (*ES*, 148).

On the subject of what makes serious, lasting art, Welty and Percy express few if any disagreements in their essays and interviews of the 1960s and early 1970s. For example, Welty's focus upon the "generality" as the necessary weapon for the crusader-novelist, which turns out to be, ironically, exactly the armament that defeats the fiction, is also a point iterated by Percy. Welty writes, "On fiction's pages, generalities clank when wielded. . . . They are fatal to tenderness and are in themselves non-conductors of any real, however modest, discovery of the writer's own heart" (*ES*, 148). In the Cremeens interview, Percy echoes her warning about fatal generalities, castigating in that conversation, as he has done elsewhere, fiction that is written to illustrate sociology. "When you start writing novels to illustrate sociology you are going to write bad novels, because sociology is a simplification, an abstraction from what is the case" (*Con.*, 19–20).

The positions Percy and Welty take during this period concerning what *is* the main function of the novelist are close, both emphasizing the creation of universal particulars that catch and reflect in fiction the "home truths" of life. As we read such fiction, writes Welty, we "see ourselves in our own situation, in some curious way reflected. . . . Truth is borne in on us in all its great weight and angelic lightness, and accepted as home truth" (*ES*, 152). "My theory," says Percy, "is that the purpose of art is to transmit universal truths of a sort, but of a particular sort. . . . What the artist does, or tries to do, is simply to validate the human experience and to tell people the deep human truths which they already unconsciously know" (*Con.*, 23–24).

During the 1960s both writers created fiction set in the contemporaneous South, fiction that embodied their theories about art, the relation of particular experience to universal truths, and the possibilities for mutual respect between the races in the South. Although neither "The Demonstrators" nor *The Last Gentleman* is concentrated exclusively upon the social milieu—these are not finally fictions of politics or manners —we can recover through these works much of the complex experience of white southerners who remained in the South during this difficult, turbulent era.

In "The Demonstrators," published in the *New Yorker* in 1966, it was very much Welty's aim to show the complexity of the southern experience of the civil rights movement, as she told Jan Nordby Gretlund in a 1978 interview. In the same year she spoke at greater length about the short story to Tom Royals and John Little, noting that the story reflected "the way we were deeply troubled in that society and within ourselves at what was going on in the sixties. . . . The effect of change sweeping all over the South—of course, over the rest of the country too, but I was writing about where I was living and the complexity of those changes. I think a lot of my work then suggested that it's not just a matter of cut and dried right and wrong. . . . I wanted to show the complexity of it all."[2]

"The Demonstrators" takes place in Holden, Mississippi, a fictional Delta town somewhat smaller than Percy's Greenville, or Ithaca of *The Last Gentleman*, more nearly resembling Yazoo City, on the edge of the Delta, a town Welty had many occasions to visit during a period in the 1960s when her mother was being cared for in a nursing home there. The central figure in the story, Dr. Strickland, moves through the town late one Saturday night, treating the aging, imperious (and impervious) Miss Marcia Pope, the terminally ill mayor, Herman Fairbrothers, one of the ruling white elite who runs the town, and finally, and most centrally and dramatically, a young black woman, Ruby Gaddy, and her lover-assailant, Dove Collins, both victims and perpetrators of a violent Saturday night stabbing. In a brilliantly visual scene, the doctor goes to Ruby Gaddy's house, where family, friends, and casual onlookers crowd in and around the bedroom where the woman lies dying. At first he does not recognize her as the maid who regularly cleans his office, so intently does he focus upon the details of the assault, her wound, her breathing—all the discrete symptoms the physician is skilled at observing. Then, like a chorus, the onlookers ask, "Don't you know her?"—as if "he never were going to hit on the right question."[3]

The central theme of this story, mirrored in the title, concerns the struggle of men and women to wrest separate selves from generic human identities. The pun implicit in the title is elaborated in the story through Strickland's perspective, through his developing sense that, although we are all "demonstrators"—one might say exemplars—of our place and time and family and ideology and all the other shaping influences that compose us as a character-self who goes through the motions of living, we are also demonstrators rebelling against anonymity and interchangeability, demanding to be recognized as a unique self, a phenomenon that cannot be known and described by the banner or headline or family name attached to us.

Patterns of duality reflecting the tension between the outer, stereotypical person and the private self occur throughout the story, but most notably in two major sections, one portraying the doctor's visit to the dying Ruby Gaddy and the other presenting a long news article, ostensibly reporting the details of assault. In this story-within-the-story, which bears the headline "TWO DEAD, ONE ICE PICK. FREAK EPISODE AT NEGRO CHURCH," with the subheading, "No Racial Content Espied," Welty satirizes small-town, white southern newspapers, prejudices, pretensions, ideologies—and, in doing so, suggests the similarity to earlier, briefer mentions in the story of a youthful Vietnam protester who burned his draft card before a camera and of another youth, a civil rights worker entertained by Strickland and his wife. The young man had given out to reporters a story that some of his group had been forced at gunpoint to pick cotton in June in one-hundred-degree heat—a statement false to the facts of cotton growing, as well as false to the facts of his case, but nonetheless true to his politics, as he points out.

As demonstrators, crusaders, racists, defenders of the faith, healers of the sick, or as those enacting any other role, ad infinitum, that men and women perform, they repress if not betray the self, Welty suggests. Living for causes, whether for other people or for ideas, is risky business, so easily can one forget or even lose the self and thus lose the medium by which one apprehends the living of life. The self must exist in the moment, aware of sensation, reflective, remembering and anticipating what is to come, always exposed to loneliness and despair, if it is to exist at all. Welty's Dr. Strickland understands the problematical self, but he is too passive or impotent to mediate successfully the claims of the Other—the transcendent claims of social roles or larger callings —and the needs of the self. He is not, however, paralyzed by despair, despite the fact that his wife has left him, his daughter has recently died, and his town is stricken by division and death. He is wearied, sick, "even bored with the intractability that divided everybody and everything"—but he still makes his calls, can still feel comforted by a kindly act of hospitality, and, in a sudden moment of human connection, can still feel the joy of being alive. Visited briefly by the sensation that "there was still allowed to everybody on earth a *self*—savage, death-defying, private," he responds with a pounding heart that "was like the assault of hope, throwing itself against him without a stop, merciless" (*CS*, 618). Here is the problematical condition of Welty's white southerner in the 1960s, in which a man or woman who would possess a self may do so only fitfully and even then, it seems, by means of an indulgent or nostalgic retreat from action.

In his 1980 study of Southern Renaissance writers, Richard King largely excluded women writers from his analysis, because, as he wrote, "they did not place the region at the center of their imaginative visions."[4] In the past, I have quarreled with King's assumptions and conclusions about southern women writers, but in one sense he is doubtless correct that a writer such as Welty does not place the South at the center of her imagination. To do so is to privilege ideology and generalization over the sentient and phenomenal—idea over experience—and in her essays and her fiction she clearly rejects this ordering. It is instructive to read "The Demonstrators" along with the two longer works Welty was engaged in writing at the same time in the 1960s—*The Optimist's Daughter* and *Losing Battles*—as explorations of the possibility of bridging idea and act, the Cartesian mind and body, or, particularly for Welty, of merging the Yeatsian dance and dancer.

In the 1960s Walker Percy was, of course, exploring similar ground, even though his coming to the writing of fiction and his sense of southern identity were very different from Welty's. A physician trained in science, student of existential philosophy, Catholic convert, and son of a powerful and respected Mississippi family, Percy imagined protagonists whose fitful, uncertain sense of self is partly the consequence of the abstracting, objectifying modern age and partly the consequence of their being simply sick, or lost, or abandoned. Distantly separated from trustworthy guides who can help to show them how to live, they exist, at least in Will Barrett's case in *The Last Gentleman*, not in life but in the state of pure possibility.

There are many interesting points of comparison one might offer in a reading of *The Last Gentleman* alongside "The Demonstrators." For example, the physician, Sutter Vaught, exemplifies the danger to the self of extreme self-consciousness and of the modern inclination to abstract and analyze life, thus losing the self to transcendence, losing the necessary connection with felt life, immanent life. By contrast, Welty's Dr. Strickland faces the danger of immanence grown lush and choking, an everydayness that numbs and distracts the self. But, as I have noted, Strickland cannot be fairly described as despairing. One might make the case that he lives in bad faith—the story allows for this possibility —but Percy's existential world is not really Welty's world, and it is just as arguable that Strickland occupies the territory William Barrett is trying to reach.

In both "The Demonstrators" and *The Last Gentleman* the authors portray a South that is halfway transformed into a generic U.S.A. and halfway holding to a distinctive past that moves increasingly toward self-parody. The prosperous Vaughts, with their Chevrolet agency and a purple castle situated beside Birmingham golf links, would be unremarkable rich Americans were it not for their eccentric children, who redeem them from ordinary consumerism. The remnants of Barrett's family in Ithaca, Mississippi, and Shut Off, Louisiana, along with the rest of the country watch television—the aunts glued to "Strike It Rich" and Uncle Fannin and the black servant Merriam enjoying "Gunsmoke" together. When Percy shows the South consciously maintaining its traditions, it is a scene of violence at the college attended by Will and the younger Vaughts, a scene closely resembling the riots at the University of Mississippi in 1962, when James Meredith was enrolled. Whereas Barrett's great-grandfather had responded to violent racism with a pistol on his hip, "like a Western hero" (*LG*, 9), Will fumbles and stumbles and finally proves victim to a thrashing flagstaff.

A well-known passage early in the novel summarizes the history of the family that has produced this last gentleman, Will Barrett. It is a family that over the years "had turned ironical and lost its gift for action," losing thereby the means by which a man could define himself —and the community could know him—as a gentleman. Lacking a mode of action, the man who would be gentleman can in no way enact himself and thus can only turn inward and go in search of his soul.

In many respects the racial matter in *The Last Gentleman* is peripheral
to the protagonist's central movement from engineer to pilgrim, though
in some significant ways racial identities and relationships give Will
Barrett important information about falsity, courage, and human connection. The episodes involving Forney Aiken, the thoroughgoing liberal who proposes to authenticate his photographic series on blacks
by darkening his skin, thus transforming himself into a "pseudo-
Negro," provide some of Percy's sharpest satire and occasions for
Barrett's zaniest bafflement. Forney Aiken's words and actions never
match—he is a parody of the doublespeaking media sociologist, agent
of deceit and disguise, a hail-fellow-well-met hyping "moral causes."
Will watches and listens intently to him and his companions, but they
seem as hopelessly dislocated as Will, offering no direction. They, along
with Sweet Evening Breeze, the black operator of the Dew Drop Inn
in Ithaca, do offer, however, a scenario that calls for courage of the
order displayed by Will's great-grandfather, facing the KKK grand wizard.

When the town deputy and his sidekick enter the inn, as if from
some familiar Hollywood scene, Barrett finally recovers a moment of
clarity such as, he imagines, his ancestor might have known. "For once
in his life he had time and position and a good shot, and for once
things became as clear as they used to be in the old honorable days"(*LG*,
325). In place of the grand wizard there is, to be sure, only Beans
Ross, but the conflict is sharp and sufficiently dangerous to galvanize
Barrett into action. The episode serves, in fact, as the initiating ritual
that allows Will to return to the house of his father, to hear again the
Brahms and the poetry, and finally to reenter the painful moment of
his suicide. Doing so, he experiences again his father's abandoning him,
seeing as an adult that his father had left without giving him any instruction that he could use to live his life.

As Will is grappling to figure out just what it is that his father had
missed, two intrusions interrupt his moment of concentration. They
are instructive here, for they signal to Barrett—and the reader—the
directions closed off to Will, leading nowhere. The laughter of the television audience, the happy group gathered in the studio of "Strike It
Rich," is utterly and transparently fake, and the appearance of a black
man, a man his own age, on the street outside the family home occasions no greeting, no exchange at all. "They looked at each other. There
was nothing to say. Their fathers would have had much to say: 'In
the end, Sam, it comes down to a question of character.' 'Yes suh, Lawyer Barrett, you right about that. Like I was saying to my wife only

this evening—' But the sons had nothing to say"(*LG*, 332–33). The old patriarchal and patronizing relation of white to black, the defining action of the southern gentleman, has disappeared.

The disappearance of roles and rules of behavior is manifest throughout the novel, an absence in part attributable to Barrett's amnesia but mainly the result of overwhelming social change and of vast moral uncertainty. Nowhere is the confusion more thorough than in Will's mistaking a group of civil rights demonstrators who have been incarcerated at the old fort on the river for a group of celebrants reenacting a Civil War battle. The spectacle is beyond Will's fathoming: "As unlikely a lot of Confederates as one could imagine—men and women! the men bearded properly enough, but both sexes blue-jeaned and sweat-shirted and altogether disreputable. And Negroes! And yonder, pacing the parapet—Good Lord!—was Milo Menander, the politician, who was evidently playing the role of Beast Banks, the infamous federal commandant of the infamous federal prison into which the fort was converted after its capture" (*LG*, 336). Shortly afterward, when Will visits his uncle, Fannin, in Shut Off, Louisiana, there is a brief reprise of the old, easy familiarity between white and black, though Fannin and Merriam's relationship is more nearly that of brothers than of master and servant. They give Will a glimpse of a loving connection, as they hunt and talk and watch television together. Still, an aura of nostalgia frames the scene, as it does when Welty's Dr. Strickland visits the house of the dying black woman. The ease of their friendship rests upon old assumptions about each one's place, and those assumptions disintegrate under the pressure of Barrett's—and Strickland's—self-consciousness, a self-consciousness about race made inevitable and inescapable by the events of the 1960s.

In a 1972 "Firing Line" interview that William Buckley conducted with Welty and Percy, Welty spoke of the increasing difficulty that self-consciousness poses for the southern writer. Pressed to talk about "the southern imagination," she was clearly uncomfortable about trying to abstract life as she has known it and offer up generalizations about the South. "The art of writing as a Southerner would now be a self-conscious thing to do," she said. "It never used to be. When we were coming along we just wrote because this is where we lived and what we knew. But to write strictly a Southern book now—I think you are quite conscious that you are seeing a segment and that people are going to look at it—" (*EW*, 96). Here and throughout the interview she was halting, tentative, and defensive. As Albert Devlin has pointed out in *Eudora Welty's Chronicle*, Percy was a more willing and forthcoming panelist than was Welty in answering Buckley's repeated questions about what composes the southern imagination. Whereas Percy recapitulated Allen Tate's thesis about the southern literary renascence and Vann Woodward's view of the burden of southern history, Welty resisted any interpretation of the South.[5] Instead, she tried to articulate what for her was most distinctive about southern culture, that is, its localized, personalized, "rooted" way of life, a culture she found particularly congenial for a writer: "If you grew up in the South when things were relatively stable, when there was a lot of talk and so on, you got a great sense of a person's whole life. . . . You get a narrative sense of your next door neighbor instead of someone you just meet in the supermarket. . . . You watch life and it is happening. Well, that is a novel" (*EW*, 97).

One senses in these comments Welty's regret for the loss of a South populated by people who know one another, a South not emptied out of particularity in the service of political positions and moral causes. There is probably more than a little nostalgia in her memory of people sitting on porches talking to one another, which is partly the nostalgia of the adult remembering her youth. Even more evident is Welty's yearning for relationships that connect human beings, yielding narratives that make life, like fiction, coherent. In "The Demonstrators" and the Fannin-Merriam episode of *The Last Gentleman*, however, both Welty and Percy suggest that old patterns of relations between blacks and whites are irremediably changed by the civil rights movement and so too the writing about these relationships. "The art of writing as a Southerner would now be a self-conscious thing to do," said Welty. What she does not say is that there is no escaping either the southernness or the self-consciousness.

In the 1960s the civil rights movement changed the way white southerners saw themselves. Whatever innocence they might have held about race relations before that decade ended with the bombing of a Birmingham church or the murder of three young men in Philadelphia, Mississippi. And, ironically, whatever good will that southern whites and blacks had built up over nearly two centuries seemed jeopardized and compromised. The civil rights movement brought needed and long-delayed societal change, but with great cost and confusion at the personal, individual level, which is the terrain available to the writer. "From a moral point of view," Percy explained in the "Firing Line" interview, "it is very simple. It's either right or wrong, and there was [in the South] a lot wrong. From a novelist's point of view, human relations are much more complex than saying that the white racist is wrong and the black protester is right" (*EW*, 99). Similarly, as Welty noted in the same interview, "the great complexity of it, how inexpressible some things are," had been the impetus for her writing "The Demonstrators."

For writer and for character alike, one has in this world only one's moment in history. The self is always partly imprisoned by social roles not of one's making and partly abandoned by a feckless past that offers one no useful direction; yet one struggles to maintain the self, struggles to have both a separate self and some transcendent connection that relieves the burden of death. It interests me that for Welty, as for so many women writers, the direct threat to the self nearly always lies in the direction of overly defining social roles and needy dependencies in relationships that overwhelm one, leaving too little of separateness or consciousness. By contrast, Percy suggests that the greater danger lurks for a self grown too solitary and egocentric, lost from daily connections and defining roles. Welty's protagonist ultimately draws upon connectedness and Percy's Will Barrett chiefly upon inwardness and self-consciousness to see them through the social trauma of their age and, at last, the pain of individual death.

In the final paragraphs of "The Demonstrators," Strickland watches the antic movements of a pair of flickers in the garden, showing off their plumage and, like the pigeons of *The Optimist's Daughter*, "probing and feeding" one another, demonstrating their vitality and their place in the natural chain. Then he thinks of his daughter, who had died the spring before, and of the dying Fairbrothers, and of his town, Holden, barely holding on. In the face of death, everywhere evident in this world, Strickland nonetheless moves toward the world. He picks up his bag and heads out, knowing that "it was all going to be just about as hard as seeing Herman and Eva Fairbrothers through."

At the conclusion of *The Last Gentleman*, Will Barrett calls out to Sutter Vaught, calls out as a son to a surrogate father, seeking instruction and understanding that will make life livable. Through his many trials he has tested and exposed the used-up forms of an earlier southern society, and he has borne witness to the death of the father and son—his father and the Vaught son, Jamie. All these have prepared Will for the next stage of the search, which will lead not so much toward the world as through it—a soul's progress toward God, or so we infer from *The Last Gentleman*. (*The Second Coming* will, of course, develop a somewhat different line of action.)

Despite the lamentable, insane state of the South in the 1960s, Percy and Welty both suggest that it yet provides a terrain where life can proceed. Their southern characters recollect the southern past with deep ambivalence, expressing an elegiac nostalgia as well as deep disillusionment, and yet it is through their recollecting the South that they go in search of those things of heaven and earth they hunger for.

Part III
Novelist and Existentialist

Marion Montgomery

Kierkegaard and Percy: By Word, *Away from* the Philosophical

In Kierkegaard's day, interviews with authors about their work were not yet the established literary genre as we know it: instant response under questioning about the secret meanings of the current book and the advance it represents over the last one. Kierkegaard submitted to endless interrogation, but with himself as questioner, even when attention is focused in the words beyond himself as writer. Nor is he much given to the pretensions of standing apart objectively to interrogate himself. His pursuit of the truth of things is much too important to him at a most personal level. Now the fiction writer, here Walker Percy, knows himself to be a personal presence in his work, no less than did Kierkegaard, knowing as well the aesthetic detachment demanded. Just what that detachment's nature is, is another matter; the arresting writer, novelist or philosopher, knows that the principle of detachment must have as its deepest intent a reconciliation of the person (the writer) with whatever purchase his words may make upon the true and the beautiful. One never escapes the "self's" entanglement in its own words. And surely it must be in part Percy's recognition of Kierkegaard's presence in his words, as well as the intellectual action underway, that proved arresting to Percy on his encounter at a crucial point, when he turned to writing, just as it was the severe detachment of Saint Thomas Aquinas in the *Summa theologica* that made Percy, early and late, declare both writers important to the development of his thinking from the outset.

We may only remark in passing the importance of Saint Thomas in orienting Percy's concerns for his own presence in his words, though we may not ignore it, given the announced concerns for Percy as novelist in relation to philosophical and theological dimensions in his novels. Still, our principal interest here is with a particular self-interview of Kierkegaard's in relation to Percy's own "Questions They Never Asked Me." Near the end of his life, Kierkegaard wrote his *Point of View for My Work as an Author*, subtitled *A Report to History*.[1] It was published posthumously. The central concern in the work is to make clear the strategy he thinks is required of himself as a writer in confronting a hostile world. Of that world he declares, in a footnote, "I have endeavoured to express the thought that the world, if not bad, is mediocre, that 'what the age demands' is foolishness and frippery, that in the eyes of the world the truth is ludicrous exaggeration; and that the Good must suffer" (n. 88). If such is one's vision of the world, then what strategy lies open to the writer who would bear an active witness to another world, to a Christian vision? Kierkegaard insists—and insists and insists—that one may do so only through an ironic indirection, by a deceit deliberately practiced against the age and its foolish demands upon an "author." Only through intellectual exercise of deliberate deceit toward inhabitants of this moment of history, persons given to foolishness and frippery, is it possible to bear effective witness to the truth. Given a world that is, if not bad, at best mediocre, it is only through a strategy of ironic indirection that an author with a Christian vision may gain a purchase upon that world.

Kierkegaard finds good precedent for his strategy in Socrates, as Percy does in Kierkegaard, a strategy he pursued with such disturbing effect upon the Danish academic establishment in his master's thesis, "The Concept of Irony, with Constant Reference to Socrates," at the outset of his intellectual career in 1841.[2] In his *Point of View*, his speaking from the grave, as it were, he defends and advances Socratic irony as the necessary device, given his fallen intellectual world as antagonist. Socratic irony allows the discomforting appearance of openness, whose effect in the end is to shock an audience —the world—into some recognition of the truth about itself. But shock whom? What audience does Kierkegaard address as primary in his posthumous speaking to the world? The subtitle suggests that his concern is focused upon an age subsequent to his own. This is a report to "history." Yet one can hardly read the book without suspecting that the actual, the primary audience is Kierkegaard himself and that he is intent upon a self-justification that "history" is welcome to overhear. He seems to be attempting, by an internal dialectical examination of his strategy and of himself as its agent—now viewed in retrospect—both to understand and to find acceptable his use of deceit, which he claims to have been divinely directed.

His writings, he asserts, are "the productions of an aesthetic character, which are an incognito and a deceit in the service of Christianity" (6). This is to say that the actual, central mind is that, not of the aesthetic person, but of the religious person. There are thus two present characters in this most singular person we call Kierkegaard. But the deceit practiced is by one of them, and the one least likely to be justified in deceitfulness—the religious person. The religious person assumes an aesthetic demeanor in the hostile world as a disguise through which to practice deceit in a purportedly magnanimous interest in the world. It is little exaggerated to say that Kierkegaard's magnanimity exhibits itself in this little book as a rage turned violently upon the object of his intended magnanimity, the world.[3] Percy differs in his address, more kindly given to human failures, which Kierkegaard treats as willful stupidities.

What this strategy intends he understands to require, to somewhat simplify, that he present himself to the world as a literary fop. Thus he would deceive the world into an encounter with the truth about itself. Not that there is no conflict between these two characters in one person, the aesthetic and the religious "selves" of Kierkegaard, for the "aesthetic always overrates youth and this brief instant of eternity," which is an individual's life in the world. And so the aesthetic person is always suspicious of the religious person. And since the world, dominated by the aesthetic, demands the foolishness and frippery of an aesthetic demeanor, that is the role the intentionally dominant religious self must play toward the mediocre intellects, mere "boys," who compose one's immediate worldly audience.

If this be so, however, is not the deception actually destructive of the truth toward which the strategy of deception intends to lead a lost age? This salient question, gnawing at Kierkegaard, he relegates to a footnote, casting the question as if it were raised to him by "a sharp witted observation" other than his own. He formulates the question: "If the notion that you are a spy is true, [is] your whole activity as an author . . . a sort of misanthropic treachery, a crime against humanity?" He responds to his own fierce formulation in a subdued manner, dependent more on paradox than on irony: "Oh yes, the crime is that I have loved God in a Christian way." He has not, he insists, attempted to give the age what it demands, having chosen to excoriate its spiritual complacency rather than soothe it. As for himself, in his own character, as opposed to his assumed role as a spy in God's service, he says, "I have nothing new to proclaim; I am without authority, being myself hidden in a deceit; I do not go to work straightforwardly but with indirect cunning; I am not a holy man; in short, I am a spy who in his spying, in learning to know all about questionable conduct and illusions and suspicious characters, all the while . . . is making inspection [of] himself under the closest inspection" (87).

In Walker Percy's "Questions They Never Asked Me So He Asked Them Himself," one encounters much the same insistence that, as author, he bears no special authority. He is not a holy man, and yet he serves a holy cause, the truth, in whose service he must conduct himself cautiously as a spy, but without such an open blowing of his cover as Kierkegaard makes in his report to history. Percy, too, walks up and down, to and fro, in his age, recording aesthetically that age for its own reflection of itself in its "aesthetic" illusions, the "author" assuming slyly, as it were, the office of devil's advocate. His indictment of the age is somewhat rescued from the intense jeremiad common in Kierkegaard by his recognition of himself as all too much a citizen of his age, though one might also conclude Kierkegaard's jeremiad to be in part a recognition of his own participation. But Percy is more open in his admissions and, in consequence, less strident. Indeed, Kierkegaard is at such temper in denying his own participation that one thinks he doth protest too much. Thus Percy accepts as a rather apt description of himself that he is "negative, . . . cold-blooded, aloof, derisive, self-indulgent, more fond of the beautiful things of the world than of God." And, being the formulator of the charge himself, he adds that he takes "a certain satisfaction in the disasters of the twentieth century" and even savors "the imminence of world catastrophe rather than world peace." His questioner who charges him with this characterization, we must remember, is Walker Percy himself, or the person of the self-interview purporting to be Walker Percy. The questioner adds, "You don't seem to have much use for your fellow Christians, to say nothing of Ku Kluxers, A.C.L.U.'ers, northerners, southerners, fem-libbers, anti-fem-libbers, homosexuals, anti-homosexuals, Republicans, Democrats, hippies, anti-hippies, senior citizens" (*Con.*, 176). (In such a catalog one imagines Kierkegaard insisting especially that junior citizens, youth, be added.) In his own name, Percy responds, "That's true—though taken as individuals they turn out to be more or less like oneself, i.e., sinners, and we get along fine." He can account for such circumstances of himself as sinner among sinners only "as a gift from God."

One could pursue similarities between Kierkegaard and Percy as self-reflecting "authors" at much greater length, but we have introduced a dissimilarity that is more profitable to discuss. In doing so, we may the better appreciate a comfort our age seems to find with Percy, in contrast to the discomfort it feels with Kierkegaard, though both may be said to be about the same Father's business in their world as each sees that business. The signal to dissimilitude is in the admission that he, Percy, is self-indulgent, more fond of the beautiful things of the world than of God. It is more pointedly present in his remark that "as individuals" those categorized and rejected through such labels as "northerners, southerners, . . . Republicans, Democrats," and so on, are suitable enough as individual company, since as individuals he and each of them are bound as sinners. There is for Percy a certain relief in the admission, as if in making it he is able to relax somewhat from what would otherwise be an elevated and severe calling as "author" that would deny him his humanity.

Kierkegaard, however, is fiercely Old Testament on the point, to which fierceness he brings a dialectic encounter that allows no moment of relaxation. One suspects that a sinner would find him an uncomfortable companion. From reading him, one would not likely choose him as a companion in strolls about Copenhagen, while Percy (one knows from his work) would be a hospitable guide to Covington, accepting one as a sinner among sinners without absolving either sinner by ignoring sin. To his own ironic view of his age and its demands, Percy brings a relieving humor out of his own sense of involvement in a fallen world, for humor almost always speaks a recognition that the individual sinner is beyond self-justification. For Kierkegaard, to judge from his witnessing words, only irony is available to allow one to participate safely in the fallen world.

Kierkegaard does recognize irony's dangers of self-entrapment, let us add at once. Irony, he says, tends essentially "toward one person as its limit." And he recalls Aristotle on the point that "the ironical man does all 'for his own sake'" (55). But if one relaxes through a humorous acceptance of oneself as sinner like all others, one forgoes the tragic dimension of the spiritual journey. Or so Kierkegaard would no doubt maintain. The sardonic, Percy's species of irony, allows pathos and humor but not tragedy, because it is so self-consciously turned upon the sardonic man as the primary object to be rescued. One must in some wise continue to be the ironical man for one's own sake as author, as God's spy, with a focus upon the age and what it demands lest a sardonic focus upon the self dissolve into self-pity or an ultimate despair of silence. Without that focus upon the age, the author in his role as prophet-spy to the age, found wandering in its spiritual wilderness, will be compromised.

Kierkegaard puts the point: "[E]veryone who has even a little dialectic will perceive that it is impossible to attack the System from a point within the System." That is a lesson he learned from Socrates, who nevertheless (we may note in passing) has a humorous streak, a playfulness one does not find Kierkegaard having learned from his hero of the dialectical. The Socrates dramatized by Plato is not above playful teasing, even in extreme moments. Thus he says, at the moment of his death (in the *Phaedo*), "Crito, we ought to offer a cock to Asclepius. See to it, and don't forget." Due to what illness suffered and recovered from does he find himself indebted to the god of medicine? Kierkegaard cannot pause for such whimsical commentary on a serious argument, the immortality of the soul and its struggle for immortality against the world.

Socrates has dealt with the world from inside it. But Kierkegaard insists that one can deal with it only from outside. "There is only one point, truly a spermatic point, the individual, ethically and religiously conceived and existentially accentuated," that is tenable, and it must be set sternly against all else. It is from such a "spermatic point" that one may declare, for instance, that "every revolt of science . . . against moral discipline, every revolt in social life . . . against obedience, every revolt in political life . . . against worldly rule, is connected with and derived from . . . revolt against God with respect to Christianity" (133). It is as if Kierkegaard must find and hold this "spermatic point" outside creation in general in obedience to a Calvinistic fatalism in him—as if to a Platonic dialectic he must superadd a strict determinism. Indeed, he is insistent that, as author, he *is* determined. He is the instrument of a consuming and unrelenting muse, meaning in one respect, as he says, that even he cannot understand his own writings in their wholeness (72), often discovering in them more than he understood them as saying when he wrote them. An intention is captured there larger than the writer's, and so the text becomes an inspired scripture.

Still, there is a "thorn" in this "spermatic point" called Kierkegaard which has to do precisely with the problem of consciousness in relation to the existence it would free itself from by moving outside the "System": the "I"—the "spermatic point"—is, alas, a system in itself that proves inescapable, enclosing at least the aesthetic and the religious persons. Kierkegaard attempts to alleviate the wound from this thorn through dialectic, through an encounter between his aesthetic and his religious selves. He wrestles, in a postpersonal way, if we may so put it, with the questions raised by consciousness about its own history, the questions we see Percy raising from time to time in relation to himself and his fictional protagonists that are projections of himself. An author, through the act of writing, may perhaps move toward a sort of self-forgetfulness that makes the spermatic point tenable. If the author were simply Percy's Tom More, the "writing" could be the dialectical exchange between More as doctor and his patient. Perhaps, then, through an interior dialectical engagement, the aesthetic self and the religious self of the writer might be reconciled, each absolved in dissolving into each other. As Kierkegaard puts it, "With regard to the movement described in a series of works as *away from* the philosophical, the systematic, to the simple, i.e. the existential, it is essentially the same movement as from the poet to religious existence" (132).

The thorn in Kierkegaard's flesh is at issue here, but it is not Saint Paul's thorn in the flesh, though it symbolically rises as such in his agitated concern over his love of Regine Olsen. That concern leads Percy to set a specific question and answer, in respect to his continuing fascination with Kierkegaard. Indeed, he recently responded in an actual (as opposed to a self-) interview that "if I had to blame [my conversion to Christianity] on someone," it would be on Kierkegaard. But in that interview Phil McCombs observes that "you and Kierkegaard don't agree on the idea of the hero getting the girl and God both," to which Percy responds, "Well, you see if he'd been Catholic he would have known better. He had this Protestant thing about sex."[4] But we must get beyond such a reduction of Kierkegaard's "thorn" to "sex," for it is the same thorn that agitates Percy himself. We come closer to this thorn when we hear Percy remarking upon the epigraphs he chose for his essay "The Message in the Bottle." He says, "One was from Kierkegaard saying that faith is not a form of knowledge; faith is something of inwardness or of something absurd. The other was from Thomas Aquinas, saying that faith is a form of knowledge. . . . I was always put off by Kierkegaard's talk about inwardness, subjectivity, and the absurd" (*Con.*, 120). One might remark here that in Thomas the forms of knowledge are more various than Percy seems to acknowledge, even as they are in Kierkegaard, who recognizes the role of systematic thought in relation to the subjectivity of instinctive faith. The movement he pursues is *away from* philosophy and toward instinctive faith, whereas it might be said of Thomas that he moves away from instinctive faith and toward systematic thought about instinctive faith.

"The Message in the Bottle," Percy goes on to say, "was a discussion, from my point of view, of the Gospel as a piece of news and how to place a piece of news in an information system, how to classify it as a serious statement." The difficulty here, in respect to Saint Thomas, lies in classifying a serious statement within an information system, as if such a statement might be certified by classification itself. It is the way more of science than of philosophy or theology, an appropriate way so long as it is understood in its limits. Saint Thomas's understanding of faith in the Gospels—the "Good News"—does not see it as fully "known" by the limits of rational knowing, whatever dangers one nevertheless finds in the inward or subjective.

One would need more words than are suitable to our present concerns to make the point substantial, so we must leave it resting at this: for Thomas, one of the forms of knowledge is the intuitive, the authority of which mode of knowing is much decayed in modern thought through impulsive distortions of inwardness and subjectivity. In such distortion, the intuitive loses its relation to its rational complement, especially in the minds who elevate the rational in opposing the intuitive—a course that science has been set upon to the extent that it has usurped the subtleties of philosophy and theology since the Renaissance. For Thomas, the form of thought is available to intellect both through the mode of knowing spoken of as *intellectus*—the mode of the intuitive—and through the complementary mode of knowing spoken of as *ratio*. One might even say that Thomas's understanding of the form of faith includes an initiating movement of intellect by intuition, so that Thomas encompasses Kierkegaard.[5]

Having introduced Saint Thomas to suggest how Percy finds him a necessary guide beyond Kierkegaard, let me suggest that Kierkegaard, like Percy, is very much troubled by the antithesis forced upon the two complementary modes of knowing, the intuitive and the rational, by modernist thought growing out of Renaissance thinkers, especially in the train of thought descending from Descartes. Rather, the rational and the intuitive are seen as contradictory, the frustration lying in the inescapable experience that we operate through one and then through the other. Intellect is seen as schizoid. Kierkegaard's concern for the dialectical struggle makes him central not only to modern philosophy but to modern science as well, most explicitly to particle physics, and we may not forget on this point Percy's intense concern for science in relation to philosophy, as both affect art. Modern science and modern philosophy are very much elements in his fiction.

Kierkegaard's concern to establish a "spermatic point" is a concern that his countryman Niels Bohr responds to, suggesting that one might pursue the presence of Kierkegaard in our world as he comes to us, not through poets and philosophers but through scientific engagements of the world, revealed tellingly in Richard Rhodes's *The Making of the Atomic Bomb*. It is a point of special interest to Percy's theme that, in *The Thanatos Syndrome*, he addresses the scientific distortions of the individual. To suggest the direction one might take in developing the point, we turn to one of Kierkegaard's countrymen by whom Kierkegaard is heavily influenced, Poul Martin Møller. In a little book that is (I am told) as popular with the Danes as the *The Adventures of Huckleberry Finn* formerly was with Americans, there is a passage very much to our purpose: "[I start] to think about my own thought of the situation in which I find myself. I even think that I think of it, and divide myself into an infinite regressive sequence of 'I's' who consider each other. I do not know at which 'I' to stop as the actual, and in the moment I stop at one, there is again an 'I' which stops at it. I become confused and feel a dizziness as if I were looking down into a bottomless abyss."[6]

One may suggest that here is the heart of the romantic agony so popular as theme to poet and critic alike since the eighteenth century. Which "I" is the real, essential I? Such is the thorn in Kierkegaard's flesh, as it is in so many of our recent philosophers and artists. Among the artists, particularly those stemming from Whitman in the American tradition, the problem is one I have called elsewhere the "infinitely recessive *I*." It leads to that counteraction whereby the poet sings the self as if it were the whole universe, as if it might thereby prevent the pull of the "I" into the abyss, our age's substitute for hell. In T. S. Eliot—and in Percy himself—the stay (the Møllerian *stop*) is found in irony, as it is found in Kierkegaard, for irony arrests the recessive "I," though one be stuck with that particular version of the self. In Eliot it was for a while the intellectual fop, even as in Kierkegaard, and there is a reduced figure of this fop in Binx Bolling of *The Moviegoer*. In that species of the sardonic as practiced by Percy, there is a craftiness whereby the stance taken teases toward a mutually sardonic encounter with the overwhelming question we have repeated from the "I" identified as Percy in his self-interview. That "I" is not the same Percy immediately on stage in "Questions They Never Asked Me *So He Asked Them Himself*." It lies behind those two fictional presences, the questioner and the answerer, though breaking into the drama at the very end: "You and I know something, don't we?" (*Con.*, 180). Very well, let us go then—you and I—to see what it is we think we know. But let us be cautious lest we suppose that the insidious discovery lies in the words of our tedious argument itself, rather than in our "selves."

Kierkegaard's attempt to arrest the recessive "I" lies in his dialectical self-interviews, as if thereby he may, through "a series of works . . . *away from* the philosophical [and] the systematic arrive at the simple, i. e. the existential." For him this is a movement from an existent "I" as poet to an existent, and presumably inclusive, "I" as religious person, for, despite his dependence upon the ironic as a mode of the "I's" journeying, he recognizes the danger of irony's arrested development. It is the danger that Eliot encounters and overcomes when he is able to surrender the ironic stance through that "awful daring of a moment's surrender / Which an age of prudence can never retract" in *The Waste Land*, for "by this, and this only we have existed" (lines 404–6). For Eliot, after this point in his life, the land of paradox opens with increasing attraction, as his ironic stance dissolves. It is a consequence of the opening of the "I" to an acceptance of the limits of its own being, an acceptance of the limits of knowing by the finite "I." We find in Kierkegaard's concern to move "away from the philosophic and systematic" a paradigm of the movement Eliot dramatizes in his dialectical poetry, from Prufrock's uncomfortable tea party to Eliot's own comfortable participation in the ambiguous mystery of the human person, the inclusive "I," in his *The Cocktail Party*. In that play, in contrast to the ironic complexity of "Prufrock," there is no longer the necessity to the "author" of an ironic dissociation from the complexities of human existence, from spiritual and intellectual creatures in the variety of their manifestations to the author, the "I" named T. S. Eliot. The point of introducing Eliot is that he is a figure intermediary between Kierkegaard and Percy, an important part of what Percy as author knows, though his relation to Percy has not been shown. We find the same movement in Percy as in Eliot, each coming to his own "fiction" by way of philosophy. One discovers parallels, I believe, between *The Moviegoer* and *The Thanatos Syndrome*, for instance, when juxtaposed to "The Love Song of J. Alfred Prufrock" and "Ash Wednesday." And the literary analogue to Percy's last novel, rich in parallels, is Eliot's *The Cocktail Party*.

The truth is that the infinitely recessive "I" is an ancient problem, inevitable to any self's self-consciousness. If this complex of the self in relation to the context of its being seems peculiarly modern, it is so for us because we have lost our grounding in our intellectual origins. In exploring Kierkegaard's intense address to the "I's" dilemma, his *Point of View for My Work as an Author*, we properly emphasize the universality of the problem. And perhaps the most suggestive way of emphasis is to observe that our quotation from Møller is not by way of Kierkegaard (who cites Møller in another point as of "pious memory") but from the passage as quoted by Niels Bohr in emphasizing the importance of philosophical meditations to science. Though perhaps detrimental to one's social existence, meditation may open the depths of being not only of the self but even of physics' mysteries, and even those of particle physics. The relation of Heisenberg to Bohr and the subsequent influence of Heisenberg's uncertainty principle (however often superficially taken) upon literary and philosophical speculations and practices leave us with the interesting irony of both philosophy's and criticism's return to problems of uncertainties in the recessive "I," out of science itself.

The presumption of an advance out of Heisenberg in respect to philosophical and literary matters, the reality that the advance proves rather a further regression, calls for ironic reflection upon the modernist dilemmas that rise up in social and political affairs out of science's potentials in the latest of science's modes of address to existence, something new confronting us with each new day. Such is the concern Percy increasingly turns to, and nowhere more explicitly than in *The Thanatos Syndrome*, the "philosophical" issues in which we discover us to ourselves as back at a beginning, despite presumptions of intellectual progress. Father Smith's sermon-confession at the novel's end underlines this point.

Kathleen Scullin

Lancelot and Walker Percy's Dispute with Sartre over Ontology

Percy wrote *Lancelot* twenty years after he wrote the essay "Symbol as Hermeneutic in Existentialism." In that essay, he disputed Sartre's ontology—his fundamental view of human being—but praised Sartre's insight into the human condition. Despite the time lapse between the two works, *Lancelot* is in effect Percy's response to Sartre in fiction. Percy's complex assessment of Sartre is helpful in examining the risks he took in writing *Lancelot* and why, perhaps, he took them. Percy credits Sartre with accurately describing the "predicament" of being human: the feeling of inner emptiness, of nothingness; the inability to know what one is, to discover an identity or name that fits; and the consequent desire to seek out ways of living in "bad faith"—assuming a false identity, an impersonation, to fill in the void. Moreover, both would agree that to live authentically means to recognize the uniqueness of one's situation, refuse to live in bad faith, and take responsibility for one's choices and actions.

Percy maintains, however, that Sartre's emphasis on the human predicament amounts to an elevation of psychology over ontology, that is, mistaking how it *feels* to be human with what it *is* to be human (*MB*, 286). For Sartre, the self, alone and empty, can sustain itself only by seizing the freedom to create a self out of its own nothingness. Other persons constitute a threat to that self-creation. For Percy, the self is rooted in connectedness with others and sustained in celebrating that connectedness—in language, in commitments to others, and in sacramental signs connecting one to God, the Other who is the ultimate ground of existence. For Percy, the other is the enemy only to an "unauthentic constitution of myself" (*MB*, 285).

Philosophically, Percy draws clear distinctions between what he rejects and what he admires in Sartre. But in writing *Lancelot*, he risked blurring the distinction by creating a protagonist who seems to dramatize a Sartrean view of the human being. Further, he risked letting Lancelot seem to go unanswered in the novel. I will argue that the novel ultimately constitutes a defense of Percy's own ontology because Lancelot's language reveals that he is not who he thinks he is. But Percy is willing to put his conviction to the test by letting the obvious elements of plot, characterization, and point of view build a case that appears to serve Sartre's ontology and not his own.

When Lancelot discovers Margot's adultery, he is jolted into a Sartrean course of action. That Lancelot needs to break out of the worn path of his life, both Percy and Sartre would agree. Before the discovery, Lancelot describes that life to the listeners: he "had done nothing but fiddle at law, fiddle at history, keep up with the news, . . . watch Mary Tyler Moore, and drink [himself] into unconsciousness every night" (*L*, 60). He had been living in bad faith, having surrendered his freedom "in order to possess, or try to possess, [his] being as a thing."[1] He had succumbed to what Percy calls "everydayness." When Lancelot becomes aware of being a self who can act, he breaks out of that pattern: he showers, shaves, does not take a drink, stays alert to watch and wait, no longer afraid of silence (*L*, 66). Catching an image in a mirror but not yet knowing it to be himself, he recognizes the "vulnerability guarded against . . . a conquered frailty" (*L*, 64). For perhaps the first time, he glimpses the elusiveness, the undefinableness, of himself. But he does not then move in a Percyan direction toward finding the center of that centerless self in another. Instead, he seizes upon a course of action as a means of coming to himself. If the self is as isolated, as fragile, and as empty as a bubble, then the ego can claim only one freedom: to set the course of that bubble.[2]

Lancelot's need to determine himself in this Sartrean fashion by discovering the "freedom to act on [his] conviction" (*L*, 156) constitutes the plot of the novel. At Belle Isle, his actions progressively remove him from others, turning them into objects, rather than partners, and that direction culminates in murder. He begins by spying on the movie company at dinner, at a remove of fifty feet, their images reflected in the hall mirror. He sets Elgin to spy on them at night at the Holiday Inn and then to record their activities on a videotape. The tape distorts the human images and voices beyond recognition. Finally, he rigs Belle Isle to blow it up. His actions, then, constitute a working out in an extreme form of the concept of freedom in Sartre: freedom to create oneself by the act of distinguishing the "I" from the threatening "not-I."

When the priest comes to Lancelot's cell one year later, he initiates a second awakening. At first, Lancelot is again numb and abstracted. He barely recognizes people, does not want to talk, cannot remember, cannot feel. But in telling his story, Lancelot again seems to come to himself. Although this second "new life" is launched by the encounter and not the solitary discovery, and this seems to be more in keeping with a genuine awakening in Percy's sense, the symptoms are still not good. Lancelot seems to be on the verge of repeating the past. As he talks about his future, he begins to sound chillingly like the Lancelot who murdered his enemies a year before. He says that he will "watch and wait"—words that in other Percy novels signal a character's break-through into the authentic posture of the symbol user awaiting signs by which he might discover a community and search for God. But Lancelot intends to "watch and wait," armed against others and in no need of God because he is taking the place of the silent God. Lancelot has not learned to value the "we" without whom there is no meaningful existence; he values only a few imaginary comrades, a morally elite "we" who will enforce their will on the "them." He chooses action as a loner rather than service, tight-lipped silence rather than the languaged encounter, freedom rather than love.

Lancelot, unanswered by anyone else throughout virtually all the novel, takes on an increasingly Sartrean voice as the point-of-view character, seeing other characters as rivals and turning them into "things" so that they do not remind him of his nothingness. For Sartre, the other poses a threat to the "I" because that other threatens to reduce the "I," the "*pour-soi*," to an object, an "*en-soi*." When two human subjects, each a separate and equivalent *pour-soi*, encounter each other, one relegates the other to a subordinate *en-soi*.[3] Merlin and Jacoby, Lancelot's sexual rivals, aggravated Lancelot's shame at his impotence, his "secret wound" (*L*, 66). Jacoby further threatened Lancelot by slighting him, by not even bothering to learn his name while staying in his home (*L*, 115). Margot rivals Lancelot by fixing him up, he thinks, with an identity (Jeff Davis at his memoirs), by being lustier than he, and ultimately by being unfaithful to him.

Although those three characters at Belle Isle actively threaten Lancelot's sense of self, and the priest and Anna do not, he also needs to deal with the latter as though they were rivals. Perhaps fearing that

Anna is a second Margot, "another woman trying to fix [him] up in a pigeonnier" (*L*, 252), he turns Anna into a mythic type: the ultimate victim and survivor, the "first woman of the new order" (*L*, 159). He also tries to dictate the terms of her recovery: if she can shoot "enough men to even the score," she can then "settle down with [him] in a barn" (*L*, 252). Lancelot also tries to relegate the listener to manageable categories, insisting on using a name that he himself once gave him, Percival, rather than using either Harry or John, his actual names. He trivializes the other's attempts to forge a self, calling them "acts" (*L*, 13, 61). He mocks the other for being a priest, standing for a church that has "the same fleas as the dogs [it has] lain down with" (*L*, 157), but also mocks him for not being priest enough, for not being whole-heartedly committed—a "screwed-up priest" who must be in some kind of trouble, who doesn't seem to have the "good news" (*L*, 10, 84).

Lancelot is a risky point-of-view character for a novelist who wants to suggest that language demonstrates what kind of creatures we are —beings inescapably connected with the other. Abstracted and isolated, Lancelot telling his story begins to sound like the Sartrean consciousness that Percy illustrates in "Symbol as Hermeneutic" with this sentence: "There is a consciousness of this chair." In contrast, Percy would say, "This *is* a chair for you and me" (*MB*, 282). Lancelot describes sex as nothing more than "the touch of one membrane against another" and the act of murdering Jacoby by cutting his throat as nothing more than "steel molecules entering skin molecules, artery molecules, blood cells" (*L*, 17, 254). He sees himself in the future keeping moral watch over the faceless others "[who] won't have anything to say about it" (*L*, 179). Lancelot's actions, his story, all seem to have somehow just happened; he does not seem to have experienced them or to have been brought to a sense of interconnectedness by them.

Yet just in this respect, where Lancelot seems utterly isolated, he is most connected. He is not soliloquizing; he is talking all the while to another. Lancelot *has* a story because his old friend comes to hear that story. To paraphrase Percy's contrast between his own and Sartre's sense of consciousness, Lancelot may feel as though he is saying, "There is a consciousness of the past," but he is actually saying, "There is a past for you and me—because there is a you and me." When Lancelot begins to talk, he does not think that the past is "worth remembering" (*L*, 3). After he has talked for several days, he says, "I've discovered that I can talk to you and get closer to *it*, the secret I know yet don't know" (*L*, 62). He acknowledges that he needs the other in order to discover who he is.

At the end of the novel, as Lancelot summarizes for the listener the results of his quest, the double vision that operates throughout the novel and contrasts Sartre's with Percy's view of human being is particularly evident. First, Lancelot says that he feels "nothing," only a "coldness." He asks the listener, "Is everyone cold now or is it only I?" (*L*, 253). Then he says that "there was no 'secret' after all, no discovery, . . . no sense of coming close to the 'answer.'" And he asks, "Why did I discover nothing at the heart of evil?" (*L*, 253). What Lancelot says here mirrors the Sartrean "predicament of consciousness": he feels only an emptiness; there was no meaning, no grail to discover. But the way he says it mirrors the Percyan sense of intersubjectivity: he asks the listener why he feels this way and whether he alone feels this way or whether others do, too. Lancelot here is asking his friend to help him understand how it is with him, to tell him whether or not he is like others, to tell him why he feels as he does. He is, therefore, asking the priest to be not what Sartre calls the other—the threat to my consciousness of self—but what Percy calls the other: "the source of my consciousness, the companion and co-celebrant of my discovery of being" (*MB*, 285). The principle behind Percy's dramatic monologue, then, is that Lancelot's need to talk with the other and his using language as the instrument of self-discovery reveal something quite different about him than what his actual language suggests.

Lancelot demonstrates Percy's view of the self by his failed attempt to define himself in isolation from others. Trying to free himself from others, he succeeds only in demonstrating his inescapable connectedness. He cannot say "I've nothing to say" until his friend arrives and he has someone to say it to (*L*, 5). He cannot rename the other Percival without linking him to himself; they are Lancelot and Percival, companions seeking the grail. Lancelot continually demonstrates Percy's intersubjective self *malgré lui*.

The priest, on the other hand, demonstrates Percy's view of the self by making a conscious choice to change. He, too, seems to have tried to define himself in Sartrean fashion. He has always been, Lancelot says, "a loner" (*L*, 10). He seems to have associated selfhood with the freedom to act independently, to have avoided the ordinary because it seemed mediocre. He joined a college fraternity but remained aloof, reading Verlaine and drinking, once leaping off the fraternity's party boat to swim alone to Jefferson Island. He later converted to Catholicism, going "from unbeliever to priest, leapfrogging on the way some eight hundred million ordinary Catholics"; but then he was "not content to be an ordinary priest" but became a doctor, served in Biafra, and returned to the United States to become a psychiatrist (*L*, 61).

When he enters Lancelot's cell, he keeps his distance: he looks out the window; he will not sit down and meet Lancelot's eyes. That he avoids the look of another is significant because for both Percy and Sartre, the gaze poses the ultimate encounter with the other as a separate and equivalent self. Sartre considers the stare to be, as Percy puts it, "the supreme aggression." Percy counters that Sartre names only one of the two possible alternatives; if it can be "hatred in the exposure of my impersonation," it can also be "love in the communion of selves." To Sartre's famous dictum "L'enfer c'est autrui," Percy replies, "But so is heaven" (*MB*, 285).

Lancelot shrewdly reads signs that the other guards his eyes and describes his look at various times as "sardonic," "hooded," "ironic," or, like one of these psychologists, "all at once abstract and understanding and leading me on" (*L*, 15, 62, 129, 159). The priest seems to fear that the look will, as Sartre says, unmask him and expose his shame or his uncertainty in his identity. The listener also withdraws by retreating into silence, by shrugging his shoulders, shaking his head, or simply declining to answer Lancelot's questions.

Lancelot also guesses that the other withdraws from a wholehearted commitment to his priesthood. He does not wear clerical clothes; he comes in the role of psychiatrist and not priest; he declines to pray for the dead when a woman in the cemetery asks him to. Lancelot seizes upon this evidence to mock the other's lukewarmness. But independent of Lancelot's need to diminish his friend's stature and his priestly vocation, the signs do suggest that the priest is a searcher who cannot bring himself to be identified as an ordinary priest. He seems to suffer from both a lack of faith in the power of prayer and of the sacraments and a mistrust of the institutional church, since he has chosen to serve people as a doctor and a psychiatrist but not as a priest.

Listening to Lancelot, however, jolts him from his withdrawal and provides the ordeal that occasions his coming to selfhood in a new way. Unlike Lancelot, he does not repeat past patterns; instead, he begins to use symbols to express his new way of seeing and being. The priest changes throughout the novel, although the most dramatic signs emerge at the end. He begins to meet Lancelot's eyes, and, as he does so, he often asks Lancelot whether he loved Margot or whether he thinks he can "ever love anyone" (*L*, 254). That juxtaposition of the look and the question about love suggests that he himself is starting to love more, to forget the boundaries between self and other, to be more concerned about meeting Lancelot in his need than about protecting himself from the dangerous gaze of the other. As Lancelot and the priest at last begin a dialogue, Lancelot exclaims, "You speak! . . . And looking straight at me!" (*L*, 256). In the ensuing dialogue, Lancelot twice remarks that he *sees* something in the other's eyes. The sign that the priest has fully entered into an encounter is his willingness not only to speak but also to let the other read his thoughts in his eyes.

Other nonverbal signs indicate the priest's conversion from life as "a loner" to life connected with others. He comes into the cell one day dressed in clerical clothes, and later, Lancelot sees him pray in the cemetery. He intends to take a parish, preach the Word of God, and, in Lancelot's words, "turn bread into flesh, forgive the sins of Buick dealers, administer communion to suburban housewives" (*L*, 256). All these signs constitute the priest's way of coming to selfhood and of dealing with evil.

To Lancelot, of course, the other's way is pitifully inadequate to combat the evil that they both agree is "out there." In his diagnosis of that evil, he speaks at least in part for both Percy and Sartre, who both deplore the forms of "bad faith" illustrated by the movie crew at Belle Isle—its pretensions, self-indulgence, materialism, and general shallowness. Lancelot recognizes and accurately names the many Sartrean forms of bad faith and self-delusion that Merlin, Jacoby, and Raine Robinette exhibit.

But the response to evil is the issue over which Percy's dispute with Sartre is crucial. Lancelot's indictments of the world are often frighteningly accurate, and yet to the extent that for him "hell is other people," he subverts the possibility of coming to an authentic self and instead becomes a satanic figure, as he half admits twice in the imagery of his narration. He describes himself being blown out of the window by the explosion as one "wheeling slowly up into the night like Lucifer blown out of hell, great wings spread against the starlight" (*L*, 246). The imagery is euphemistic—Lucifer was cast down from heaven, not up from hell—but Lancelot's connecting his destruction of Belle Isle with the fall of Satan is significant. In the final scene of the novel, Lancelot urges the listener to come to the window with him; when the other declines, Lancelot says, "Why so wary? You act as if I were Satan showing you the kingdoms of the world from the pinnacle of the temple" (*L*, 254).

Lancelot as a Satan figure constitutes Percy's warning about the dangers of an ontology that is grounded in the self alone. Although Sartre would not ultimately approve of his concept of freedom, Lancelot lives out an ethic opened by the Sartrean ethic of freedom. As Thomas Anderson points out, choosing freedom as the basis of a meaningful existence does not necessitate choosing a logical, consistent freedom. One could as well value "irrationality" or "nonrationality" to achieve meaning.[4] Thus a Sartrean ethic could function as the basis of Lancelot's delusive plan to establish a utopian society in Virginia.

Lancelot is the moralist morally bankrupt; but there is a further irony in Percy's portrayal of him: his "way" does not actually prevail in the novel. Lancelot's way of action, moral outrage, and of hostility to the other is not ultimately reflected in the dynamic of this novel. Rather, the dynamic points to the priest's intent to live centered in the symbolic encounter, in forgiveness, and in love. In the present-tense encounter that centers the novel, Lancelot does not act; he speaks to another. The primary "action" of the novel, then, is the discovery of the self in symbol making. In addition, Lancelot admits to the other that neither action nor right convictions are in themselves efficacious in meeting the problem of evil in the world. He says to the other: "I can see in your eyes it doesn't make any difference any more, as far as what is going to happen next is concerned, that what is going to happen is going to happen whether you or I believe or not and whether your belief is true or not" (L, 256). Having said this, Lancelot has already conceded the failure of the Third Revolution which he plans.

Moreover, the whole context of Lancelot's narration constitutes a second concession to the priest's way. Lancelot's narration is, in effect, a confession. He defies the priest to say so, and he denies that he wants forgiveness. But he does tell his story to a priest because he knows that he is not well, saying at one point, "A fox doesn't crawl into a hole for a year unless he is wounded," and a little later, "But what went wrong with the other new life last year? I must find out so I won't make the same mistake twice" (L, 108). Thus while Lancelot spews out moral outrage, he is engaged in a quite different sort of action: he is being revived and confronted with his own failures through talking, through accepting the gift of another's listening to his long and terrible story.

In the final exchange in the novel, Lancelot makes a third concession to the priest by asking, "Is there anything you wish to tell me before I leave?" (L, 257). It is his question as much as the priest's answer of "*Yes*" that initiates the dialogue that begins as the novel ends. All of Lancelot's questions before this last one are carefully controlled to limit the listener's intrusion into Lancelot's monologue by evoking nothing more than a yes or no. But at this final moment, Lancelot opens himself to the full intersubjective encounter by inviting the priest to say *anything* he thinks Lancelot should hear. In asking this question, he voices Percy's conviction that the other is not the threat but the "companion and co-celebrant of my discovery of being" (*MB*, 285). The priest's way has prevailed in the novel. Percy's final triumph is not just having the priest get the last word and making that word an affirmation to counter Lancelot's negations. It is having Lancelot ask at last the question of a man who seeks his being not through himself alone but through the dialogue with the other.

Linda Whitney Hobson

The "Darkness That Is Part of Light": *Lancelot* and "The Grand Inquisitor"

In the concluding scene of Fyodor Dostoevsky's *The Brothers Karamazov*, Alyosha Karamazov and a group of schoolboys reflect on the death and funeral of their friend, Ilusha Snegirov. Young Kolya says to Alyosha, "'It's all so strange, Karamazov, such sorrow and then pancakes after it, it all seems so unnatural in our religion.' 'They are going to have salmon too,' a boy observed in a loud voice." Sorrow and pancakes is one metaphor of comic pattern which offers an illustration of Walker Percy's possible intention for his fourth novel, *Lancelot*. That the characters and patterns of Dostoevsky's novel have shaped Percy's thinking is clear in his 1987 introduction to *Walker Percy: A Comprehensive Descriptive Bibliography*:

> A novelist is not used to thinking of his novel as an actual book in hand, but rather as ghost stuff coming out of his head. But after all that is what one reads, books in hand. So I got to thinking about the mysterious connection between the two, the book in the writer's mind and the thing in the reader's hand. There is a connection. How can I not connect *The Brothers Karamazov* with the big fat Random House edition, fat as a bible, its pages slightly pulpy, crumbling at the corners and smelling like bread? Is this bad? And how can I disconnect Ivan and Mitya from reading about them sitting in a swing on my grandmother's porch in Athens, Georgia, in the 1930's? Should I? (xviii)

A book read during adolescence, when one is seeking both signposts and hitching posts, will be remembered for decades, at least subliminally, so that by 1983, Percy can tell John Griffin Jones that Dostoevsky has influenced his own writing "in his idea of people obsessed with . . . some idea or something, [as they] find themselves in a certain situation, a terrible predicament, and behave accordingly" (*Con.*, 275). And in 1988, Percy commented on the right of novelists to issue "warnings": "It's in a noble tradition, going back to Dostoevski. . . . I guess that great saying of Dostoevski he put in the mouth of Ivan Karamazov. Ivan was arguing with his younger brother Alyosha, who was a young monk. Alyosha was trying to convert Ivan. Alyosha says, 'You don't believe in God' and Ivan says, 'If God does not exist, all things are permitted,'" an almost verbatim passage from *The Brothers Karamazov*'s story-within-a-story, "The Grand Inquisitor."[1]

Percy rewrote *Lancelot* several times, the early versions based on the dialogue in Albert Camus's *The Fall* (*Con.*, 146). But that form was ideological, so Percy thought, "Why not have the silence serve as a sort of dialogue?" (*Con.*, 146). The result is much like Ivan Karamazov's "poem," "The Grand Inquisitor," in that Percival speaks only at the end of the novel and Christ speaks not at all.

Like those who suffer from "angelism" in *Love in the Ruins*, mankind as portrayed by the Grand Inquisitor is only too eager to give up its "sovereignty" to "experts" in the church who offer to guide its conscience. Ivan has such a set of circumstances in mind when he poses a riddle to Alyosha, a riddle similar to one Lancelot poses to Percival. Before Ivan begins the story of Christ's coming to Seville, he baits his brother: "Do you find acceptable the idea that those for whom you are building that edifice of human destiny would gratefully receive a happiness that rests on the blood of a tortured child, and having received it, should continue to enjoy it eternally?" Alyosha does not "find that acceptable,"[2] nor does Percival when Lance asks a similar question: "Didn't one of your saints say that the entire universe in all its goodness is not worth the cost of a single sin? Sin is incommensurate, right?" (*L*, 139). Thus, in *Lancelot*, too, Percy is concerned with the same problems of freedom and evil that haunted Dostoevsky. As in "The Grand Inquisitor," *Lancelot* takes place in a prison, which in this case is also a hospital, suggesting perhaps that only in such a dual-functioned place of the possessed body and mind may a despairing soul be spoken to and touched. However, unlike Dostoevsky's plot, in *Lancelot* the prisoner is the spokesman for evil. The agent of God, Percival, is free to leave, though the speaker is the Satan figure in both stories.

Like the Grand Inquisitor of Dostoevsky's last novel, Lancelot Andrewes Lamar plays "Satan showing [us] the kingdoms of the world from the pinnacle of the temple" (*L*, 254), and the fictional device works a comic aesthetic reversal. The powerful representation of evil strengthens the appeal of *caritas* in a world that today seldom considers the issue, as Percy maintains in "Notes for a Novel about the End of the World" (*MB*, 101–18).

Percy's Catholicism allows him to represent the divine-human drama as a comedy, albeit a dark one, wherein there is no permanent destruction and man, in all his guilt, is continuously accepted by God. And since one's deepest experiences often come in the form of Kierkegaardian contradictions, "The religious individual has as such made the discovery of the comical in largest measure."[3] This discovery informs Walker Percy's novelistic study of madness, along with the equally comic notion Percy learned from Dr. Harry Stack Sullivan—every patient carries within himself the seeds of his own cure (*TS*, 16).

The art that depicts the spiritual conflict between good and evil has its roots far back in history. "Comedy is a primal rite; a rite transformed to art," writes Wylie Sypher, glossing Aristotle. "Comedy began with a scene of sacrifice and a feast," he continues. The sacrifice gradually became invective and later a "dramatizing of the ridiculous." There were two players in the drama—the *eiron* (the intruder, devil, villain, or man of irony) and the *alazon* (young god-hero); they engaged in what Sypher calls "double action," an ambiguous blend of "rational debate and phallic orgy."[4] Thus, after the serious action, the comedy ended in a celebration or generalized revelry. Such is the comic pattern of agony and revel inherited by the authors of "The Grand Inquisitor" and *Lancelot*.

But one might argue that these two fictions are tragic. No, concludes Sypher, because it is impossible to have a Christian tragedy.

From the anthropologist's view the tragic action, however perfect in artistic form, runs through only one arc of the full cycle of drama; for the entire ceremonial cycle is birth: struggle: death: resurrection. The tragic arc is only birth: struggle: death. Consequently the range of comedy is wider than the tragic range—perhaps more fearless—and comic action can risk a different sort of purgation and triumph. If we believe that drama retains any of the mythical values of the old fertility rite, then the comic cycle is the only fulfilled and redemptive action, and strange to think, the death and rebirth of the god belong more fittingly to the comic than to the tragic theatre. Is this the reason why it is difficult for tragic art to deal with Christian themes like the Crucifixion and the Resurrection? Should we say that the drama of the struggle, death and rising—Gethsemane, Calvary, and Easter—actually belongs in the comic rather than the tragic domain? The figure of Christ as god-man is surely the archetypal hero-victim. He is mocked, reviled, crowned with thorns—a scapegoat King.[5]

As a Catholic writer, then, Percy finds in comedy his natural mode for expressing both his sacred and his secular concerns. As Sypher says of such concerns: "If the authentic comic action is a sacrifice and a feast, debate and passion, it is by the same token a Saturnalia, an orgy, an assertion of the unruliness of the flesh and its vitality. Comedy is essentially a Carrying Away of Death, a triumph over mortality by some absurd faith in rebirth, restoration, and salvation." Though the audience may register shock and disgust, "The comedian can perform the rites of Dionysus and his frenzied gestures initiate us into the secrets of the savage and mystic power of life. Comedy is sacred and secular."[6]

The comic hero is always complex and ambivalent, because he must be reviled before he is renewed. One type of comic hero is the devil or tempter, a "deputy of God." Since evil is inherent in good, the imposter, profaner, or devil is a "darkness that is part of light." For instance, Goethe binds Faust to such an "impudent spirit" in the character of Mephisto. In realizing that Mephisto is only his darker self, Faust exclaims, "Why must I be fettered to this infamous companion who battens upon mischief and delights in ruin?"[7]

Another type of comic hero is the mocker, blasphemer, and offender. "He embodies . . . the side of the god that must be rebelled against before the god can be worshiped." Falstaff is such a figure, for example. Yet another type of fool is "the Seer, the prophet, the 'possessed,' since the madness of the fool is oracular, sibilline, delphic. He may be the voice crying in the wilderness, an evangelist or Baptist, or an Imbecile-Prince like Muishkin. . . . Thus in almost all his roles the fool is set apart, dedicated, alienated, if not outcast, beaten, slain. Being isolated, he serves as a 'center of indifference,' from which position the rest of us may, if we will, look through his eyes and appraise the meaning of our daily life."[8] As the crazed, lonely, dedicated prophet of a Third American Revolution, Lancelot Lamar embodies many of these traditional attributes of the devil in Percy's cautionary tale.

Like Walker Percy, the skeptical Ivan Karamazov is a comic poet who uses all the wiles of his craft in "The Grand Inquisitor" to provoke his brother, Alyosha, and presumably the reader as well, to consider life as man-God drama, with the Inquisitor and his flock playing the role of the suffering fool—reviled, despised, and despising. The hatred in both cases stems from failed idealism and loss of faith, a form of fear. However, Alyosha, the listener, who has perceived the comic aesthetic reversal, does not interpret Ivan's story this way. He perceives the tale as proof of God's power over evil through acceptance of it, despite Ivan's long-winded "poem" to the contrary. And as the brothers argue over the meaning of the story, they personify the polarized critical response to *Lancelot*, a response that no doubt pleased Walker Percy. In arguments similar to the Karamazov brothers', readers confront and duplicate the man-god drama themselves, giving the drama a cogent immediacy not found in theological debate per se.

As Ivan and Alyosha talk in the upstairs room of a tavern, Ivan confides that he has written a "poem," and though it is still rough, he would like his brother's opinion of it. Alyosha loves a good story, and asks Ivan to tell it. In his story of sixteenth-century Seville and the auto-da-fé of the Inquisition, Ivan uses the traditional battle of good and evil, invective and blasphemy, prophecy, and the endurance of good to form his story.

Ivan begins his story on an evening after the day when one hundred heretics had been burned to death by order of the Grand Inquisitor. After the terrible deaths, Christ "came unobserved and moved about silently but, strangely enough, those who saw Him recognized Him at once," though Ivan stresses that this was not the Second Coming "in which He had promised to appear in all His heavenly glory at the end of time" (*BK*, 299). Walking in silence up to a crowd of mourners for a seven-year-old girl, Christ smiles, and the people sense the "sun of love [which] burns in His heart. . . . The funeral procession stops. They put the coffin down at His feet. He looks down with compassion, His lips form the words '*talitha cumi*'—arise, maiden—and the maiden arises. The little girl sits up in her coffin, opens her little eyes, looks around in surprise, and smiles. She holds the white roses that had been placed in her hand when they had laid her in the coffin" (*BK*, 300).

But just at that moment, the Grand Inquisitor, a cardinal of the Spanish church, emerges with his train of followers. He is ninety years old, with a "withered face and sunken eyes, in which there is still a gleam of light" as he confronts Christ. After a darkly comprehending glance at what has just taken place, the old priest "points his finger and orders his guards to seize Him." Still silent, the prisoner allows himself to be taken to prison, where later that night the Grand Inquisitor visits his cell to confront him with the magnitude of his crime. He should not have come again and thereby reduced the hard-won authority of the church (*BK*, 300).

Asserting that "there has never been anything more difficult for man and for human society to bear than freedom," (*BK*, 304) the cardinal harangues his prisoner in an extended monologue that chilled Dostoevsky himself, who commented in his notebook, "Even in Europe there are not and have not been atheistic expressions of such force" (*BK*, xiii). In December 1879, Dostoevsky read his "Legend" to the students of Saint Petersburg University, but he prefaced it with a short introduction in which he explained his view of the poem.

> An atheist who is suffering in his unbelief writes during a spell of misery a curious, fantastic poem, in which he portrays Christ in conversation with one of the foremost priests of the Catholic Church—the Grand Inquisitor. The author's sufferings are so intense because in this priest he sees a true and genuine servant of Christ, even though the priest has a Catholic world outlook which has clearly grown remote from the orthodoxy of the old Apostolic faith. The Grand Inquisitor is really an atheist. What the poem is saying is that if the Christian faith is combined and corrupted with the objectives of this world, then the meaning of Christianity will perish. Human reason will abandon itself to unbelief, and in place of the great ideal of Christ a new Tower of Babel will be built. Where Christianity had an exalted view of mankind, under the new order of things mankind will be viewed as a mere herd, and behind the appearance of social love there will arise an open contempt for humanity.[9]

It is clear that Lancelot Lamar and the Grand Inquisitor share many characteristics: both are dedicated to an altruistic cause—the welfare of "the herd"—and both are dead wrong in utilizing science to that end. They seek a materialistic solution to a spiritual problem.

Continuing his argument for the prosecution, Dostoevsky's atheist first reviews the three temptations put to Christ in the desert by "the wise and dreaded spirit of self-destruction and non-existence" (*BK*, 307). Christ should have taken up Satan's offer of power over man by feeding man, by giving him one to worship without contention, and by wielding political power to seal his authority. Christ's reticence in accepting this bribe stemmed from his love for man and the acting out of that love—not from wanting to rob man of his free will. But people want bread, not freedom, the Inquisitor repeats again and again.

"Do You Know," he asks the prisoner, "that more centuries will pass, and men of wisdom and learning will proclaim that there is no such thing as crime, that there is therefore no sin either, that there are only hungry people?" (*BK*, 304). Percy's speaker for that position, Lancelot, maintains that such a time has arrived: the late twentieth century. Lance cannot perceive sin, he admits. He sees society as being psychopathic, too, and believes that even the church no longer values the difference between good and evil: "Come here, Percival, I want to tell you something. It is not a confession but a secret. It is not a sin because I do not know what a sin is—Bless me, Father, for I have done something which I don't understand. . . . I might have tolerated you and your Catholic Church, and even joined it, if you had remained true to yourself. Now you're part of the age. You've the same fleas as the dogs you've lain down with" (L, 155–57).

Until the notion of crime is erased, the church has stepped in to fill the void left by the fastidious Son of God, says the Inquisitor: men need bread, gods or idols to worship, and mystery and authority. The Roman church has answered all of these needs, thus proving its compassion. Of course, since there is no heaven and men are just natural creatures, when they die, they will not discover everlasting life. That is a pity, he tells Christ, but at least during their lives, the church has kept the weak from knowing the truth, and this ignorance is better than the painful freedom held out to them by Christ: "You overestimated men, for they are certainly nothing but slaves, although they were created rebels by nature. Look around and judge for yourself. Fifteen centuries have passed. Examine them. Who have You raised up to Yourself? I swear that man is weaker and viler than You thought" (BK, 308).

This harsh speech is similar to what Lance tells Percival in several instances, the last of which is nearly word for word what Dostoevsky has written. Lance has contempt for what he sees as others' inability to make up their minds and act: "Here is an incidental discovery: If you tell somebody what to do, they will do it. All you have to do is know what to do. Because nobody else knows" (L, 196). At other times, his contempt takes in great categories of people, though later he wants to save the "good" ones under his authority in a new colony in the Shenandoah Valley. Lance despises tourists from Michigan and Ohio, who are too dull to be insulted when he makes fun of them (L, 60); women, whom Lance believes are so contemptible that they enjoy being raped (L, 222–23); and Yankees, southerners, Californians, Russians, Chinese, and a panoply of others, all abstracted into scientific types for easy dismissal (L, 220). Lance's character plays the traditional role of the comic fool here because he, like the Inquisitor, sees himself apart from other men and superior to them: just before his contempt takes the form of murder, Lance recalls, "I was alone, far above, . . . upright and smiling in the darkness" (L, 235). Both Percy's and Dostoevsky's satanic speakers believe that such an "upright" stance allows them with all impunity to ask their listeners/confessors to assume with them a superior position from which to regard lowly man. Lance's words echo the bitterness of the Inquisitor's when he says to Percival: "You say we are redeemed. Look out there. Does it look like we are redeemed?" (*L*, 224).

Throughout the Inquisitor's fiery monologue, Christ is silent, just as Percival is in *Lancelot*. The Inquisitor, having become uneasy at the prisoner's silence, asks, "Why do You look at me silently with those gentle eyes of Yours? Be angry with me. I do not want your love, because I do not love You myself" (*BK*, 310). His self-destructive words imply his membership in Satan's party. Then the old priest summarizes the third necessity of man, another need he says Christ wrongly underestimated: "someone to worship, someone who can relieve him of the burden of his conscience, thus enabling him finally to unite into a harmonious ant-hill where there are no dissenting voices" (*BK*, 310). The Inquisitor prophesizes that "there will still be centuries of chaos, in which men will be guided by their own unbridled thinking, by their science, and by their cannibal instincts, for, since they started building their tower of Babel without us, they will end up devouring each other" (*BK*, 311). Cannibalism is the end result of men trying to live in secular freedom, without God (or Satan).

When this has failed, the church will be waiting to take unruly, rebellious man back under its protection, the cardinal explains.

> We shall prove to them that they are nothing but weak, pathetic children, but that a child's happiness is the sweetest of all. They will grow timid and cling to us in fear, like chicks to a hen. They will admire us, be terrified of us, and be proud of the strength and wisdom that enabled us to subdue a turbulent herd of many millions. They will tremble abjectly before our wrath; they will become timorous; their eyes will fill with tears as readily as those of women and children; but at the slightest sign from us, they will just as readily change to mirth, laughter, and untarnished joy, and they will burst into a happy children's song. Yes, we shall force them to work but, in their leisure hours, we shall organize their lives into a children's game in which they will sing children's songs together and perform innocent dances. (*BK*, 312)

In his own Gnostic vision of the utopia he will create in Virginia, Lance uses many of these same images of children, singing, innocence, and verifiable categories of good and evil. But the most important quality shared by the two synthetic Edens is simplicity, as Lance describes it to Percival:

There will be leaders and there will be followers. There are now, only neither knows which is which. There will be men who are strong and pure of heart, not for Christ's sake but for their own sake. There will be virtuous women who are proud of their virtue and there will be women of the street who are there to be fucked and everyone will know which is which. You can't tell a whore from a lady now, but you will then. You will do right, not because of Jew-Christian commandments but because we say it is right. There will be honorable men and there will be thieves, just as now, but the difference is one will know which is which and there will be no confusion, no nice thieves, no honorable Mafia. There are not many of us but since we are ready to die and no one else is, we shall prevail. (L, 178–79)

The Inquisitor has no respect for the "Jew-Christian commandments" either, though he admits that when he was younger, he tried to follow Christ's teachings; they came to seem impossibly comical and absurd to him, and he gave them up. Finally, as he says, "I came to my senses and would not serve a mad cause. I turned away and joined those who were endeavoring to correct Your work" (BK, 313). To prove the truth of what he has told the prisoner, he invites him to watch the eagerness with which the very people whose child Christ had raised from her coffin come tomorrow, at a signal from their priest, to light the fire that will consume the prisoner. For, coming to hinder both the church and the people it "serves," no one has ever deserved immolation more than Christ.

Besides the Gnostic prophecies in both stories, both also feature sacrificial victims of fire. Christ is threatened with death, and one hundred of the townspeople have already died in the auto-da-fé. In Lancelot, too, four people are burned to death after Lance's proud judgment upon them. Margot lies on her bed, in the abject, fetal position of a sacrificial lamb, just before she is burned in the explosion and conflagration of Belle Isle. Lance's last glimpse reveals her "lying on her side . . . , knees drawn up, cheek against her hands pressed palms together, dark eyes gazing at me" (L, 245–46). As the methane explodes, Lance finds himself separated from Margot, and "wheeling slowly up into the night like Lucifer blown out of hell, great wings spread against the starlight" (L, 246); in this Lancelot-Lucifer coupling, Percy repeats the Inquisitor-Satan identity in which the priest confronts Christ with the same questions Satan did in the desert.

Margot's violent death-as-sacrifice is prefigured in the plot of the film being made at Belle Isle. The end of the film, in fact, owes much to the plans the Grand Inquisitor has for Christ, his prisoner, whom he intends to burn at dawn. Though simpleminded and stereotypical in its Tobacco Road plotting, the film is to end with a burning, too. When Lance asks the director what he has planned for the ending, Merlin answers, "The stranger is immolated by a town mob who think they hate him but really hate the life forces in themselves that he stirs. He is the new Christ, of course" (*L*, 153).

In *The Brothers Karamazov*, after Ivan, an unbeliever and an intellectual, appears to end his poem with Christ consigned to the flames, he leans back in his chair and smiles at Alyosha. Waiting patiently throughout, Alyosha is agitated and moved to speak: "'But it makes no sense!' he crie[s], turning red. 'Your poem is no disparagement of Jesus, as you intended—it is in praise of Him!'" (*BK*, 313) Several of Percy's reviewers were not as perspicacious as Alyosha, failing to see in *Lancelot* Percy's comic reversal of positing the existence of God by depicting the impudence and power of his opposite. In this way both the Inquisitor and Lancelot continue the ancient Greek tradition of the comic tempter, profaner, fool, and seer. Such a "devil" confronts the hero-king, who may himself play the fool upon another occasion, they debate under fiery and abusive conditions, the hero triumphs, and a celebration follows—the "sorrow and pancakes" aesthetic.

Lancelot's querulous voice, emanating from a prison cell representing the mind, speaks for man's free will to do evil, whereas Percival speaks for the other, the good. The traditional *eiron*, or evil figure, is not only allowed by but needed by the *alazon* to exist, like Goethe's Mephisto, "who explains how he is 'the spirit that endlessly denies'; he is also 'part of a power that would alone work evil, but engenders good.' The Imposter, Profaner, or Devil is 'darkness that is part of light.' Evil is inherent in Good, and to reach salvation man must pass through a 'negation of negation.'"[10] Such a negation of negation is the comic result Percy effects as Lancelot's angry diatribe runs its course and Percival begins to speak, perhaps, of *caritas* and grace, the equivalents of Christ's kiss on the ancient and pale lips of the Inquisitor before the old one sets him free.

In his study of language and consciousness, Walker Percy has concerned himself with questions such as "Where do I end . . . and where does the listener begin?"[11] *Lancelot* is in one way a fictional exploration of that question within the traditional comic structure given similar content in "The Grand Inquisitor," for the nineteenth-century treatment raises the same issue of freedom in posing the old priest against his prisoner, Ivan against Alyosha. Within the scope of the dialogue, each of these characters is trying to define his own limits, confined by the limits of the other. Setting both stories in prison creates a tension between captivity and freedom in a material, visceral sense which undergirds the intellectual dialogue. Within this prison of the mind, the story then becomes a one-sided infernal dialogue between the speaker, for whom man is the measure of all things, and his own better nature, which sits in the corner of the cell and regards him silently with big, dark eyes full of sadness tempered by patience. Both Dostoevsky's and Percy's stories, therefore, are spiritual dialogues in the form of a psychomachia of doubt and belief, restraint and freedom, hate and love.

Several critics have argued about whether *Lancelot* is Percival's story (declining faith catalyzed by confrontation with evil) or Lancelot's (despair brought to confrontation with faith). If we regard the story as a one-sided dialogue, both parts of which are necessary for communication, then this argument is irrelevant. There is no need to choose, just as a portrayal of beauty implies the existence of ugliness. Whether the reader focuses on Lance or on Percival, by the comic aesthetic reversal the story leads outrageously but ineluctably to God.

Lancelot Lamar's voice speaks seductively as he upbraids Percival for being one of Christ's party, but Percy's own line-editing for punctuation subtly reinforces the identity. In several places Lance calls Percival "Christ" or "Jesus" under cover of an expletive: "Jesus, come in and sit down. You look awful. You look like the patient this morning, not me" (*L*, 84). The author, as a careful student of language, must know that the more conventional way of writing expletives into dialogue is: "Jesus! Come in and sit down." Yet Percy did not do that. In this subtle way, even the mechanics of the text allude to Dostoevsky's parable.

The concluding sentence of Ivan's poem describes Christ's response to vilification: a kiss, which "glows in his heart. . . . But the old man sticks to his old idea" (*BK*, 316). Here Ivan, the proud unbeliever yearning to believe, skews his story to the obduracy of evil, in spite of the holy kiss glowing in the Inquisitor's heart. Like Ivan, Walker Percy says he also considers his hero unredeemed at the end of the story: "In the end I regarded Lancelot as demented, as a man who has gone into the religious stage in a demented way" (*Con.*, 209). Dostoevsky's old priest may also have gone demented into the religious stage in order to take God's law into his own hands and decide what is best for his "flock." Yet Percival's final *"Yes"* (*L*, 257) is as good to hear as post-funeral pancakes are comforting to eat; both could partly redeem Lance's anger, which is born of cowardice, helplessness, and a feeling of abandonment. Moreover, after the holy kiss, instead of sending Christ to his immolation, the Inquisitor sets Christ free. Whether or not Ivan would admit it to Alyosha, that action inevitably continues the gracious dialogue between darkness and its surrounding light—all the way down to 1977, and beyond.

John F. Desmond

Language, Suicide, and the Writer: Walker Percy's Advancement of William Faulkner

Walker Percy has insisted repeatedly on separating himself from the tradition of southern letters epitomized by Faulkner, a tradition he sees as concerned mainly with memorializing the past through storytelling. However, Percy makes one exception to this general disclaimer: his interest in a Quentin Compson who did not commit suicide.

> I don't fit into the southern pattern. . . . All my characters . . . find themselves in a here-and-now predicament. And the whole backdrop is this historical scene which is drawn so well by Shelby, Eudora, and Faulkner. It's *there*, all right, but my character is looking in the other direction; he's not looking back. And that's why I've always felt more akin to Faulkner's Quentin Compson than to anybody else in his fiction because he's trying to get away from it. He is sick of time, because time means the past and history. . . . So, I suppose, I would like to think of starting where Faulkner left off, of starting with the Quentin Compson who *didn't* commit suicide. Suicide is easy. Keeping Quentin Compson alive is something else. (*Con*, 299– 300).[1]

Percy's declarations of independence from the Faulkner tradition are, of course, oversimplified; his protagonists are looking backward *and* forward, their lives shaped by the inescapable past. Yet his interest in Quentin Compson and suicide is a defining point for understanding his relationship to Faulkner and his transformation of the southern hero from suicidal despairer to creature of hope. Percy transforms the theme of literal suicide into the theme of spiritual suicide and focuses that theme in the predicament of the modern writer, whom he defines as an "ex-suicide." It is possible, I think, to see the evolution of this development from Faulkner to Percy by concentrating on two central aspects of the suicide theme: language and sexuality. Percy's definition of spiritual suicide is Kierkegaardian, the despair of refusal to be a self "transparently under God."[2] Conversely, one who relinquishes an inauthentic existence to live transparently under God can be called an ex-suicide. Percy adds a semiotic dimension to Kierkegaard's idea of selfhood and suicide by insisting that language—naming—makes the self uniquely human. Though language suffers devaluation, Percy emphasizes the literary artist's power to redeem it: "A recovery is possible. The signified can be recovered from the ossified signifier. . . . A poet can wrench signifier out of context and exhibit it in all its queerness and splendor"(*LC*, 105). Combining these existential and semiotic perspectives, one can define an ex-suicide as one who, as a namer, affirms selfhood transparently under God and a suicide as one who refuses to become such a namer: by choosing the introversion Kierkegaard calls "shutupness"; by deferring completely to another's language and vision, which Kierkegaard calls being "defrauded by another"; or by affirming a self defiantly without God, which Kierkegaard calls "Stoicism" (*The Sickness unto Death* 166 ff).

It is also clear from Percy's novels, especially *Lancelot*, that sexuality defines selfhood as intrinsically as language does. Like language, sexuality is rooted in the mystery of human origins and man's relationship to the divine; hence it is conjoined to the mysterious power of naming. Again using Kierkegaard: to become an authentic self transparently under God is to become a unique sexual self, understanding sexuality as a mystery rooted in the paradoxical finite/infinite nature of man. Conversely, strictly historicist or scientific views of sexuality are reductive because they deny the unique mystery of the finite/infinite sexual self. Just as naming is a triadic event for Percy, so also is the authentic sexual relationship—concelebration of creation with another, in mutual recognition of the other's mystery, under God. I am looking forward, of course, to *The Second Coming*, but there is a long road back through Faulkner and Quentin Compson before we reach that point.

Lewis P. Simpson, Louis D. Rubin, Jr., and other Faulkner scholars have already demonstrated how Quentin Compson in *The Sound and the Fury* can be understood as Faulkner's figure of the modern literary artist.[3] Simpson in particular shows how the nexus of sexuality, creativity, and history focused in Quentin represents Faulkner's own attempt to understand his vocation as a writer. As an artist figure Quentin fails to wrest permanent meaning from his situation. His failure eventuates in literal suicide, but his spiritual suicide as incipient artist figure occurs long before this, when he capitulates to the fatalistic vision of his father. Mr. Compson's cynical vision is at one with his rhetoric, and Quentin's failure to refute the language tradition is shown by his increasing appropriation of his father's language and vision, to the point of total union of father and son by the end of the Quentin section.

Mr. Compson's vision and language embody that defiant despair Kierkegaard terms Stoicism. His rhetoric is characterized by devaluation, by closure to mystery, and by denial of a transcendent spiritual order. Moreover, it relativizes language itself, denying any ultimate source of truth expressible in words. Thus the collapse of values Mr. Compson voices is coextensive with his sense of the collapse of language into meaninglessness. His Stoic rhetoric likewise includes an explicit rejection of logocentric Christianity and a historicist view of sexuality. Christ is a "stuffed doll" on the trash heap of history; women are a "delicate equilibrium of periodic filth."

Quentin tries to counter his father's fatalism by affirming an equally Stoic code of honor, one that ironically drives him as storyteller to imagine a tale of incest with Caddy to give the family collapse some meaning. But his imagined story fails, not only because his father would find him incapable of such an act but also because to Mr. Compson the words themselves have no meaning. Overwhelmed by Mr. Compson's fatalism, Quentin succumbs to his father's view of language and sexuality as he approaches suicide. Fittingly, his last colloquy with his father concerns the bankruptcy of language itself, echoed in the word that sums up the historicist compulsion: "temporary." So Quentin succumbs, a would-be artist figure drowned into silence by an act that consummates a lifelong extinguishment of the self.

Percy's fictional preoccupation with a Quentin Compson who didn't commit suicide is central to his self-definition as a southern writer. This preoccupation involved subsuming, yet passing beyond, Faulkner's portrait of the artist in Quentin Compson to create a portrait of the artist as an ex-suicide. It meant moving beyond both the closure of Stoicism and the limits of Faulknerian humanism into the mystery of the religious mode. And it meant coming to terms with the two central elements in Quentin's suicidal despair—language and sexuality.

Percy's first three novels contain intimations of actual suicide and depict a general milieu of spiritual suicide, and the themes of language and sexuality are also present as recessive, ironic strains. But only with *Lancelot* did Percy begin to explore fully the meaning of spiritual suicide in direct relationship to language and sexuality, and *Lancelot* is the novel that most clearly echoes the situation of Quentin Compson as artist figure in *The Sound and the Fury*. The problem of spiritual suicide and the writer is not fully settled in *Lancelot*, but the novel is a crucial turning point from which Percy was then able to resolve the "matter of Quentin" in *The Second Coming*.

Important differences notwithstanding, the parallels between Quentin Compson and Lance Lamar are apparent even from a cursory glance. Both are sensitive, half-mad narrators, the offspring of weak fathers and self-indulgent mothers. Both are obsessed with the past and the collapse of values, specified by sexual betrayal within the family; and both long to retrieve lost honor through Stoicism.[4] Both are involved in symbolically incestuous relationships with family members. Both agonize over the failure of love and, more deeply, over the historicizing of sexuality. Both are governed by dualistic, mechanistic views of women. Both face crises over the meaning and value of action and choose obverse forms of violence—suicide and murder—to escape their situations. More importantly, both are storytellers who try unsuccessfully to convince fatherly listeners of the rightness of their views. Quentin finally identifies in failure with his father, but Lance is unable either to seduce Father John to his neo-Stoicism or to accept the Christian position implied in the priest's actions, a crucial difference in the two novels. Both books deal centrally with language and sexuality as keys to defining the self as spirit. Finally, like Quentin, Lance can be seen as a symbolic artist figure, through whom Percy explores the meaning of his own vocation and the predicament of the modern writer faced with what Lewis Simpson calls the historicism of the mind.[5]

As Faulkner did in Quentin's case, Percy focuses the predicament of the artist figure in *Lancelot* on the conjoined themes of sexuality and language. Quentin cannot make Caddy's acts of lust commensurate with his abstract, rhetorical concept of honor and virginity. For his part Lance argues that the sex act is "incommensurate" with any other experience and therefore is indefinable. It is "unspeakable" because it involves the mystery of personality; it is an "ecstasy" in which the self may paradoxically lose itself yet find itself in the other. Because the self is spirit, the sex act involves divine and demonic potentialities, which Lance notes when he overhears Margot and Jacoby utter "God" and "shit" while lovemaking. Yet though he affirms the mystery and unspeakability of the sex act, Lance finally embraces the historicist view of sex and women just as fatally as Quentin does. Like Quentin, Lance regards women as either idealized ladies or whores, a truth revealed when he claims to have found the "great secret of life"—that is, that men and women are born to violate and be violated by each other. His view, of course, totally collapses the ontology of sexuality into a purely mechanistic vision. Unlike Quentin, Lance seems to overcome his literal and symbolic impotence by a sexual assault on the actress Raine. But even though he claims to "know" her in the sex act, his bestial possession of Raine is a perverse corruption of human communion through sex, a mystery that literally escapes him.

Lance rages against the collapse of the meaning of sexuality even as he tries to affirm a blasphemous pseudoreligious view of his sexual pleasures with Margot. As a symbolic artist figure, he therefore attempts to destroy mystery even as he affirms the incommensurability and unspeakability of sexual experience. Lance presumes to define evil by his search for sin as surely as he tries to define sexual experience as violation. In this role as autonomous knower and sayer, he would supplant God, act independently of any divine source of naming. But in this attempt to know all in order to say all, he becomes the demonic rationalist whose vision and rhetoric take on all the marks of closure and Stoic reductiveness seen in Mr. Compson. Viewed in this light, Lance can be seen as Percy's dramatization of the namer as autonomous rationalist, one who defiantly refuses to become the artist as "nought," the ex-suicide under God. Thus, near the end of the novel, Lance is linked with Satan, the demonic "anti-namer" whom Father Smith later calls the "depriver of meaning."

Like Quentin, Lance would assume the symbolic role of artist as world savior through his plan to revive the lost code of honor and female virtue in the new colony in Virginia. But his utopian ideal, based on sexual dualism and Gnostic pride, is as unworldly as Quentin's desire to create a private world for himself and Caddy by persuading his father that they have committed incest. Like Quentin, Lance is driven by the illusory figure of the ideal feminine and the stoical father. It is his duplicitous mother, Lily, who guides Lance to revenge and to "overcome" the impotence of his father, in which he ironically fulfills Mr. Compson's admonition to Quentin that "no Southern gentleman ever disappoints a lady."

As a figure of the artist, Lance's reductive view of experience is coextensive with his reductive deployment of language in his savage, univocal condemnation of his age. But Percy balances Lance's monologue with the silent "voice" of Father John, which embodies the religious dimension that finally separates Lancelot from Quentin. Faulkner's doomed hero is engulfed by his father's Stoicism, but Lance has available to him a fatherly voice and vision that avoids closure. Father John rejects Lance's Stoicism and prods him toward deeper levels of "unformulable" meaning and self-understanding, particularly about love. About God he is largely silent, but his opposition effectively undermines Lance's self-vindicating narrative. In the end, Lance is damned out of his own mouth, but Father John's presence and few words offer an alternative religious vision of reality, signified by the very openness of the novel's ending.

Nevertheless, this possibility of a way out of the closure of Stoicism —the possibility of the religious, that is—is still presented obliquely in the priest's role in *Lancelot*. So also the possibility of escape from spiritual suicide, defined through language and sexuality, exists only marginally in the role of Anna. Only in *The Second Coming* does Percy fully explore the triadic relation between language, sexuality, and the self as spirit "transparently under God." Will Barrett becomes Percy's most developed figure of the writer as ex-suicide, the prophetic "nought" who explores man's spiritual predicament in the century of Thanatos. Barrett triumphs over both the temptation of actual suicide and the condition of spiritual suicide which is the real legacy of his Stoic father, triumphs focused specifically in the defining elements of selfhood—language and sexuality—manifested in his relationship with Allison Huger.

Parallels to Quentin Compson's situation abound in *The Second Coming*, but Percy's move beyond *Lancelot* is decisive. Like Quentin, Barrett struggles against his father's deadly Stoicism, but he is much more self-conscious of his predicament than either Quentin or Lance. Barrett knows he and his father are not "pals," and in his repeated references to him as "old mole," he ironically recognizes their reenactment of the archetypal struggle between that other son who anguished over the emptiness of words, the "fall" of female sexuality, and suicide and the all-demanding father figure—Hamlet himself.[6] Moreover, unlike Quentin, Barrett is aware that although his father literally missed killing him on the hunting trip, he infected him with a despair that has governed most of his life. "By now I have learned . . . that he didn't miss me after all, that I thought I survived and I did but I've been dead of something ever since" (*SC*, 324). Will discovers, in short, that he is a spiritual suicide.

Again, as in the case of Quentin, the suicidal vision of the father is embodied in a mechanistic view of sexuality. Eros without love equals Thanatos, a total inversion into narcissism and symbolic onanism. Barrett sees this as he recalls the hunting episode.

I cleaned the gun when I got it back from the sheriff in Mississippi. Both barrels. Wouldn't one have been enough? Yes, given an ordinary need for death. But not if it's a love of death. In the case of love, more is better than less, two twice as good as one, and most is best of all. And if the aim is the ecstacy of love, two is closer to infinity than one, especially when the two are twelve gauge Super-X number eight shot. And what samurai self-love of death, let alone the little death of everyday fuck-you love, can match the double Winchester come of taking oneself into oneself, the cold-steel extension of oneself into mouth, yes, for you, for me, for us, the logical and ultimate act of fuck-you love fuck-off world, the penetration and union of perfect cold gunmetal into warm quailing mortal flesh, the coming to end all coming, brain cells which together faltered and fell short, now flowered and flew apart, flung like stars around the whole dark world. (*SC*, 148–49)

As suicide is equated with a solipsistic sexual orgasm, so also is living in the fallen world equated with impotence, impotence culminating in suicide, the only violent alternative to despair. "'*You're one of us*,' his father said. Yes, very well. I'm one of you. You win. Where does such rage come from? from the discovery that in the end the world yields only to violence, that only the violent bear it away, that short of violence all is in the end impotence?" (*SC*, 171). Lance chooses violence in his attempt to overcome such impotence, but it is not the alternative chosen by Will Barrett. Unlike Quentin and Lance, Barrett finds a locus of meaning—an authentic self—by discovering the secret to overcome suicide. The secret is not only his love with Allison Huger, transforming Eros into *caritas* through a new language of communication, but also the gift he receives to name, and break free of, the destructive influence of his father's Stoic rhetoric, as neither Quentin nor Lance could do. Will names death in all its forms and so becomes the figure of the artist as ex-suicide, one who gains power over creation by his acts and words. Will's conversion occurs after his thwarted "attempt" at suicide in the cave and comes in the form of God's oblique "answer" to his quest and in the gift of Allison herself.

Percy resolved the paradoxes of sexuality and language in the relationship between Will and Allison by linking the mystery of language explicitly with the mystery of sexual love. As she listens to Will speak, Allie thinks, "She could not hear his words for listening to the way he said them. . . . Was he saying the words for the words themselves, for what they meant, or for what they could do to her? . . . Though he hardly touched her, his words seemed to flow across all parts of her body. Were they meant to? A pleasure she had never known before bloomed deep in her body. Was this a way of making love?" (*SC*, 262). Indeed, in their lovemaking, Allie and Will's words are as integral to the act as their physical union. Allie's previous sexual experiences were simply physical exchanges, literally selfless acts of despair. But with Will it is different. In love they discover a new, fresh language, not the deadly rhetoric of convention. They indeed "make it new" and "sing a new song," something Percy insists the writer must do to overcome the dead weight of rhetorical convention. As they join together, Allie explicitly links the linguistic and the sexual in their feelings: " 'The good is all over me, starting with my back. Now I understand how the two work together.' 'What two?' 'The it and the doing, the noun and the verb, sweet sweet love and a putting it to you, loving and hating, you and I'" (*SC*, 263). The conjunction of the "it and the doing, the noun and the verb," in the mystery of love enacts the triadic mystery of language which for Percy defines the self as human. In *Lost in the Cosmos*, he says, "A particularly mysterious property of [language] is the relationship between the sign (signifier) and the referent (signified). It is expressed by the troublesome cupola "is," when Helen [Keller] said that the perceived liquid 'is' water (the word). It 'is' but then again it is not" (*LC*, 96). Allie's recognition of this mystery of language—the mystery of the "troublesome cupola" seen now in their union—transforms their experience of sex into the mystery of love. The dualism of a Quentin or a Lance is left behind.

But it is in his final break with his father that we see most clearly Will's assumption of the figurative role of artist as ex-suicide. Descending into the cave, Will challenges God to prove his existence. His suicidal quest is an inversion of Lance's demonic quest for the meaning of sin, its passive form reminiscent of Quentin's suicide by drowning. Although Will receives no direct answer to his quest/question, the signs he does receive are enough to convert him from suicide to ex-suicide. Saved by a toothache and cared for lovingly by Allie, Will returns to become the namer who triumphs once and for all over the Stoic vision of his father by affirming his selfhood against the forces of death. The secret he discovers, the revelation given him, is one that Quentin and Lance failed to find—the knowledge of this century's, his father's, and indeed his own love of death. Now he can stand over against it and name it.

Ha, there is a secret after all, he said. But to know the secret answer, you must first know the secret question. The question is, who is the enemy? Not to know the name of the enemy is already to have been killed by him.

Ha, he said, dancing, snapping his fingers and laughing and hooting, *ha hoo hee*, jumping up and down and socking himself, *but I do know. I know. I know the name of the enemy.*

The name of the enemy is death. . . .Not the death of dying but the living death.

The name of this century is the Century of the Love of Death. Death in this century is not the death people die but the death people live. (*SC*, 271)

After naming the many forms of death that is this century, Will proclaims his allegiance to life by explicitly rejecting his father, now equated with the "old Father of lies," Satan himself. Simultaneously, Will as artist figure discovers his authentic voice, and in this Percy implicitly affirms the religious connection between earthly manner and the ultimate source of word and vision. "You gave in to death, old mole, but I will not have it so. It is a matter of knowing and choosing. To know the many names of death is also to know there is life. I choose life" (*SC*, 273–74). But to knowing and choosing must also be added the central act of the prophetic writer as ex-suicide— naming.

Death in the form of death genes shall not prevail over me, for death genes are one thing but it is something else to name the death genes and know them and stand over against them and dare them. I am different from my death genes and therefore not subject to them. My father had the same death genes but he feared them and did not name them and though he could roar out old Route 66 and stay ahead of them or grab me and be pals or play Brahms and keep them, the death genes, happy, and so he fell prey to them.

Death in none of its guises shall prevail over me, because I know all the names of death. (*SC*, 274)

Quentin's imaginary colloquy with Mr. Compson ends in the identification of son with father; Lance's colloquy with Father John is unreconciled; but Will's colloquy with his father's spirit ends in his total rejection of Mr. Barrett's Stoicism. Yet in separating himself from this earthly father Will implicitly finds another. In an apocalyptic vision that immediately follows his litany against death, Will intuits the presence of an Other—a gift-giver—as the source of his power to name. In this strange vision, Will comes to himself amidst a scene of desolation.

When he came to years from now, he was lying on the spot. The skylight of the mall was broken. The terrazzo was cracked. Grass sprouted. Somewhere close, water ran. Old tax forms blew out of H & R Block. A raccoon lived in the Orange Julius stand. No one was there. Yet something moved and someone spoke. Maybe it was D'lo. No. Was it Allie? No, nobody. No, somebody was there all right. Someone spoke: Very well, since you've insisted on it, here it is, the green-stick, Rosebud gold-bug matador, the great distinguished thing.

The ocean was not far away.

As he turned to see who said it and who it was, there was flash of light then darkness then light again. (*SC*, 277)

The revelation, with its allusion to many fatal "endings," is the answer Will received to his demand for a sign from God when he entered the cave. It is this knowledge of all the ways of death over against which he declares his being. The revelation is mysterious, yet clear, enabling him to renounce the "Father of lies," and to love and act freely in the world, not death-ridden by his past or by Stoicism. It also marks explicitly Percy's clearest declaration of his difference from Faulkner on the matter of Quentin and as a southern writer himself. Percy moves beyond Faulkner's humanism, recognizing its inadequacy as a response to spiritual suicide in the age of despair. Through his creation of Will Barrett as figure of the artist as an ex-suicide, he demands the sign of an ultimate namer and giver, made flesh in the word and in the world of human love. Loving Allie, Will asks, "Is she a gift and therefore a sign of a giver? Could it be that the Lord is here, masquerading behind this simple, silly holy face? Am I crazy to want both, her and Him? No, not want, must have. And will have" (*SC*, 360).

Percy's answer is yes, yes.

John Edward Hardy

Man, Beast, and Others in Walker Percy

The gift of language is in Percy's orthodox scientific view a faculty uniquely human. In recent decades a goodly number of researchers, some with excellent academic credentials, have reported at least rudimentary success in their efforts to converse with birds and beasts. Percy's responses to such claims are scarcely more respectful than his noble namesake's comments on Glendower's boasts of calling spirits from the vasty deep.

The celebrated key-tapping exercises of Duane Rumbaugh's chimpanzees and B.F. Skinner's pigeons (*LC*, 92–94)—actually nothing more than tricks performed for specified rewards, bananas and backscratching, grains of corn—are examples of what Percy, adapting the terminology of C.S. Peirce, calls "the 'dyadic' behavior of stimulus-response sequences," radically different from events having "the 'triadic' character of symbol-use" in human language (*LC*, 85). Claims of the kind that Percy attributes to Rumbaugh—of having provided "'the first successful demonstration of symbolic communication between two nonhuman primates'" and "the all-too-frequent use . . . in a loose analogical sense," of terms such as *"language, symbols, sentences"* in reports by various investigators on the communicational activities of other creatures such as dolphins and humpback whales (*LC*, 92–93)—are evidences, perhaps, of some fundamentally *anti*scientific spirit of intellectual *despair* disguising itself as a relatively harmless and correctable excess of zeal, that rules in the entire field of such research.

Why, Percy asks, is it true that not only "people in general" these days but many scientists "want so badly to believe that chimps can speak that they will compromise their own science?" The case is much like that of Carl Sagan, who "has written whole volumes promoting the probability of the existence" of ETIs, while admitting that not one shred of evidence has yet been produced to support the hypothesis. Intolerably lonely in their state of a transcending intelligence which their symbolic activity itself constantly asserts, at the same time that the basic tenets of their sciences require them to deny the truth of that assertion, primatologists, on the one hand, are desperate to identify at least a few other earthly creatures who share with human beings the faculty of language, while the more fastidious Sagan, on the other, holds out for news of "other transcending intelligences from other worlds" (*LC*, 169, 172–73).

Despite Percy's cautious willingness to admit the possibility that "triadic behavior [may not] be unique in man" (*LC*, 95), I think it is hardly necessary to define the enormous fund of theological hope and conviction that he has at stake in the effort to discredit the work of people such as Rumbaugh and Skinner. In any event, the point I want to emphasize here is that while in his nonfictional writings Percy is concerned with the behavior of all other creatures almost exclusively in the interest of demonstrating its collective difference from human behavior, in the vast world of words, world of symbolic creation, that is his novels, animal behavior is represented as much more complex than anything that can be accounted for on the basis of the human/nonhuman, speaking/nonspeaking distinctions with which he is preoccupied as a philosopher. Human beings and other animals live together in Percy's novels much as they do in our common, workaday world, in circumstances of association at once remarkably intimate and remarkably ill defined and in which the myriad differences among various kinds of nonhuman creatures, even those between one and another member of the same species, often count for at least as much as the likenesses.

In Binx Bolling's vividly detailed recollection of how the idea of "the search" first occurred to him, when he regained consciousness in the Korean forest after being severely wounded, he notes that he "came to [him]self under a chindolea bush," that his shoulder "didn't hurt but it was pressed hard against the ground as if somebody sat on [him]," and that "six inches from [his] nose a dung beetle was scratching around under the leaves." More, in fact, than a matter simply of "regaining" consciousness, the experience is one that Binx remembers as a distinctly new state of awareness. He "came to [him]self" with a sense, it is suggested, of having been previously separated from himself, not just for the minutes or hours since he received the wound in his shoulder but for all the days of his life until that awakening. And the sense of self-discovery, the new awareness of the reality of his own existence, is inseparable from the new awareness of the ground upon which he is lying and of the other living things with which he shares his space there.

Finally and most emphatically, his attention is fixed upon the close but obscure movements of the beetle. "As I watched," he says, "there awoke in me an immense curiosity. I was onto something. I vowed that if I ever got out of this fix, I would pursue the search" (*M*, 10 –11). In an interview some ten or twelve years after the publication of *The Moviegoer*, Percy compared this visionary experience of Binx's to that of Tolstoy's Prince Andrey as he lies wounded on the battlefield, gazing up into the sky. As Percy puts it, Andrey "*sees* the clouds for the first time in his life." Percy goes on to remark that Binx, in his so distinctly earthbound fascination with the beetle, is "the opposite of Prince Andrey" the cloud-watcher. But when the interviewer is tempted then to pursue the question of an "irony" in the contrast, emphasizing suggestions of "magnificence" in Andrey's clouds as opposed to the "ugly little dung beetle" that Binx "zooms in on," Percy acknowledges only in passing that "maybe there is a little twist there" and prefers to stress the similarity of the two experiences, as instances of the "recovery of the real through ordeal." In that context, "the beetle is just as valuable as a cloud" (*Con.*, 81).

Neither in the novel nor in the interview does Percy indicate precisely what it is about the beetle that awakens the "immense curiosity" with which Binx regards the little creature. And it strikes me as a bit odd that both Percy and the interviewer neglect comment on what is surely one of the most important distinctions between cloud and beetle, namely, that the latter is itself a sentient being, capable in some rudimentary fashion of observing, as well as exciting observation, and of locomotion. It is difficult to tell whether Percy meant us to surmise that the wounded Binx was thinking of the possibility that the beetle's movements were in any way affected by his presence, as an unfamiliar element of the environment, something that cast a strange shadow upon the ground or emitted a strange odor, perhaps alarming, perhaps enticing. But one can hardly imagine its not being a matter of authorial design that Binx's committing himself to "the search" is somehow provoked by his observation of the beetle's own obscure quest, "scratching around under the leaves."

The importance of all other distinctions notwithstanding, the paradigm is clear. The beetle may have no power of language, no memory and no foresight, no conscious intention in its seeking, and the very thought of what it seeks may be, for a human being of normal adult sensibility, disgusting. But the beetle can and does move about from one place to another, albeit within a narrow range, can and does go in search. And if we note that Binx, recalling the incident many years later in his Gentilly apartment, experiences the same strangely heightened sense of wonder, of *seeing* for the first time, as he stands looking at the little pile of inanimate, manufactured objects lying on top of his bureau—wallet, keys, slide rule, and so on, instruments of symbolic consciousness, inanimate but intimately personal, familiar, strange now precisely in and by virtue of their familiarity (*M*, 11)—the reference to this paraphernalia of civilized existence may serve only to underscore the importance of the fact that in the original, wartime episode the object of his intense scrutiny was most precisely not inanimate, not manufactured, not, in McLuhanese, a mere "extension" of himself as human being, but a distinct, independently existent organism.

There are other invertebrates of complex fictional significance in the Tom More novels: the garden spider in the opening scene of the epilogue section of *Love in the Ruins* and, near the beginning of *The Thanatos Syndrome*, the cicadas that inhabit the live oaks outside the old tin-roofed "Cajun cottage" building, once his coroner father's office, where More now conducts his desultory psychiatric practice. The description of the cicadas especially well exemplifies the subtle, characteristically understated artistry of Percy's use of flora and fauna in creating a sense of time and place. Further, both passages are notable for the "humanizing" tendency of the tropes used to present the nonhuman life forms. The deceptively benign spider is "like a child on a swing." Proceeding from a description of the sparrows who have taken over "[his] father's martin *hotel*" in the yard of the departed coroner's office and incorporating the architectural then in a musical metaphor, idling Tom goes on to speak of how "the cicadas start up in the high *rooms* of the live oaks, *fuguing* one upon the other" (*TS*, 12–13, emphasis added).

In innumerable instances, quite as often as the nonhuman is humanized, the figurative order is reversed. "Poppy" Vaught on the golf course goes "hopping along like a jaybird" (*LG*, 194). Binx entertains a mental picture of sexologists Dr. and Mrs. Bob Dean "at their researches, as solemn as a pair of brontosauruses" (*M*, 190). Old Father Weatherbee, alarmed at his importunate visitor's bending toward him with excited and incoherent demands for religious enlightenment, rolls backward in his chair watching Barrett "as if he were a cobra swaying atop his desk" (*SC*, 358).

All Percy's fiction, of course, is quest fiction. Not surprisingly—along with tales of amorous pursuit, detective work, scientific and historical research, fire watching and map reading, hazardous travel, meetings with dubious wise men (and women) in desert places, and so on—there is much about hunting and fishing.

Poppy Vaught, trying during his first conversation with Will in the New York hospital corridor to sort out recollections of his past acquaintance with the Barrett family, momentarily confuses Will's father with his uncle Fannin, trainer of prizewinning bird dogs (*LG*, 51). Much later in the same novel (337 ff), Will visits Fannin, at his forest retreat near the town of Shut Off, Louisiana, and goes with the old man and his black servant and companion, Merriam, on a brief quail-hunting expedition. In *The Second Coming*, the long story of Will's father-search reaches its climax when he succeeds at last in clearly recalling the details of a shooting "accident" during another quail hunt, in his boyhood, and realizes for the first time now, in middle age, that his father had probably meant to kill them both.

Memorable references to fishing include the episode of Binx Bolling's early-morning colloquy with his mother on the dock of the Smiths' camp at Bayou des Allemands (*M*, 149 ff), Tom More's lyrical reflections upon the bountiful life of the waters near the apartment in the old slave quarters where he has taken up residence with his second wife and their children (*LR*, 382), and, in the sequel novel, the tense, fake camaraderie of Tom's dialogue with John Van Dorn about the arcana of bridge bidding conventions and angling for sunfish in southern Louisiana.

Throughout the studiedly companionable conversation of the two men in the little boat (*TS*, 56–64)—cuckold and cuckolder, More the faithless defender of Christian humanism, disgraced and self-doubting champion of the rights of human selfhood, Van Dorn the sinister neo-Nazi visionary, prophet of the coming triumph of human engineering, himself clearly suspect as avatar of the fallen angel Azazel, for whom one of the bidding conventions is named—the undercurrent of deadly enmity is readily apparent. Fishing and the game of bridge both serve as extended metaphors of contest, communication, and inquiry, at once revealing and obscuring the more profound issues of the encounter. For one moment, as they gaze together in wonder at the evanescent beauty of the sunfish Van Dorn has caught—"the amazing color spot at his throat catching the sun like a topaz set in amethyst," More thinking how "the colors will fade in minutes, but for now the fish looks both perfectly alive yet metallic, handwrought in Byzantium and bejeweled beyond price, all the more amazing to have come perfect from the muck," Yeats and Hopkins, Darwin and Moses most marvelously reconciled—a boyish innocence and peace almost as of the first days of the world possesses them, before they lapse again into the familiar patterns of adult civilized existence, with its unrelenting wariness and insincerity, inescapable time consciousness, and myriad deceits of word and gesture.

This episode is in various ways reminiscent, one may assume deliberately so, of the two in the earlier novels I have mentioned. Binx Bolling is not and never has been an ardent fisherman. More is obviously an expert. For all his satiric detachment, Binx on the dock at Bayou des Allemands is deeply affectionate with his mother, while More is surprised to discover, even for an instant, any trace of geniality in his attitude toward Van Dorn. But, on these occasions, both our heroes notably confine themselves to the role of spectators, both refusing suggestions that they take a more active part, questioning and watching, rather, angling in media darker even than the murkiest of bayou waters, while their companions busy themselves with more immediately practical matters.

Binx, searching for self-knowledge, any possible clue to his own destiny, not direct advice certainly, but any chance hint of guidance in the choices he must make, encourages his mother to talk to him about his dead father. Tom More, concerned for his own and his wife's and his patients' welfare and for that of the community at large, maneuvers adroitly "by indirections [to] find directions out," trying to determine exactly what John Van Dorn is up to and how to thwart him. Van Dorn, of course, is onto More's game and is quite consciously playing it himself all the while that he displays his skill with rod and reel. But there is never any doubt that Tom—on his home territory in more senses than one, as psychoanalyst and amateur linguist as well as expert in such matters as the preference of Louisiana sunfish for such live bait as the catalpa worms—has the upper hand.

Elements of myth and mystery, such we have seen here in the heavily allusive description of the sunfish and the references to Azazel—resident demon of the desert, it should be further noted, where Aaron's "scapegoat" was driven forth to perish[1]—are more or less readily observable in all the passages of Percy's fiction concerning waters and the creatures that live and are preyed upon in and near them. Binx's mother at Bayou des Allemands, herself an eminently mythic presence, talks half cajolingly, half threateningly to the unseen fish she is trying to catch. In a typically Percyan mode of complex symbolic irony, the scene foreshadows the Smith family's churchgoing a few hours afterwards—where only Lonnie takes Communion, while the rest sit through the mass as if totally unaware of one another, "each . . . lapsed into his own blank-eyed vacancy"—and still later in the day, back at the camp, during a pause in the conversation with Lonnie about sin and the efficacy of the Eucharist, Binx's rather uncannily happening to look down from the dock just at the moment when a swimming snake "glides through the water without a ripple, stops mysteriously and nods against a piling" (*M*, 149–59, 160, 164).

The theme is most explicitly stated in Tom More's paean on the beauties of his new simple life in the old slave-quarters apartment, on the secret joy especially of the solitary fishing excursion upon the misty waters with which he begins each day: "Water is the mystical element! . . . As the trotline is handed along, the bank swiftly disappears and the skiff seems to lift and be suspended in a new element globy and white. Silence presses in and up from the depths come floating great green turtles, blue catfish, lordly gaspergous" (*LR*, 382).

Later in the day, listening to Colley Wilkes's fervent report of his having seen an ivory-billed woodpecker, the first such sighting recorded in some eighty years, covert millenarian Tom inevitably recalls his own portentous experience that morning of "hauling up a great unclassified beast of a fish" and thinking "of Christ coming again at the end of the world" (*LR*, 387).

Perhaps more frequently than all other nonhuman creatures, it is the birds that excite Percy's fictive imagination, at the levels both of natural curiosity and of sacramental and prophetic consciousness.[2] The Hopkinsian kingfisher that "goes ringing down the bayou" as Tom More sits musing in his collard patch is a notable example (*LR*, 382). And even the most casual reader of *The Last Gentleman*, one who knows little or nothing of the symbolic traditions upon which Percy so elaborately draws here, is unlikely ever to forget the peregrine falcon that is the first object of Will Barrett's telescopic quest in Central Park. His pursuit of the bird leads, "accidentally," to his pursuit of Kitty, and that in turn—with our hero all the while, even at the end, little aware of what it is he seeks—leads to his pursuit of Sutter and Jamie to Santa Fe. There, having witnessed and willy-nilly assisted at the boy's deathbed baptism and then seeking enlightenment from Sutter, he appears, instead or besides, as the reader is left to decide, about to become the instrument of the despairing doctor's salvation.

Percy's new bestiary, appropriately, no doubt, for our scientistic era of unprecedented religious ignorance, is a good deal more reliable as natural history than are the medieval models but is never so clear in the dimensions of its moral and theological meaning. Still, a plainly labeled *significacio* is hardly required for us to see, at least in retrospect, an emblem of Christ in the triumphant falcon—something, to return to modern sources, a shade more Hopkinsian than Yeatsian, though accommodating both—and perhaps, even in the victim pigeons, another aspect of the Godhead. Associated as it is with Valerie Vaught, herself so plainly identifiable as the chief of Will Barrett's divinely appointed guides on his spiritual journey, and in a scene, at her Tyree County mission school, involving much talk of language and dumbness, of vocation and teaching, and of the recreation of the world through language, the bedraggled southern chicken hawk, although ingloriously caged and fed on offal, is unmistakably another predator avatar of Christ. Indeed, Percy is embarrassingly heavyhanded here simply in having Barrett himself, as he looks at Val's hawk, "remember the falcon in Central Park" and reflect on how "he could see him better at one mile than this creature face to face" (*LG*, 301). Surely we might have been spared the authorial rib-nudging of the very next sentence: "Jesus," the agitated and apprehensive engineer thinks of a sudden, "my telescope: is it still in the camper?"

A diving hawk, here identified as "a dagger-winged falcon" but clearly meant to remind us of the two of other species in the earlier novel, is repeatedly described in a way that gives its flight the character of a portent of the middle-aged Will Barrett's first meeting with Allison early in *The Second Coming*, the book in which girl-search and God-search finally coincide. And, once past the fence that encloses the country club's property and into the enchanted forest in pursuit of his errant golf ball, coming ever closer to Allison before he is quite sure that anyone is there, Barrett is greeted by still another winged harbinger: "A tiny bird, no larger than his thumb, lighted on a twig not three feet away, stared at him with a single white-goggled eye, then turned its head clean around to look with its other eye" (*SC*, 71).

At another level of the "fabulous," the narrator's word for it in *The Second Coming*, the habits and names of birds are a prominent topic of folkloristic interest. The "dagger-winged falcon" whose appearance foreshadows Will's first encounter with Allison—the bird "fly[ing] across the fairway straight as an arrow and with astonishing swiftness . . . then fold[ing] its wings and drop[ping] like a stone into the woods" (*SC*, 47), one of the same kind about whom a Negro had once told Will the story that it "could fly full speed and straight into the hole of a hollow tree and brake to a stop inside" (*SC*, 48)—is clearly reminiscent also of the "blue-dollar hawk" featured at the beginning of Percy's essay "Metaphor as Mistake" (*MB*, 65). In the anecdote of the essay it is "a black guide" who furnishes the fascinatingly "mistaken" name of the hawk ("blue dollar" for "blue darter"), and the description there of its straight, arrow-swift flight, from which it "dropped like a stone into the woods," is reproduced almost word for word, more than twenty years later, in the novel.

Something approaching the ultimate mode of grossly naturalistic, late-twentieth-century comedy of southern interracial manners is offered in white Uncle Hugh Bob's account of how Vergil Bon, the university-educated young black man of refined modern sensibilities, reacted to the sight of a freshly killed woodcock as the still living worms it had swallowed just before it was shot came wriggling out of the bird's mouth. Vergil, the uncle contemptuously informs Tom More, "ain't ever touched a woodcock since," despite its being locally well known as "the best eating of all" game birds (TS, 183).

Birds and beasts are associated in various ways with human sexual behavior. Lance and Margot take acutely decadent delight in the old pigeonnier as setting for their first coupling, accompanied by the faint, soft cooing of the birds in the loft above them and, after the rain, a joyous chorus of frogs outside. Having been humiliatingly denied the private audience with God he sought in the darkness of Lost Cove Cave —the absent deity emblemized in the saber-toothed tiger whose fossil remains have been removed to a state museum[3]—Will Barrett, smeared head to foot with bat guano, tumbles out of the cave into Allison's greenhouse, there to be tenderly cleansed and nourished by her, restored first to full sexual vitality, and seized at the end with a vision of the union of Eros and agape. The menus of profane love feasts feature the flesh of sundry creatures. For breakfast at Pantherburn, after her late-night visit to cousin Tom's bed, contented hostess Lucy produces generous servings of Hugh Bob's quail—"half a dozen hot little heart-shaped morsels per plate, six tender-spicy, gamy-gladdening mouthfuls" (TS, 169).

When a presumptuously amorous male hiker sits down to talk with Allison at her woodland retreat and puts his hand on her thigh, the big stray dog who has appointed himself her guardian has only to growl, "his eyes turning red as a bull's," to persuade the young man he should leave (SC, 240). Earlier, in obvious contrast, when the dog has charged Will Barrett as he approaches the greenhouse, even taking the man's hand in his jaws for an instant before Allison calls out to stop the attack, the beast's immediate obedience is a kind of certification of Barrett's worthiness to become her lover. In The Thanatos Syndrome, one of Tom's rich women patients of the horsey set, after a messy attempt at seducing

an underage groom, goes berserk and shoots several of her thoroughbreds, including a prize stallion. Lastly, in the same novel, the continuing story of More's observations on the strangely regressive, apelike
behavior of women in the community, including one of his patients
and his wife, who "present" rearward to invite sexual intercourse, culminates in the bizarre satiric fantasy of Van Dorn's metamorphosis and
his subsequent redemption by the love of Eve, the language-trained
gorilla.

I shall leave it to feminist critics to deconstruct Percy's chivalrous,
male-supremacist rhetoric in all this. Women, no doubt, are one group
of the "others" that some readers might see as covered by the title of
my essay. "Angelism/Bestialism," of which Percy speaks so often,
would appear to be principally, if not exclusively, a manly affliction.
In any event, the fate of Van Dorn, fallen angel turned into a beast
and restored then to health and prosperity as a best-selling author and
a favorite guest on the big-time TV talk shows, is obviously appropriate
to the interlinking evils of the scientistic ideals he has promoted in
his roles as bridge expert, codirector or chief technical consultant,
whichever it is, on the Blue Boy project, and progressive-pedophile
schoolmaster. His prophetic zeal in the cause of sexual liberation is all
of a piece with his enthusiasm for research in artificial intelligence.

There is, of course, no suggestion that computers are evil in themselves. Tom and Lucy's use of the terminals at her house, with access
to the state health department's files (*TS*, 146), is the first essential step
in their campaign against the Blue Boy conspiracy. But the equipment
can be put to legitimate use only as an instrument of unimpaired human
intelligence. What Van Dorn and Comeaux have done instead, with
the heavy-sodium additives in the public water supply, is to tamper
with the normal brain functions of their victims, so that the people
themselves become walking computers of a sort, equipped with moder-
ately efficient data storage and retrieval systems, responding first, not
as they ordinarily would to a question such as Tom's to Donna about
the location of Arkansas (*TS*, 19), with some counterquestion—probably about why he wants to know—but entirely automatically and disin-
terestedly, as if at the touch of his fingers on an electronic keyboard.
Then there is Ella, the patient who has been fired from her job at a
nuclear utility plant after complaining that "her superior" there, "a person called Fat Alice," had physically attacked her. When Tom gets the
facts in the case from an old friend who holds a managerial position
at the plant, he is told that the accused "Fat Alice" is actually "a rather
low-grade robot," officially designated "FA413–T," not a flesh-and-

blood "person" at all; but Ella remains unpersuaded that the distinction is substantially relevant to her complaint of abuse (*TS*, 77–78).

It is by no means coincidental that, only a few minutes later during the same session in which Donna has answered his question about the location of Arkansas, she should go into her "rearward presenting" routine with More. That and the computerlike behavior are presumably but two manifestations of the same dehumanizing, depersonalizing, "odd suppression of cortical function" that Tom has already begun to suspect, well before he gets wind of the Blue Boy project, is afflicting both Mickey and Donna. "I'm thinking particularly," Tom say, "of the posterior speech center, Wernicke's area, Brodmann 39 and 40. . . . It is not only the major speech center but, according to neurologists, the locus of self-consciousness, the 'I,' the utterer, the 'self'—whatever one chooses to call that peculiar trait of humans by which they utter sentences and which makes them curious about how they look in a mirror—when a chimp will look behind the mirror for another chimp" (*TS*, 22).

Van Dorn—the man of no certain origins, no dependable identity; computer-language expert reduced first to enraged gibbering and chest thumping, then to craven, depressive silence; comic, demonic embodiment of the premillenial zeitgeist; spokesman for our age in its despair of language as adequate to the needs of human communication, despair of the self—is consigned to the care of Eve and her mentor, the zoo semioticist Dr. Rumsen Gordon, as offering the last possible hope for his deliverance (if deliverance it is, to join the high intellectual company of Phil Donahue and his guests).

It works, to repeat, only as a device of satiric fantasy. Percy means, I assume, only to say that computers offer no more realistic hope than animals do for those of us who yearn to escape the uniquely human state of language competence and language dependence. Computers are no more likely than gorillas are ever to be able to carry on a real, volitional conversation and are no doubt still less apt to "interface" satisfactorily with human beings in sexual congress.

So much is clear, and it is amusing enough up to a point. But I find it gratifying that direct statements of the human/nonhuman distinction, so wearisomely predictable from the essays, appear rather infrequently in the fiction. In *The Second Coming*, for example, we are treated to an account of Will Barrett's reflections concerning the selfless beatitude of a cat dozing in a patch of sun on the garage floor. An organism "with its needs satisfied, for whom one place was the same as any other place as long as it was sunny, . . . the cat was exactly a hundred percent cat, no more no less" (*SC*, 16). This by contrast, of course, to the suicidal, memory-haunted man, who is never more than somewhere between 2 and 47 percent himself, "caught in the great suck of self" with no idea most of the time who, where, what, or why he is, but with an irresistible need to know.

One might fear that what is coming next is a full-dress disquisition on dyadic and triadic behavior models, complete with diagrams. That does not happen. And Barrett's reading of the cat's behavior is to some extent offset by his observations on the later incident of his encounter with Allison's dog. The man was silent, making no show of resistance, but the girl had shouted something an instant before the beast halted his charge. "Did he stop," she asks afterward, "because of my saying or because of your not saying?" Most people experienced in such matters would be likely to doubt that Allison has had the dog long enough to train him to obey her voice commands. But Barrett is fairly confident in his response to her question: "Probably because of your saying." Moreover, the dog is described as "embarrassed" in the situation, a word that suggests a highly complex sense of social self-awareness (*SC*, 107). In sum, it would appear that no such simplistic, behaviorist doctrine as that invoked in the case of the cat—or of chimpanzees or pigeons—is applicable here.

Yet, not only in the essays but in the novels, despite the numerous and varied expressions of his fascination with animals we have noted in the latter (I use the term "animals" now in the commonplace sense of reference to all nonhuman members of the animal kingdom) there are few indications that Percy has thought very seriously about other problems of animal behavior, and of animal-human relationships, to which his preoccupation with the speaking/nonspeaking distinction is only remotely relevant. For a novelist otherwise so acutely observant of contemporary ideological controversy, both popular and academic, he appears to be little interested in a vast range of hotly debated issues involving animals and human dietary practices, animals and the law, animals and economics, animals and the ethics of industrial and medical research, and so on, with or without regard to troublesome theological implications.

Tom More's first wife had installed on their patio a birdbath statue of Saint Francis, who was "Doris's favorite saint, not because he loved Christ but because he loved titmice." If Doris is only a relatively harmless sentimentalist, fake fakir Alistair Fuchs-Forbes, her spiritual seducer, is a contemptible hypocrite. He and his companion, Martyn, entertained at the Mores' house with a grilled dinner on the patio, "spoke of Hindoo reverence for life, including cattle, and fell upon [Tom's] steaks like jackals" (*LR*, 67). A humor at once more complex and more indulgent marks the characterization of old black Merriam, with his compassion both for the foolish young dog called Rock, whom Fannin Barrett peppers with birdshot to correct his mistakes in the hunt, and for the quail they are hunting. But there is little or nothing in the actions of any of the principal, sympathetically portrayed white male characters to suggest Percy's inclination to scrutinize seriously the ethical implications even of "sport" fishing and hunting, not to speak of laws governing commercial enterprises in the provision of flesh for human consumption.

Toward the end of *The Thanatos Syndrome*, Tom More expresses pity for Eve, the forsaken gorilla, in her homeless plight after she has outlived her usefulness to Dr. Gordon and Van Dorn. "Having lapsed into silence upon Van Dorn's departure, she was returned to Zaire, where it was hoped that she would be accepted by other mountain gorillas, who, however, were members of an endangered species on the verge of extinction. She was last seen squatting alone on a riverbank, shunned by man and gorilla alike" (*TS*, 344–45). And Percy himself, referring in a later interview to this passage of his novel, chastises certain unnamed real-life investigators for the same sort of callous behavior in getting rid of animals they have used: "Some of the primatologists have had to send the primates back where they came from. Or to zoos. Either way it's tough on the gorillas."[4] And so it is, very tough. But when the offenses of these few investigators he speaks of, against these few beasts, are compared to what goes on every day at the "factory farms" that furnish our supermarket meat counters and in the laboratories of universities and cosmetics manufacturers alike, to what has been going on throughout the long history of mankind's ingenious exploitation of all manner of other animals, Dr. More's and Dr. Percy's protest, though well-intentioned and praiseworthy as far as it goes, is hardly such as to kindle a worldwide demand for reform.

Still, at least in the novels, there is a recurrent tone of profound respect, of something approaching awe, in human contemplation of the very *existence* of other creatures, their unreckonable multitude and variety, that does much to redeem the shortcomings of Percy's anthropocentric scientific outlook and the primitive moral theology of man's earthly "dominion" to which he implicitly subscribes. Given his thematic preoccupations and the general intolerance for gentleness that marks our literary age, "on-stage" acts of violence of any kind are remarkably rare in Percy's fiction, and those untempered by wit or humor or a poetic virtuosity in the telling are rarer still, even in *Lancelot*. And the victims of Lance Lamar's crimes are other human beings. The nearest thing we get to a confession of perversely pleasurable human cruelty in an attack upon an animal is Binx Bolling's account of his spiteful relations with his landlady's dog. The cur has bitten him once, without warning, and "now and then" thereafter, when Mrs. Schexnaydre is away, our charming hero finds occasion to "give him a tremendous kick in the ribs and send him yowling" (*M*, 77). Perhaps in the very violence itself Binx is acknowledging, however perversely, old "Rosebud's" definite individuality. Having "taken it personally" when the beast bit him, he reacts in unpatronizing kind, holding a grudge against the dog just as he might against another man.

But the moral atmosphere of Binx's underground life in Gentilly is stifling at best. Let us revisit, in conclusion, the Smiths' fishing camp at Bayou des Allemands.

I think again of the swimming snake, of how it "stops *mysteriously* and nods against a piling" (*M*, 164, emphasis added). The primary mystery here has nothing necessarily to do with traditional symbolism. It is, rather, astonishing in its freshness, a mystery of natural being, mystery of this particular creature's doing a particular thing that no herpetologist, no mythographer, certainly no moral theologian, could satisfactorily explain. Explain away, in one way or another, but not explain. The awe I speak of, the sense of endless mystery, is something generated in human awareness of the very *proximity* of the wild creatures, the nearness of their irreducible, ungovernable otherness.

I think again of the snake, so near, though untouchable, in so clear a light, that the man looking down "can see the sutures between the flat plates of its skull" (*M*, 164). I think of the egret, departing its perch on the tree limb over the water, who "pumps himself up into the air and rows by so close [Binx] can hear the gristle creak in his wings" (*M*, 159).

Robert H. Brinkmeyer, Jr.

Lancelot and the Dynamics of the Intersubjective Community

Walker Percy has long been fascinated by the dynamics between psychological therapist and patient. In a number of his novels, interactions between analysand and analyst crucially shape the narrative and its structure, and in a real sense this dynamic also defines the relationships of the author and the reader to the text. Each of Percy's novels, for instance, has at least one important character who by society's standards is mentally sick, and it is the task of the other characters to come to grips with this person's sickness (or, as the case may turn out, his or her sanity) and along the way perhaps to discover their own. The reader's task is similar: challenged by these strange characters to discover the nature of their illness, the reader must decide what constitutes sanity and insanity. If characters in and readers of Percy's fiction are in a sense diagnosticians of the disordered self, so too is the author; in his discussions of his role as artist, Percy frequently compares himself to a therapist, his fiction, his diagnostic instrument.

Besides his novels, many of Percy's essays, particularly those on the mysteries of language and communication, also focus on the relationship of patient and therapist. The overriding significance of this charged interplay to Percy's thinking is suggested by the number of important issues to which Percy has the relationship speak: psychoanalytic theory and technique; the position of the scientist in the world; the layperson's relationship to science; the interpersonal dynamics occurring in a language exchange between two people; the conflict between behaviorism and phenomenology as a means of understanding the human condition; the problem of how contemporary people can "recover being." At the end of "The Symbolic Structure of Interpersonal Process," Percy's statement that "the existential modes of human living" can be derived from only one type of human interchange—"one man encountering another man, speaking a word, and through it and between them discovering the world and himself" (*MB*, 234)—echoes the patient-therapist encounter and suggests that such an encounter ultimately emerges for Percy as a paradigm of both the human condition and the process by which the self comes to know itself.

The patient-therapist interaction that Percy has in mind for this paradigm, however, differs significantly from that which is traditionally accepted in psychological therapy. Percy's critique of traditional therapy centers on what he sees as the skewed understanding of self that underlies the two primary psychological theories of human behavior—the "analytic-psychical" (typified best by Freud) and the "organismic-behavioristic" (typified best by B. F. Skinner). Percy finds both severely limited in their ability to understand consciousness because the foundation of each theory rests on a dyadic model of behavior—that is, on an interpretation of the self that sees its development primarily in terms of energy exchanges and interactions between fields of force, best illustrated by the stimulus-response model. Simply put, the psychoanalyst sees these exchanges and interactions occurring between unconscious forces and drives within the psyche, while the behaviorist sees them occurring between forces and drives within the larger environment. Both approaches, Percy argues, drawing on distinctions developed by Charles S. Peirce, fail to grasp that the workings of consciousness are irreducibly triadic. A triadic event occurs when a signifier is *interpreted* by an organism to mean something else, the signified. Triadic events cannot be reduced to dyadic exchanges because what establishes the relationship between signifier and signified is an independent—and finally unexplainable—act of interpretation, not a stimulus-response mechanism. Percy argues that the process whereby a chimpanzee learns that pushing a red button in a cage will bring food is far different from that whereby Helen Keller realizes that the letters w-a-t-e-r spelled on one of her hands "is" the water spilling over her other.

Interpreting human activity as merely dyadic exchanges, as Percy charges most therapists do, relegates the role of psychologist to that of objective observer and decoder of forces in the patient's life in order to resolve conflict. The irony in the therapist's situation—and Percy finds this in the stance of the objective scientist in general—is that while the therapist can interpret the patient's activities, he cannot, by the dyadic model, say anything about the activities he is engaged in to reach and put forth these conclusions, that is, about acts of interpretation and communication. As Percy argues in "Culture: The Antinomy of Scientific Method," this silence undermines the very foundations of the scientific method: "The ineluctable reality upon which the scientific method founders and splits into an antinomy is nothing else than the central act of science, 'sciencing,' the assertions of science . . . . It is ironical but perhaps not unfitting that science, undertaken as a total organon of reality, should break down not at the microcosmic or macrocosmic limits of the universe but in the attempt to grasp itself"(MB, 233).

The therapist's attempts at objectivity only compound the problems of the therapeutic model. Although Percy acknowledges that the therapist in all likelihood understands himself as both involved in and detached from the diagnostic encounter (as participant-observer), he notes, in "The Symbolic Structure of Interpersonal Process," that even so, "there is hardly a second when [the therapist's] own objective placement in the world is not operative" (MB, 210). "The stance of the pure scientist," writes Percy, and he is speaking of the therapist here, too, "is that of objectivity, a standing over against the world, the elements of which serve as specimens or instances of the various classes of objects and events which comprise his science (MB, 210). This perception of objectivity by the therapist necessarily limits his understanding of the more active and participatory role he actually plays in the therapeutic encounter. The therapist, in other words, remains ignorant of the dynamics which his simple presence has in shaping the patient's responses.

Percy believes that to understand a conversation a person must understand its context, and particularly the ways that the participants' assertions interpenetrate, but he holds that the therapist, in his presumed objectivity and detachment, downplays if not dismisses altogether such an understanding. As a good scientist, the therapist attempts to exclude himself from the world he studies. For Percy, as he writes in "Toward a Triadic Theory of Meaning," understanding a therapeutic encounter entails much more than merely grasping the analyst's diagnosis: "We want to observe this conversation not through the analyst's eyes, which see the patient as a psychic malfunction, but through a zoom camera which zooms back in order to see the encounter as it occurs, between two sentence couplers, in a world, in an office where a certain language game is played, next to a street where other language games are played" (MB, 184).

Context is so significant for Percy precisely because he sees the funda-

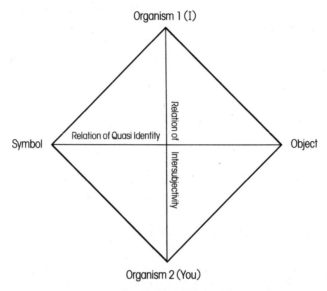

Symbol Tetrad: Generic Type of Symbolic Behavior

mental nature of consciousness as intersubjective. Citing the etymology of "consciousness"—"Consciousness: *Conscious* from *con-scio*, I know with" (*LC*, 105)—Percy argues that both the origin and the development of consciousness arise from interactions with other selves; or, as Percy says in a note in *Lost in the Cosmos*, citing his debt to Charles S. Peirce and George Mead, "The self becomes itself only through a transaction of signs with other selves—and does so, moreover, without succumbing to the mindless mechanism of the behaviorists" (*LC*, 87). The myth of the Cartesian autonomous self is for Percy just that—a myth; and he suggests in "Symbol as Hermeneutic in Existentialism" that the basic formula for intersubjective consciousness is "not the Cartesian *I am conscious of this chair* nor the Sartrean *There is a consciousness of this chair* both of which *presuppose* consciousness but *This is a chair for you and me* which joint act of designation and affirmation *is itself* the constituent act of consciousness" (*MB*, 282).

Percy's understanding of consciousness embodies a tetradic model; to the triad of signifier-person-signified, Percy adds a second triad with a second person sharing in the act of consciousness. Intersubjectivity, embodied in the model and defined by Percy in "Symbol, Consciousness, and Intersubjectivity" as "that meeting of minds by which two selves take each other's meaning with reference to the same object beheld in common" (*MB*, 265), is the foundation act of consciousness.

And as Percy makes clear, all acts of consciousness are by their very nature intersubjective, even thinking to oneself or writing in a diary, since such acts are always done with another person in mind and are shaped by that person's anticipated responses. "Even Robinson Crusoe," Percy declares in "The Symbolic Structure of Interpersonal Process," "writing in his journal after twenty years on the island, is nevertheless performing a through-and-through social and intersubjective act" (*MB*, 200).

Traditional psychological therapy, both behaviorist and psychoanalytical, Percy believes, ignores the dynamics of intersubjective encounters, perverting the I-Thou interplay of two free and independent subjects into the I-It relationship of the all-knowing subject (therapist) interpreting—but not engaging in intersubjective interpretation and interplay —the object (patient, whose behavior is understood to be dyadically determined). In "Toward a Triadic Theory of Meaning," Percy argues that the only alternative to behaviorist and psychoanalytical models of therapy is what he calls, significantly, the "novelistic." By this he means, quite simply, that the therapist must view the patient as a triadic creature and must understand that therapy, in the end, is essentially getting to know the patient well. To achieve this understanding of the patient, the therapist must interact with him in an I-Thou relationship and must be forever aware of the intersubjective dynamics and context of their conversation. Percy's conception of therapy is clearly more demanding of the therapist than that of traditional models, since intersubjective encounters with the patient—rather than I-It encounters —entail active engagement by the therapist so that his thoughts and views are put under constant pressure and resistance by the patient's words—as are, in like manner, the patient's ideas by the therapist's responses. The dialogic interplay between therapist and patient, embodying the formative acts of consciousness, thus becomes a process of growth in awareness and self-consciousness not only for the patient but for the therapist. Therapy, then, the intersubjective encounter of two people, is finally the primary model of cognition, the basic way we have of understanding ourselves and the world.

That Percy calls his therapeutic model "novelistic" unmistakably underscores the connections he sees between the therapist and the fiction writer and, more generally, between the dynamics of therapy and the dynamics of fiction. In his essays and interviews, Percy has consistently argued that fiction's primary purpose is cognitive, both for the reader and for the author. For the reader, fiction presents concrete particulars —specific characters in specific situations—of humanity's universal situation and specifically the condition of suffering and alienation. In this presentation the novelist assumes the role of therapist, naming for the reader the disorder of the self and thereby providing the means for the reader's understanding of his own condition. Percy describes this process in an interview with Carlton Cremeens as "telling the reader . . . something he already knows but which he doesn't quite know that he knows, so that in the action of communication he experiences a recognition, a feeling that he has been there before, a shock of recognition. And so, what the artist does, or tries to do, is simply to validate the human experience and to tell people the deep human truths which they already unconsciously know" (*Con.*, 24).

But the artist's role as therapist is not merely to communicate something he already knows but to learn and grow through the narrative process. Percy believes that writing fiction entails not the imposition of meaning but the discovery of it; fiction is a means to investigate the nature of humanity, a method, as he told John C. Carr, "as valid as any science, just as cognitive." In this interview, Percy draws explicit connections between the artist and medical scientist: "In fact, I see my own writing as not really a great departure from my original career, science and medicine, because . . . where science will bring you to a certain point and then no further, it can say nothing about what a man is or what he must do. And then the question is, how do you deal with man? And if you are an anthropologist in the larger sense, interested in man, how do you study him? And it seemed to me that the novel itself was a perfectly valid way to deal with man's behavior" (*Con.*, 60). In "The Diagnostic Novel: On the Uses of Modern Fiction," Percy argues that both the physician and the novelist diagnose and treat illness, in the novelist's case the patient being culture itself, its malady the breakdown of the modern self. The novelist, Percy says, hopes "to discover, or rediscover, how it is with man himself, who he is, and how it is between him and other men."[1]

What the novelist as therapist discovers is, in Percy's terms, not knowledge but news—that is, not information that can be ascertained at any time and any place and that is therefore irrelevant to the knower's predicament of self (knowledge for knowledge's sake), but instead information on a specific state of affairs that affects the hearer's existence and that is therefore crucially relevant to the understanding of his self and its placement in the world.[2] Percy's novelist, in other words, is not the objective scientist who stands apart from the world, detached and excluded from whatever he sees. Rather, his novelist is the "novelistic" therapist who participates in intersubjective encounters

with his works' characters; he understands that their own concrete pre-
dicaments speak tellingly to his own situation and challenge him to
see himself as mirrored in the characters. Only by openly and freely
engaging these characters in a dialogue where he responds to their pressures and challenges (rather than silencing them as irrelevant to his
own condition) can the author become conscious of self and world
and resist the destructive temptation to see himself as all-knowing and
autonomous. Percy's words to John Griffin Jones on what he hopes
the reader will bring away with his engagement with his protagonists
—"The reader is supposed to recognize the outsider in himself, and
to identify with the alienated values of those characters. Maybe I try
to design it so that it will cross the reader's mind to question the, quote,
'normal culture,' and to value his own state of disorientation" (*Con.*,
281)—also speak to the recognition and identification that Percy himself
discovers in the text. In "Metaphor as Mistake," Percy writes that we
"know one thing through the mirror of the other," and nowhere is
this more true than in the knowledge of the depths of the self.

In his fiction, the dynamics Percy envisions between therapist and
patient and between novelist-text-audience are most clearly evident in
Lancelot. At the center of the novel stands the encounter between Percival and Lancelot—doctor and patient—and in Lancelot's storytelling
we have a version of the interplay between storyteller (novelist), text,
and audience. The dynamics of intersubjectivity, and the resistance to
those dynamics, crucially shape both encounters.

First, the encounter between Lancelot and Percival. Lance, until the
end of the novel, embodies what Percy sees as perhaps humanity's most
destructive resistance to intersubjectivity—the myth of the autonomous
self. According to Percy, with the collapse in the Western world of the
traditional Judeo-Christian framework of belief and order, the
postmodern self turns inward to itself as the seat of all knowledge and
value. Percy describes the autonomous self in *Lost in the Cosmos*: "The
self sees itself as a sovereign and individual consciousness, liberated
by education from the traditional bonds of religion, by democracy from
the strictures of class, by technology from the drudgery of poverty, and
by self-knowledge from the tyranny of the unconscious—and therefore
free to pursue its own destiny without God" (*LC*, 13). The solipsism
of the autonomous self becomes particularly dangerous when the self
embraces, with unyielding commitment and without regard for the
rights and even the lives of other people (since all value is located within
the isolated autonomous self), extreme ideologies calling for the remak-
ing of society. In an unspoken reference to Hitler (and others, such

as abortionists and euthanasiasts, whom Percy sees as following in Hitler's footsteps), Percy writes in *Lost in the Cosmos* that no one "is as murderous as the autonomous self who, believing in nothing, can fall prey to ideology and kill millions of people—unwanted people, old people, sick people, useless people, unborn people, enemies of the state—and do so reasonably, without passion, even decently, certainly without the least obnoxiousness" (*LC*, 157).

Lance's plans for his new order—his Third Revolution or his New Reformation, as he calls it—for all its apparent decency, embodies just this type of murderous thinking; it is representative work of the autonomous self gone mad with ideology, in this case a version of southern Stoicism based on honor and chivalry in a fallen world. (In an interview with Jan Nordby Gretlund, Percy said that Lance carries the southern ethic "to its logical conclusion" [*Con.*, 209].) Violence will have its place in ushering in this new order, accompanied once the order is established by strict allegiance to an authoritarian—fascist, actually—elite, with Lance himself, of course, at the center. "You will do right," Lance says, speaking of those who will live in his envisioned society, "not because of the Jew-Christian commandments but because we say it is right" (*L*, 178). Lance's desire for ruthless domination of others surfaces most revealingly in his attitude toward women; when Percival suggests that women may not like the choice of roles the new society will dictate —lady or whore—Lance bluntly replies: "The hell with them. They won't have anything to say about it. Not only are they not strong enough. They don't care enough" (*L*, 179).

As hard as Lance strives to become a fully autonomous self, free from the past and from others, he has trouble achieving his goal. At one point Lancelot brags to Percival that his plans for a new society are founded on the freedom to act on his conviction, yet it is clear that Lance lacks such freedom. This is true not merely because Lance is a prisoner in a psychiatric hospital; it is also true because he is haunted by the past, nagged by an awareness that something went wrong on his quest for evil and that he must figure out what it was. "There is something I don't understand," he tells Percival. "And you are both my leverage point and my companion" (*L*, 108). Lance's need for Percival's presence—and, indeed, merely the act of conversing with Percival—underscores Lance's own insufficiency. If he were truly the autonomous self he desires to see himself as, he would have no need to speak with, indeed, confess to, Percival. "It's strange," he confides to his friend: "I have to tell you in order to know what I already know" (*L*, 85).

Percival's presence jars Lance's security for a number of reasons: their past friendship, their many shared adventures, Lance's lingering resentment of what he sees as Percival's betrayal of their fellowship by joining the priesthood and going to Africa. But what strikes him most forcefully is his recognition that in Percival he looks at a mirror image of himself. "When I saw you yesterday," Lance says to Percival in their first meeting, "it was like seeing myself" (L, 5). Whatever kinship he at first feels with Percival becomes sorely strained as the novel progresses and Percival actively asserts his Christian faith. Now, rather than as a vision of himself as abstracted modern man, Lance sees Percival as a mirror image of what he might have become had he found God on his quest —and, indeed, what he still *might* become. This awareness only increases his rage, for Lance is determined to smother all threats to his autonomous self; he wants to silence all voices that fail to echo his own chosen attitude.

Lance's attacks on Percival and his faith merely mask his disturbing awareness of his own insufficiency as all-powerful self (the presence of Percival does indeed teach him what he already knows) and signal his eventual downfall as stoic hero and new-world leader. By the end of the novel, Lance's conception of the autonomous self has been shattered, and he now asks Percival for answers rather than dictating them to him. The charged intersubjective dynamics of their conversation (Percival has been far from silent in the novel, even though we don't hear his voice directly until the final pages) have brought him a larger awareness of self and world, an enlightened level of consciousness—a knowledge of self in context and communion with others.

Likewise, as several critics have noted, Percival himself, the therapist, gains in consciousness.[3] Early in the novel Percival appears as a priest who has lost the way: he wears street clothes, he seems lost in abstraction, and he apparently rejects an appeal for prayer for the dead on All Souls' Day. As Lance sardonically notes, as a priest-physician he is either a "screwed-up priest or a half-assed physician" (L, 10). But through his interactions with Lance, not as detached observer but as active participant, Percival grows and develops, seeing, as Lance saw in him, a mirror image of himself—an image of what he might become were he to continue the directionless drift of his current life. Lance and the story he tells thereby help Percival to name his despair and indeed to (re)discover God and his role as priest. From the abstracted therapist who says little and for the most part stares out the window as Lance talks, Percival becomes the involved sharer of experience with his friend, now looking him in the eye and actively probing him about his past and his future plans, particularly the place (actually, the nonplace) in his life of loving relationships, the most charitable and meaningful expressions of intersubjective communion. Percival's decision to wear his clerical garments signifies his redefined identity both as priest and as therapist: he is no longer the objective observer and interpreter of psychological forces but the involved counselor of the mysteries of self and God. Percival will continue his shepherd work, we learn, as a parish priest in rural Alabama.

Besides embodying the potentially rewarding intersubjective dynamics between patient and therapist, the Lancelot-Percival interaction also speaks crucially to the dynamics Percy envisioned for the novelist in the creation of fiction. Lance, of course, is a storyteller, and his struggles with narrative represent much of what Percy sees as the weaknesses and limits of modern fiction. In his essays and interviews Percy identifies two significant temptations, in terms of technique, for modern writers: to write entirely from the perspective of a single consciousness and to write to assert a particular ideology. Both have potentially destructive effects. According to Percy, writing from the point of view of a sole consciousness, while not necessarily a skewed fictional technique, nonetheless is generally a telling symptom of the author's own reductive solipsism that discourages intersubjective growth. Modern writers, Percy said in an interview with Carlton Cremeens, "are much more locked into themselves" than were writers of the eighteenth and nineteenth centuries, so that in modern fiction "what is being presented now is not so much the action on the stage as the experience of the spectator in the privacy of his box" (*Con.*, 25). The second temptation, writing to champion a particular cause, is almost always fatal to fiction because the narrative manipulates rather than explores reality: fiction becomes reductively didactic rather than enrichingly cognitive.

Lance's narrative suffers from both of these faults. As storyteller, Lance remains firmly mired in his solipsism, convinced of the supremacy of his autonomous self and driven by his commitment to his revolutionary ideology. Because of his pride and his elevation of self, he stands detached from the narrative and its characters—even, and most significantly, the character of himself—oblivious to whatever challenges the discourse might present to his already complete views. Lance, in other words, resembles Percy's scientist who stands apart from the world that he or she observes; he reduces the humanity of the people about whom he speaks, turning sovereign and free people into dyadic creatures to be observed with scientific detachment and explained with scientific certainty. All life, for instance, Lance claims at one point, can be ex-

plained by the perverse workings of the libido. "The great secret of
the ages," he tells Percival, "is that man has evolved, is born, lives,
and dies for one end and one end only: to commit a sexual assault
on another human or to submit to such an assault" (L, 222). The irony,
of course, is that Lance does not apply these words to his own actions,
despite his assault on Raine, nor does he realize that his theorizing
cannot explain the very act of interpretation that has brought him to
this conclusion. His commitment to the ideology of his Third Revolution
further isolates him in his own consciousness and from his narrative:
his story is less an exploration of reality than an effort to convince
himself and Percival of the justice of his ideology and to convert his
friend to the cause. "No, it is not you who are offering me something,
salvation, a choice, whatever," he says to Percival. "I am offering you
a choice. Do you want to become one of us? You can without giving
up a single thing you believe in except your milksoppery" (L, 179).

Lance's position as storyteller speaks tellingly to Percy's own, for
Lance's faults—his utter confidence in his own perspective and his
evangelizing—are two temptations to which Percy as Catholic novelist
is given. In seeing a version of himself as author in Lance, which I
am sure he does, much as Percival sees himself mirrored in the madman, Percy thus gains a disturbing perspective on himself; but it is a
perspective that challenges him to further growth and awareness because it frees himself from the confines of his limited vision and gives
him a perspective and context for understanding his position in the
world. His very involvement with Lance embodies the active dialogic
stance that Percy believes authors must have with their works; rather
than standing apart from their narratives, as Lance does, Percy believes
that writers must be crucially engaged with their stories, knowing that
their meaning is news, not knowledge, and so speak significantly to
their creators' situations.

All of this brings us back to the therapist-patient relationship and
what Percy calls "novelistic" therapy. Percy's conception of an actively
involved therapist, who gets to know the patient well and along the
way also himself, is indeed precisely Percy's conception of the novelist,
whose relationship with the text must be thoroughly intersubjective.
Consciousness of one's self, Percy believes, arises from turning not inward but outward; these intersubjective encounters between self and
other consciousnesses shape not merely the best therapy and art but
the best lives, for to live for and with other individuals is to live by
a charity at once enlightening and ennobling. Father Smith's admonishment of Tom More near the end of Love in the Ruins, when Tom refuses

to express sorrow for his sins, embodies such charity: "Meanwhile, forgive me but there are other things we must think about: like doing our jobs, you being a better doctor, I being a better priest, showing a bit of ordinary kindness to people, particularly our own families—unkindness to those close to us is such a pitiful thing—doing what we can for our poor unhappy country—things which, please forgive me, sometimes seem more important than dwelling on a few middle-aged daydreams" (*LR*, 399). Father Smith's admonition speaks not merely to Tom More but also to Walker Percy and indeed to us all—patients and therapists, writers and readers, individuals all in an intersubjective community.

Part IV
Novelist and Moralist

Ashley Brown

Walker Percy: The Novelist as Moralist

In a letter written to Caroline Gordon in 1962, soon after *The Moviegoer* was published, Walker Percy said, "My main problem as a fiction writer" is that "I do not consider myself a novelist but a moralist or propagandist. My spiritual father is Pascal (and/or Kierkegaard). And if I also kneel before the altar of Lawrence and Joyce and Flaubert, it is not because I wish to do what they did, even if I could. What I really want to do is to tell people what they must do and what they must believe if they want to live."[1] As Walker Percy well knew, he was making a distinction between the aesthetic and moral qualities of fiction that Caroline Gordon would not easily accept. He was surely aware that she was sometimes very critical of Catholic novelists such as François Mauriac and Graham Greene, who slighted the natural order in their zeal to pursue a theological theme. In an article called "Some Readings and Misreadings," published in the *Sewanee Review* in the summer of 1953, she praised instead such writers as Joyce and Flaubert and Faulkner, whatever the state of their theological beliefs: "That kind of patient, passionate portrayal of natural objects is a recognition of the natural order which I can only call Christian, 'Christian in hope.'" Moreover, Caroline Gordon was not exactly receptive to the existentialist mode represented by Pascal and Kierkegaard, and she could be almost harsh in her remarks about Sartre and Camus, two novelists whom Percy has repeatedly mentioned with admiration.

For many years it has been evident that one of Percy's main assets as a writer is his extraordinary observation of the social scene in the South. He seems almost deliberately to locate his fiction in the midst of a postwar consumer society where appearance is everything. Posterity will find his novels a rich source of information about the houses and automobiles, the artifacts and the brand names that constitute the mise-en-scène of American life in the late twentieth century. The following, for example, is a typical passage from *The Moviegoer*:

> The closer you get to the lake, the more expensive the houses are. Already the bungalows and duplexes and tiny ranch houses are behind me. Here are the fifty and sixty thousand dollar homes, fairly big moderns with dagger plants and Australian pines planted in brick boxes, and reproductions of French provincials and Louisiana colonials. The swimming pools steam like sleeping geysers. These houses look handsome in the sunlight; they please me with their pretty colors, their perfect lawns and their clean airy garages. But I have noticed that at this hour of dawn they are forlorn. A sadness settles over them like a fog from the lake. (*M*, 84)

But more important is Percy's depiction of manners at every level of southern society; he knows exactly how people behave, and he has some understanding of the historical forces that have led to their behavior. Like George Eliot, like Proust, but unlike most novelists, he was a critic before he turned to fiction, and some of his early essays and reviews in such magazines as the *Commonweal* already set up the attitudes about human behavior that would emerge in his novels. His comments about southern Stoicism, for instance, are brilliantly realized in the famous confrontation between Binx Bolling and his aunt in *The Moviegoer*. Aunt Emily's great tirade concerns "the one heritage of the men of our family, a certain quality of spirit, a gaiety, a sense of duty, a nobility worn lightly, a sweetness, a gentleness with women—the only good things the South ever had and the only things that really matter in this life" (*M*, 224). But what brings off the scene (as Caroline Gordon used to say) is Aunt Emily's letter opener, "the soft iron sword she has withdrawn from the grasp of the helmeted figure on the ink-stand." As the scene builds up on the strength of her feelings about his treatment of Kate—has he behaved responsibly toward this self-destructive girl?—the letter opener becomes a symbol of Aunt Emily's ancient Stoic authority: "We watch the sword as she lets it fall over the fulcrum of her forefinger; it goes *ta't't* on the brass hinge of the desk. Then, so suddenly that I almost start, my aunt sheathes the sword and places her hand flat on the desk. Turning it over, she flexes her fingers and studies the nails, which are deeply scored by longitudinal ridges" (*M*, 222). As the scene reaches its climax, the letter opener brings a certain guilt into the situation: "I cannot tear my eyes from the sword. Years ago I bent the tip trying to open a drawer. My aunt looks too. Does she suspect?"(*M*, 224).

This scene is a superb example of the way in which moral attitudes are projected through the minutiae of behavior, and it tells us that Walker Percy, if he chose, could easily be a novelist of manners. He has all the social experience and the wit required for this mode of fiction. The novel of manners has not been typical of southern writers, at least until recently. Many years ago, when he was still defending book-culture, Marshall McLuhan described the "passionate" nature of traditional southern life, in a society dominated by rhetoric rather than dialectic or self-questioning. *Passion*, he said, "makes for the tragic in art and life just as *character* tends toward satire, comedy and the play of manners."[2] This formulation well describes most southern novelists from William Gilmore Simms to Robert Penn Warren, and it is especially true of the finest novels of the 1930s, from *Light in August*, to *Night Rider*.

At the same time one can see the novel of manners emerging during the so-called southern Renascence. Ellen Glasgow, in *The Romantic Comedians* (1926) and *They Stooped to Folly* (1929), is probably the pioneer; but these novels, which are rather deliberate exercises in this mode, are not typical of her best work. An interesting figure of the period is Grace Lumpkin, a radical novelist from South Carolina, who moved from the social propaganda of her early fiction, such as *To Make My Bread* (1932), to *The Wedding* (1939), a novel of manners that in a sense is based on the class struggle but whose main interest is the comedy produced by such a situation. Another South Carolina writer who ended up in social comedy was the poet Josephine Pinckney. Her neglected novel, *Three O'Clock Dinner* (1945), is a perfect if slight example of this genre. More important is Caroline Gordon, who was to be the mentor of Flannery O'Connor and Walker Percy. Her early novels, from *Penhally* (1931) to *Green Centuries* (1941), constitute a tragedy of historical ruin in the South that she knew. But beginning with *The Women on the Porch* (1944), she moves, with a serious Christian purpose, into contemporary social comedy. *The Strange Children* (1951) is a roman à clef that candidly reexamines the life she and her friends knew during the 1930s, their agrarian period. It is a novel of manners in every sense, but it also suggests that there was something futile (or at least ironic) about the effort to perpetuate a history already ruined. Here, and even more so in *The Malefactors* (1956), originally subtitled *A Comedy*, she is saying that redemption must lie in another order of existence, and of course she finally makes no secret of her Christian emphasis. Caroline Gordon was perhaps too restless to be satisfied with the novel of manners, but she practiced it well on at least one occasion.

I seem to be suggesting that the general movement of modern southern fiction has been from the tragic to the comic, somewhat along the
lines of Marshall McLuhan's formulation. That does seem to be the
case. Eudora Welty was moving in this direction from the beginning,
and what she attempted with some success in *Delta Wedding* (1946)
she brought to perfection in *The Optimist's Daughter* (1972), one of the
finest short novels of our time. One could say much the same thing
about Peter Taylor and Elizabeth Spencer, whose best work has come
very recently. These writers are well aware of the tragic issues that were
dramatized by their great predecessors, Faulkner and the novelists of
the 1930s, but they live in another world, one of fluctuating and uncertain values, where the tragic mode could not easily be realized. (There
are always exceptions to any formulation; one I easily think of is Madison Jones, who has brought something of the tragic power of the southern novel of the 1930s into the recent past.)

This seems to me the background for Walker Percy's fiction. He was
a late starter among southern writers, but he had the advantage of
being on the edge of his generations's literary culture, and by the time
he published *The Moviegoer* in 1961 he had thought out his basic conception of the modern scene. He easily accepted Gabriel Marcel's Catholic
version of existentialism, as he has said to several interviewers, and
he frankly begins with the assumption that the contemporary city of
man is an "alien place." The South, he once said, "is now almost as
broken a world as the North, and we must learn to live in it." There
is no lament for a lost community, southern or otherwise, in his novels,
and some of his most sardonic pages are devoted to the meretricious
instant community offered to the public by the real estate industry.
Percy's world may still contain the residue of something tragic, but it
is essentially a world of incongruities. Comedy is always based on incongruity, that is, on the discrepancy between the way people behave
and the way we think they should behave.

As a literary mode comedy always involves a social situation, people
played off against each other in different combinations; but this situation
is typically resolved by a public occasion, a secular ritual. *The Moviegoer*
takes place against the background of Mardi Gras week in New Orleans.
Binx Bolling deliberately avoids the public occasion, which he may
well regard as a travesty of the real thing, but he is very conscious
of it, and eventually he establishes for himself and Kate a "komos"
—that being the Greek term, meaning revel, which is the original of
our term, "comedy." In this respect *The Moviegoer* is a comedy of manners, like Josephine Pinckney's *Three O'Clock Dinner* or Eudora Welty's

Delta Wedding or Caroline Gordon's house party in *The Strange Children*. But with Walker Percy the ritual occasion is somewhat suspect; it is no longer easily taken for granted. The characters in his novels must establish some meaning in their lives out of the shards of belief that still seem authentic. They must find some basis for mutual trust out of their own limited experience.

Walker Percy clearly does not look upon the social scene he knows so well as something self-sufficient. Writers like the Byron of *Don Juan* and Pushkin and Chekhov have been willing to do that. As he told Caroline Gordon in the letter already cited, "What I really want to do is to tell people what they must do and what they must believe if they want to live." Since I have just mentioned two of the greatest Russian writers, this is the place to introduce another, namely, Dostoevsky, because Percy mentions him several times in this same letter. He evidently thinks that Dostoevsky was more daring in his approach to a religious thesis than any other novelist before him had been: "The conclusion has almost forced itself upon me that one cannot write a religious novel in this day and age. It has to do with the threadbareness of religious words, to say the least. God is a word I will have nothing to do with. Nobody but Dostoevsky can use it. When the holy has disappeared, how in blazes can a novelist expect to make use of it? . . . Perhaps the craft of the religious novelist nowadays consists mainly in learning how to shout in silence."

Now, there may be a slight discrepancy between the moral intention and the social occasion—the idea and the image—in Percy's fiction. One sometimes senses that the moralist is getting the upper hand. I have virtually said that he is our most ambitious novelist of manners, and that description will probably do in assessing his work. He is something like the early Evelyn Waugh, another novelist-convert who brilliantly dealt with the absurdity of the social scene that he happened to know at first hand. Good comic writers always assume that they live in a fallen world, but they are willing to accept its incongruities. That, I think, is the case with the Waugh of such novels as *Decline and Fall* and *Vile Bodies* and the Percy of *The Moviegoer*. But already with his second novel, *The Last Gentleman*, the comic writer is on the way to becoming the satirist, and with his third, *Love in the Ruins*, that is altogether the case. I was rather astonished, when that novel came out in 1971, that Percy had chosen a title and indeed a fictional situation so close to Waugh's *Love among the Ruins*, which had been published in 1953. Both, of course, are satires set in the near future. I see by Percy's conversation with Charles T. Bunting, which took place in 1971 but which I have just recently read, that the issue was raised at that time. Percy claimed not to have been aware of Waugh's novel, but he mentioned Browning's poem "Love among the Ruins," which was probably the source for both Waugh's and Percy's titles. But no matter. Waugh, like Percy, practiced the satiric mode on occasion, but he was not at home in it. The good satirist is always a moralist; he would have the world other than what it is; he finds it difficult to accept its imperfections. That, I think, is very much the case with writers such as Swift, the Dostoevsky of *Notes from Underground* (an important book for Walker Percy), and George Orwell, different though they are in other ways. They all set themselves against the world as they had experienced it. I suggest that the comedian and the satirist are sometimes at odds; they practice essentially different literary modes.

Percy's boldest fiction, for me at least, is *Lancelot.* Here he returns to the first-person narrator that he used as a governing device in *The Moviegoer.* (In *The Last Gentleman* and *Love in the Ruins* he shifted to the omniscient narrator, perhaps because Caroline Gordon had made some comment about his use of the first-person and its attendant "armor," its air of self-protection, in *The Moviegoer.*) The general model for this novel is Camus's *La Chute,* as Percy himself noted in an interview with Herbert Mitgang when *Lancelot* appeared in 1977. The French would probably call *La Chute* a *récit* rather than a *roman;* that is, it has the form of a monologue, a confession, which Northrop Frye claims is a literary mode in itself. In Camus's novel the central figure, Clamence, lives in Amsterdam, where he has a kind of death-in-life existence following his flight from Paris, where he has been a witness to a suicide. His feeling of guilt in this matter is obsessive and repetitious; in his monologue the same images return with variation. (Camus's model for this narrative procedure was very likely Dostoevsky's *Notes from Underground.*) Amsterdam is a city almost surrounded by water; its rings of canals suggest the circles in Dante's *Inferno* to Clamence and, of course, provide the setting for his death in life. I suppose he is a kind of Trimmer, an unbeliever, as in Dante's canto 3. Caroline Gordon, in some comments that she made about the novel in 1957, the year in which it appeared in English, said that the action is never resolved. But if Camus were seriously imitating Dante, that problem would only follow: those in the *Inferno* do not move; they are fixed in their positions of torment forever.

I find it interesting that Walker Percy uses, as an epigraph for *Lancelot,* a quotation from the *Purgatorio:*

> He sank so low that all means
>   for his salvation were gone,
>   except showing him the lost people.
> For this I visited the region of the dead.

His hero, Lancelot Lamar, is certainly in a purgatorial state, but that already makes him different from Clamence. Looking out at a tiny fragment of the world from his cell in a mental institution, he would seem to have no hope of moving on, of resolving his situation. But the narrative technique allows him to recreate his life in a kind of cinematic montage: in his peculiar, mad way he understands what he has done, and in the end he moves on to Virginia with Anna, the girl in the next cell, to create another kind of life, one different from the stoicism that he tried to perpetuate in his youth. The technique of the novel, as Percy described it in an interview with Jan Nordby Gretlund in 1981, was something that he only gradually arrived at. It began as another third-person narrative, essentially a dialogue between Lancelot and his old friend, Percival the priest. But Percy was evidently dissatisfied with the "threadbareness of religious words" (to use his phrase, already quoted), and in the final version the priest is only a silent listener. It is a daring fictional tactic, and I think of what Percy wrote to Caroline Gordon in 1962: "Perhaps the craft of the religious novelist nowadays consists mainly in learning how to shout in silence." This is the best comment that one could apply to the novel. At any rate, Walker Percy the satirist has arrived at another stage with this book—the satirist himself (Lancelot) is satirized. This is the stage that was reached by Shakespeare in *Timon of Athens*, by Molière in *Le Misanthrope*, by Swift in *Gulliver's Travels*. The problem for Walker Percy is that the novel of manners is not a convention that lends itself very easily to satire of such deeply felt conviction. George Orwell abandoned it completely in *Animal Farm*, just as Flaubert had in *Bouvard et Pécuchet*. But this is a striking work of a certain sort, and Lewis A. Lawson and other critics have demonstrated the intricate patterning of its references to movies, crime novels, and other phenomena of our culture.

Incidentally, there is a comparison yet to be made between Walker Percy and his near contemporary, John Cheever. Cheever was an early starter who made a considerable reputation with his short fiction, but his best work came fairly late. Like Percy, he was a novelist of manners who operated within what was left of a regional culture, in his case, New England. He also gradually turned to satire, and in *Falconer*, which was published in 1977, the same year *Lancelot* was published, we find a remarkably similar book, the monologue of a sinner who is serving time in prison. There is also a marked religious dimension to Cheever's work, but he has probably not thought out the issues as thoroughly as Percy has. Although Percy takes his place with such writers as Peter Taylor and Elizabeth Spencer as a novelist of manners, he simply is not content with this role; he would be a Dostoevsky rather than a Chekhov. We must honor him for bringing so much intelligence to bear on the art of fiction.

François Pitavy

Walker Percy's Brave New World: *The Thanatos Syndrome*

This is the most humanitarian century in history. . . . But at the same time it is the century in which men have killed more of each other than in all other centuries put together.

WALKER PERCY

In *The Thanatos Syndrome*, Father Smith complains to Dr. Tom More of a loss of sense—things no longer seem to signify: "If it is a fact that words are deprived of their meaning, does it not follow that there is a depriver?" (118). Contrary to what Father Smith implies, however, the depriver is no Satan. The *diabolos*, the slanderer of sense, who divorces the word from the thing, or the signifier from the signified, and man from himself, is man himself. That is why Percy the survivor, the ex-suicide, commits himself to a search for sense by passionately, and more and more satirically, exploring and exposing the American dream, indicting American culture, or civilization at large, and ultimately man's dream of perfection in our Judeo-Christian tradition. Just as Binx Bolling has produced what he calls a "document" and Lance Lamar a confession, Percy wrote six novels to that effect, the last being the most ambitious because the indictment, as it does in Huxley, takes the form of a dystopia, that is, a distorted, grotesque reflection of what the dream has become and must become if some survivors are not left to warn us.

On formal grounds, *The Thanatos Syndrome* is not Percy's best piece of fiction. The novel needs tightening, and despite its almost too visible centrality, "Father Smith's Confession," and even Father's Smith's very presence, can be seen as redundant (the confession and footnote were in fact added after the first manuscript stage): that tenderness leads to the gas chamber is already clearly suggested in Comeaux's and Van Dorn's elated visions of a totalitarian brave new world and in the Belle Ame Academy episode that is the core of the thriller. Evidently playing for larger stakes than just a thriller, however, Percy seems to have emphasized his main plot with this loosely integrated subplot, as though fearing that his message might not be obvious enough. But this structural strategy is also an index to his ambition: despite its formal flaws, *The Thanatos Syndrome* may be regarded as Percy's most didactic and also most ambitious piece of fiction; and precisely because of them, the author's intentions stand out the more clearly.

Unlike Faulkner, who went back to the foundation of the city in the first prologue of *Requiem for a Nun*, or Fitzgerald, who re-created the original moment of the American dream at the end of *The Great Gatsby* in the vision of the Dutch sailors, Walker Percy need not hark back to the origins and attempt to retrieve that moment of splendor when the dream still appeared possible, existing brightly as long as it remained short of realization. The undercurrent of nostalgia that runs through Faulkner and Fitzgerald does not run through Percy. He does not see the failure of man's dream as foreordained; despite his pessimism, he still hopes and thinks he can do something about man's predicament. Like Flannery O'Connor, he looks forward, not backward, attempting to come up to the threshold of transcendence: his ruthless indictment of the follies of men leads up to that point, but, as in O'Connor, it must stop there. What lies beyond is no longer a matter of fiction, but of faith, and it must remain unknowable. "Whether or not the catastrophe actually befalls us, or is deserved—whether reconciliation and renewal may yet take place—is not for the novelist to say," Percy writes at the end of his "Notes for a Novel about the End of the World" (*MB*, 118). At the end of *The Moviegoer*, it remains "impossible to say" whether the black person seen entering a church on Ash Wednesday has been touched by grace or has even received ashes.

O'Connor was fond of quoting Saint Cyril of Jerusalem: "'The dragon sits by the side of the road, watching those who pass. Beware lest he devour you. We go to the Father of Souls, but it is necessary to pass by the dragon.'"[1] Since the Father of Souls must remain outside the realm of fiction, the roadway is precisely the subject matter of both O'Connor and Percy; they are concerned with evil, with the absurdity or grotesqueness of man's predicament, with the dragon (and so are, significantly, other Catholic writers, such as François Mauriac, Paul

Claudel, and Julien Green). Essentially, man in his lifetime remains to them a *Homo viator*, and their fiction takes the form of a quest for sense amid the seeming senselessness of life, or the death-in-life Percy calls "everydayness"—in the last analysis, death itself, the syndrome of which he tracks in his last novel.

Tom More, the narrator-psychiatrist-detective of *The Thanatos Syndrome*, uncovers evidence of a conspiracy to chemically alter the behavior of the inhabitants of Feliciana Parish, to create in Feliciana a brave new world—an experiment those sorcerers' apprentices would readily extend to the rest of America, in their idealistic-cum-totalitarian longing for perfection. Indeed, these southern Drs. Strangelove venture into regions where man is made to regress into disturbing patterns of behavior, which also have the all too familiar ring of recent historical nightmares.

Heavy sodium (Na–24), added to drinking water, depresses or suppresses the superego, that is, the voice of conscience—the interdicting agency, in Freud's topology. The neutralization of the superego entails the end of anxiety and guilt, a sharp decrease in aggressive tendencies and the demythification of sex, which is then reduced to acts devoid of significance. Intoxicated by his elated vision of the new *Homo americanus* he is on his way to re-create, or rather to create, since in the American psyche such a perfect man has never been any more than a dream, Bob Comeaux experiences a sense of illimitable, Promethean power: "What would you say," he asks Tom, "if I gave you a magic wand you could wave over there . . . and overnight you could reduce crime in the streets by eighty-five percent?" (*TS*, 191)—not only crime in the streets, but also child abuse, teenage suicide and pregnancy, wife battering, depression and chemical dependence, and, what appears to him of even greater import, a telltale index to more profound obsessions, AIDS, anal intercourse, homosexuality, and pornography.

On closer inspection, Comeaux's dream appears to be twofold: one aspect is social and "cultural," even sectional, and thus nostalgic and backward looking, historically and socially regressive; the other aspect, more ambitious and more threatening, is at once biological, intellectual, spiritual, and thus forward looking: it aims at the creation of a new man, thereby achieving the mythical dream of man's perfection and of a perfect society, transcending even the Puritan ideals of the first settlers and those of the idealistic Quakers in William Penn's colony, who very well knew, or finally came to accept, that man is not perfect but ineradicably tainted by the Original Sin, so that society cannot do without prisons (as appears at the opening of *The Scarlet Letter*). The first aspect of Comeaux's dream has to do with the restoration of a mythical past and is designed for the lower segments of society; the second is concerned with the creation of a new superior being and is thus designed for the higher segments of society (with token blacks, of course). Comeaux wants not only to stabilize society but also to improve upon it. He then envisions no less than the achievement of the original American dream of a new Adam, a dream the first settlers had failed to realize: such is his ambition in his chemical New Zion.

That Comeaux's dream harks back to the past is obvious in his conversations with Tom.

> "Tom, would you laugh at me if I told you what we've done is restore the best of the Southern Way of Life? Would you think that too corny?"
>
> "Well—"
>
> "Well, never mind. Just the facts, ma'am. Here are the facts: Instead of a thousand young punks hanging around the streets in northwest Baton Rouge, looking for trouble, stoned out, ready to mug you, break into your house, rape your daughter, packed off to Angola where they cost you twenty-five thousand a year, do you want to know what they are doing . . . of their own accord?"
>
> "What?"
>
> "Cottage industries, garden plots, but mainly apprenticeships. . . . Tom, Baton Rouge is the only city in the U.S. where young blacks are outperforming the Vietnamese and the Hispanics." (*TS*, 197–98)

However elated, Comeaux's vision is clearly (and unwittingly) racist. The elegance and graciousness of the southern way of life can be restored only by a return to the time-honored view of a rigidly stratified society, with clear-cut separations between the strata. To Comeaux, the contemporary evil, the new "plague" threatening America, is social (and moral) disruption: when the strata are fissured, outbursts and eruptions can no longer be contained, and the responsibility for such disruptions, as is unambiguously shown in his speech, is shouldered by the blacks. The stereotypical image is immediately recognizable ("rape your daughters") even before the "young punks" are designated by their color. The restoration of the old order means that the blacks (as well as the other minorities, since this is, unfortunately, contemporary America) must return to where they belong, that is, underneath, to the lower strata. The comparison of the blacks with the newer minorities may be meant to be comical here; it has a damning double-edged racist ring.

Later, when Tom is temporarily back in prison, Bob Comeaux makes an even more revealing remark: "There is still grace, style, beauty, manners, civility left in the world. It's not all gone with the wind" (*TS*, 265). The use of the word "grace," the first and most important in the series, and the reference to Margaret Mitchell hark back to the 1930s and *Gone With the Wind*. Comeaux's words here echo Ashley's yearning for the "slow grace" of bygone days, that is, for a motionless society, and they recall Sutpen's desire to freeze time in *Absalom, Absalom!*, published just a few months after Mitchell's best-seller (surprisingly, Ashley is more clearsighted than Comeaux or Sutpen, who believe the restoration is possible). The disruptive elements must be controlled and immobilized in their proper places. Comeaux's vision is in fact ahistorical: he does not dream so much of the antebellum society proper as of the escapist regressive images propounded by revisionist historians in the 1920s and 1930s and, above all (judging by his culture as a self-adopted southerner), of the never-never land of the southern plantation novel, in which the plantation has become the paradigm of that golden age—of paradise lost. Such a dream is now relayed by Hollywood: that is why Belle Ame, "restored to its 1857 splendor, a slightly vulgar splendor, showy and ritzy," is "now the creation of Texaco and Hollywood" (*TS*, 213). No longer a working plantation, Belle Ame, rather than the Paramount back lot, is now used by Hollywood, because it appears more genuine or more "cultural" than Los Angeles, as the dream here is seemingly sanctioned by actual history—revisited, of course. Ritzy and showy indeed, it is the proper place to try to make the spurious dream come true in its pristine and illusory simplicity. Binx Bolling's early remark should be recalled at this point: "The movies are onto the search, but they screw it up" (*M*, 13).

In Comeaux's vision, the blacks are made safely to return to where they come from—their African origins, as evinced in their garden work for the city:

"One of the anthropologists on our board noted a striking resemblance to the decorative vegetation of the Masai tribesmen—and guess what they've done with the old cinder-block entrances?"

"What?"

"They're now mosaics, bits of colored glass from Anacin bottles, taillights, whatever, for all the world like—can't you guess?"

"No." . . .

"Do you remember the colorful bottle trees darkies used to make in the old days?"

"Yes," I say, wondering how Bob Como of Long Island City knows about bottle trees. (*TS*, 198–99)

The black is then made to regress to his original nature, which is good
—for him. He is again the good savage—not, however, Rousseau's
child, but an American version. There certainly lies at the back of the
unreconstructed southerner's mind (of whom Bob Comeaux is the current ironical avatar, since he is a Como from Long Island) a subconscious desire to keep the black at a convenient distance by restricting
him to a racially specific activity, such as, for instance, the practice of
his native arts. Labeled a native artist (with the usual derogatory con-
notations), the black is safely back where he belongs. The southern
sense of place, not just geographical but mostly social and cultural,
is thereby restored as a rampart against any disruption—and against
time (which is also the dream of the "innocent" Sutpen).

A revealing evidence of the nature of Comeaux's dream is the way
he has it sanctioned by Jefferson: "We're not talking about old massa
and his niggers. We're not talking about Uncle Tom. We're talking about
Uncle Tom Jefferson and his yeoman farmer and his yeoman craftsman"
(*TS*, 198). This is, however, a revised view of Jefferson, who never made
the black a yeoman craftsman, let alone a yeoman farmer. Look at
Monticello. The admirably graceful mansion seems the perfect metaphor of the antebellum southern society: the black craftsmen and ser-
vants are kept underneath, supporting the aristocratic grace, half buried
and invisible when you look at the mansion from the front lawn. The
foundation of southern society must remain that: a foundation. Which
is exactly what Comeaux has in mind. Whether or not this is a carica-
ture of Jefferson is not the point. Comeaux needs the sanction not so
much of the actual Jefferson as of the usable Mr. Jefferson for his dream
of an orderly society in which everyone knows where he belongs and
works in his own place toward the common good.

The other aspect of Comeaux's dream, oriented toward the future
creation of a new man, is more ambitious and much more threatening.
Heavy sodium affects the female biology, effecting a regression from
menstrual cycle to estrus: while the female human is in heat 75 percent
of the time, the percentage falls to 9 percent for the female mammal.
Not only is this a "marvelously built-in natural population control"
(*TS*, 196), but more significantly it means the end of "useless" sex:
"Goodby pills, rubbers, your friendly abortionist. Goodby promiscuity,"
Comeaux says, waxing enthusiastic (*TS*, 197). By neutralizing the superego, that is, the voice of conscience, by demythifying sex and reduc-
ing it to a mere biological function necessary only at certain appointed
times, as it is with animals, in other words by doing away with sex
and sin (a synonymous pair), Comeaux at last realizes in his brave

new world the Adamic, prelapsarian dream, then come true in America. The price, however, is not progression but regression to animality, as Tom More will discover.

Another effect achieved by breaking down the inhibitory function of the superego is the "average twenty percent increase in I.Q.—plus an almost total memory recall," Comeaux claims (*TS*, 192). Inconsequently, but revealingly, he never mentions any such effect at the Angola prison farm. The blacks are left to their native arts and their love of apprenticeship— their subservience—but Ellen has become a bridge champion, Comeaux, Jr., has a stunning and effortless memory recall, and the students at Louisiana State University systematically win football matches (a singular achievement!) and "no longer use calculators. They are as obsolete as slide rules. They've got their own built-in calculators" (*TS*, 195). This entails a different type of communication —a minimal, paratactical language with very few words, not even making up proper sentences. It also means new modes of computerlike reasoning and even new objects of thought—the most profound alteration of man's mind: "Tom, these kids are way past comic books and *Star Wars*. They are into graphic and binary communication—which after all is a lot more accurate than once upon a time there was a wicked queen" (*TS*, 197). In other words, exit fiction (or literature), indeed an inaccurate fantasy, a lie, according to etymology; enter the binary, either/or computer mind, with no literary frills attached. The Faustian desire to improve upon creation or, according to Van Dorn, to correct the aberrant evolution of man's brains therefore also means the discarding of imagination, the end of art. No contradiction here, however, with the development of native arts among the blacks: those are the mere repetition of what they once knew and had forgotten.

The American dream of success and man's dream of perfection are ironically epitomized in the Belle Ame Academy. There, admittedly, the children (that is, the new race to come) outperform themselves physically and intellectually, but in no way spiritually. The plantation, outwardly an exemplar of excellence, has its skeleton in the cupboard, that is, its upstairs facilities, where the mind-altering cocktail is prepared and where the self-proclaimed educators use and abuse the children sexually: the plantation is also a bordello, where the victims not only do not retain any sense of decency (or indecency, for that matter), no longer have the fine souls their "academy" proclaims by its very name to develop in them, but have no souls at all.

So Comeaux and Van Dorn's dream of perfection condemns itself by the very excesses to which it leads. The exposure, or the self-deflation, is here achieved in different ways, ranging from an ironical musical counterpoint to dark comedy and satire and to the linking of the experiments of the Feliciana scientists to those of the Nazi eugenicists.

The fantasy of the ancien régime willed by Comeaux must, of course, be graced by beauty and music. Paradoxically, however, the paradigm of beauty is to be found in the state prison farm:

> We look out over the vast prison farm. Rows of cotton, mostly picked, stretch away into the bright morning sunlight. Hundreds of black men and women, the men bare-chested, the women kerchiefed, bend over the rows, dragging their long sacks collapsed like parachutes. Armed horsemen patrol the levee.
>
> "Listen, Tom," says Bob Comeaux softly.
>
> From all around, as murmurous as the morning breeze, comes the singing.
>
> > *Swing low, sweet chariot,*
> > *Coming for to carry me home.* (TS, 266)

This beats Mitchell's description of the blacks at Tara, who sing on the way back from work (they are never seen actually working in the fields). Here they sing *while* working, as of course they should in this brave new world. Fifty years after *Gone with the Wind*, this must have a comical, deflating effect to most readers.

In a more subtle and significant way, music works as an ironical obbligato accompaniment to Comeaux's words. While driving with Tom among the balmy pines "in the gold autumn sunlight" of Louisiana, "surely as lovely as the Vienna woods" (TS, 194), his inflated dream is pricked by the counterpoint of music he has himself chosen: waltzes by Johann Strauss. Tom first notices "The Artist's Life," then "Wiener Blut," then "Tales from the Vienna Woods" (TS, 191, 192–93, 194): this is no haphazard order, but a manner of comment upon the experiments of the sorcerer's apprentices, understood in the light of "Father Smith's Confession." Then come the triumphant strains of "The Blue Danube" (TS, 201), blue like the Blue Boy Project, of course. The loud, fantasy-inducing music prevents Comeaux from apprehending the profound meaning and the consequences of his beautiful blue vision. Similarly, in *The Rosenkavalier*, the waltzes stressing the vulgarity and blindness of Baron Ochs expose the character's pretensions and subvert his endeavors. Such ironical use of music Percy may very well have learned from Richard Strauss himself, whose opera he had already significantly used in *The Moviegoer*.

Another deflating device is, of course, achieved with the end of the

Belle Ame Academy episode. The side effects of this experiment in excellence are so obvious in the molestation of the children and the sexual perversions of the educators revealed by the photographs that the best weapon Percy can use here—short of being a moralist or a preacher (a defect, however, he seems less and less able to avoid)—is comedy, in the hilarious, even if somewhat too explicit, ending. The Prometheuses of the project are literally exposed in their nakedness and driven back to animality when forced to do to themselves what they had done to others. Van Dorn, the founder of the academy, the descendant of the gallant Civil War hero who, however, did not die the death of a hero, is all along superbly satirized by Percy and awarded the worst punishment: an ape in a cage, the spurious and cynical new Adam will be redeemed to humanity by Eve, an actual chimpanzee. As for the homosexual coach, he is condemned to take tender care of terminal AIDS patients.

The photographs taken at Belle Ame also play a function of exposure (*TS*, 298–99). The bare, emotionless description of them by the narrator (with the proper scientific terms in Latin) has a surreal effect far beyond the mere sexual perversion. Tom is struck here by the formality of the participants' attitudes, "the archaic pose of old group photographs": "The photographs, I can't help but notice again, exhibit the same Victorian propriety, the decorous expressions, every hair in place, bobbed in the women, old-fashioned 1930s high haircuts in men, a British sort of nakedness, white-as-white skins and vulnerable backs, unlike tan-all-over U.S. California nakedness, and the children above all: simpering, prudish, but, most of all, pleased" (*TS*, 299, 330). It looks as if the American psyche could never rid itself of its Judeo-Christian heritage, of guilt and Original Sin. The very formality of the poses contradicts the neutralization of the superego, claimed as the primary effect of heavy sodium: the little girl, partly penetrated by Van Dorn, may have her legs "kicking up in pleasure" and be somehow unaware of what she is submitted to, yet she is "looking at the camera with a demure, even prissy, expression" (*TS*, 298). And even though the educators occasionally drink a glass of the school cocktail, the photographs reveal that theirs is no Edenic, innocent nakedness; they have retained, as if it were clothing of which they can never divest themselves, a white, self-conscious sort of nakedness, a Victorian sense of propriety in their very improper behavior. You cannot eradicate the fall from grace and return to Eden. You cannot go home again. The Adamic dream must remain just that: a forever receding dream, forever contradicted by the principle of reality.

The most sinister side of the scientists' desire for perfection is evidently their so-called Qualitarian Center, where they do away with imperfection simply by eliminating the unfit infants and the useless old, that is, those who never will, or no longer can, measure up to the model of perfection set up by the scientists: "'What we're doing . . . is following the laws of the Supreme Court, respecting the rights of the family, the consensus of child psychologists, the rights of the unwanted child not to have to suffer a life of suffering and abuse, the right of the unwanted aged to . . . a death with dignity'"(*TS*, 199). Apparently a blander form of a brave new world, this is indeed more insidious, for it shifts the responsibility for euthanasia to the victims themselves, conditioned to exercise a pseudoliberty that entails no choice—a liberty to choose what has been set for them by court decisions or the consensus of psychologists and scientists, as if the law, or even reason or science, were not contingent, as if the unwanted child were responsible for being unwanted and freely accepted to live, or rather to die, by the unwritten rules of that consensus. This is nothing else than rhetorical legerdemain.

At this point, the scientists' vision unambiguously harks back to the Nazi dreams of perfection. Fascination with Germany has indeed long been a part of the southerner's mind. His grand tour led him as a matter of course to the Rhine, the Lorelei, Cologne, and Heidelberg, where Faulkner's Gavin Stevens spends one year; and as Father Smith tells Tom, "being a student at Heidelberg was as much a part of the Southern tradition as reading Walter Scott" (*TS*, 240). To the southerner, the vision of an orderly medieval society (also evinced in the taste for Scott and Dumas) must have appeared as a mirror image of the motionless ancien régime of his dreams and a compensation for Appomattox and Reconstruction.

At the end of his long discussion with Tom at Belle Ame, Van Dorn already prepares the way for the confession of Father Smith: "We've got the highest SAT scores in the state and the most National Merit scholars. You know what the answer is, Tom, the only answer? Excellence? We give them the tough old European Gymnasium-Hochschule treatment. We work their little asses—"(*TS*, 219). A perfect instance of unwitting double entendre, in which the spurious Van Dorn gives himself away.

"Father Smith's Confession" tells of his grand tour to Germany in the 1930s as a young man. That his fascination for virile strength and the Nazi dream of perfection is not just a compensatory southern dream but also a quest for the despised, and thus absent, father does not change anything in the threatening intimations of what is yet to come. The implicit and logical consequences—that so-called tenderness leads to the gas chamber—are definitely there, though not clearly understood by Rinaldo Smith at the time. The footnote, the narrative of his second visit to Germany in 1945, with the discovery of the children's division in a Munich hospital and its geranium-lighted death chamber, just confirms what was already latent a little more than ten years before, were he perceptive enough to have read the signs. As he says in the end, "We've got it wrong about horror. It doesn't come naturally but takes some effort" (TS, 254).

The Thanatos Syndrome, however, is no book about the Holocaust, and it has nothing of the complacent and neatly timed commercial enterprise of William Styron's Sophie's Choice. The Nazi dream of excellence is anatomized here to emphasize (admittedly, almost too clearly) the implications of Comeaux's brave new world and, more generally, to reveal what our civilization, even with the avowed best intentions, is necessarily coming to, if one does not make some effort to see clearly ahead.

"The barbarians at the inner gate and who defends the West?" Aunt Emily had asked in Percy's first novel (M, 33). The answer of The Thanatos Syndrome is that the enemy is not outside, in the civilization that man has created for himself, but at the inner gate of his consciousness, in that fascination for death man harbors in his heart of hearts, and in the death of conscience and consciousness that Comeaux and Van Dorn engineer in their brave new world. This is where the confession of Father Smith is essential to the full understanding of the novel. The fascination for death is indeed the result of senselessness. In Percy's own case, that lack of sense goes back to the tradition of paternal demise in the family, that is, to the solution in the continuity of sense, experienced generation after generation—which also applies to Rinaldo Smith. The achievement of Percy the survivor, the ex-suicide, is that he has here succeeded in integrating his own despairing quest into an anatomy of our Western civilization. Though the structural economy of the novel may appear formally flawed, though "Father Smith's Confession" may appear redundant, the thematic integration is achieved and the message comes out of the bottle, even though somewhat heavy-handedly. There is a mirror structure between the main plot and that central confession, which in the last analysis can be seen as a *mise en abyme* of the main plot, for the novel is indeed an epistemological quest, cognitive—self-cognitive.

The "well well well" of the end of the novel means that at the provisional end of his wayfaring the narrator accepts Mickey LaFaye and himself as ordinary, suffering humans, ready to talk and listen, to communicate, as the only way of overcoming senselessness and despair, just as, for Percy, communicating with his readers in his writing may have been the rampart against death.

To reach that point, he had to go through this Thanatos syndrome, so threatening that it could be faced only through irony and grotesqueness, that is, by way of distortion, of "seeing near things with their extension of meaning and thus of seeing far things close up," in O'Connor's words.[2] In his dystopian fable, *The Thanatos Syndrome*, Percy once more decenters, or ex-centers, his stance, the better to recenter his vision. Like O'Connor, he had to be an eccentric in the American house of fiction in order to warn us against the brave new worlds threatening to destroy man in this end of the twentieth century.

William Rodney Allen

"Father Smith's Confession" in *The Thanatos Syndrome*

The powerful narrative-within-the-narrative entitled "Father Smith's Confession" is unquestionably the centerpiece of Walker Percy's last novel, *The Thanatos Syndrome*. Though part of a flawed book of mixed results, Rinaldo Smith's vividly recounted reminiscence of his visit as a young man to Germany in the mid–1930s conveys Percy's most direct fictional warning that contemporary American culture is moving toward an open expression of the death wish. "Father Smith's Confession" is striking for several reasons: for the way it conforms to a classic pattern in American literature originating in colonial times, the jeremiad; for its ties to the narrative strategies of Percy's most intense novel, *Lancelot*; and for its appropriation of the typical Percyan protagonist's anger at his weak father. Yet precisely because it usurps the dramatic tension of the father-son conflict that has heretofore been so important to Percy's protagonists, "Father Smith's Confession" overpowers the rest of the novel, leaving the reader with a rather bland Dr. Thomas More of diminished psychological complexity. Moreover, as charged as the confession is with Percy's deepest psychic conflicts, its grim insistence that abortion is the logical precursor to genocide is both unfounded and at odds with the novel's comic, even farcical ending and so points out not only structural problems in *The Thanatos Syndrome* but also a shift in Percy's later writing away from fiction as philosophical quest and toward fiction as religious polemic.

Sacvan Bercovitch identifies the jeremiad as "America's first distinctive literary genre."[1] The term comes from the Old Testament prophet Jeremiah, who, like Isaiah and others, denounced the moral failings of the Jews whenever they appeared to be forgetting their identity as God's chosen people. In medieval times, Bercovitch explains, the European jeremiad "decried the sins of 'the people'—a community, a nation, a civilization, mankind in general—and warned of God's wrath to follow" (*J*, 7). Both the Old Testament and European forms of the jeremiad "held out little hope, if any" (*J*, 7), but something distinctive happened when the jeremiad appeared in New England in the seventeenth century. Puritan ministers taught that

> their church-state was to be at once a model to the world of Reformed Christianity and a prefiguration of New Jerusalem to come. To this end, they revised the message of the jeremiad. Not that they minimized the threat of divine retribution; on the contrary, they asserted it with a ferocity unparalleled in the European pulpit. But they qualified it in a way that turned threat into celebration. In their case, they believed, God's punishments were *corrective*, not destructive. Here, as nowhere else, His vengeance was a sign of love, a father's rod used to improve the errant child. In short, their punishments confirmed their promise. (*J*, 8)

Thus the American jeremiad serves a cultural function analogous to the habit of individuals who constantly criticize themselves in front of others: in both cases, the deepest impulse underlying the self-criticism is the desire for self-aggrandizement. As Bercovitch observes, through this ironically uplifting mode, the Puritan preachers succeeded "in transmitting a myth that remained central to the culture long after the theocracy had faded" (*J*, 17).

It is not hard to see the modern, secularized form of the jeremiad present in such novels as *The Great Gatsby* and *All the King's Men*, in which the unfulfilled promise of America is celebrated even as it is lamented. And it is easier still to see the jeremiad underlying the Christian postmodern fiction of Walker Percy—especially in his novels from *Love in the Ruins* on. Though his Catholicism places him at a distance from such early Protestant ministers as John Winthrop and John Cotton, his Christianity places him at an even greater distance from most of his secular contemporaries. Thus the tensions between Catholic versus Protestant and colonial versus postmodern America have helped generate Percy's novels. In Percy's fiction, no matter how depraved the country seems to be at the moment, underlying the criticism is the old Puritan vision that through a reawakening of faith America can yet be an example for the whole world—it can still become Winthrop's "shining city on a hill."

In *The Thanatos Syndrome*, however, set sometime in the late 1990s, the times seem dark indeed. As in so many dystopian novels, the central issue is the manipulation of the human psyche by scientists, either inside or outside government. Like Anthony Burgess's *A Clockwork Orange*, *The Thanatos Syndrome* asks whether the ostensibly "good behavior" imposed on individuals by technocrats using chemical and other suspect means is in fact superior to the social chaos of individuals acting on their own good or, more frequently, evil, impulses. While Dr. More admits the results of Bob Comeaux's and John Van Dorn's Blue Boy experiment (of putting heavy sodium in Feliciana's water supply) are impressive, he is troubled by the flatness of emotional affect he sees in his patients. Sterilization, abortion, pedeuthanasia, and gereuthanasia are all proceeding apace in the government's Qualitarian Centers with little or no dissent from a population zonked out on drugs, sex, and stereo-v. In this amoral landscape, Winthrop's shining city on a hill has been reduced to the laser-glare of Disney World, where Tom takes his family near the end of the novel in an attempt to reclaim Ellen from heavy sodium and Van Dorn and his children from his own neglect. The trip is a sad parody of a religious pilgrimage. As Dr. More concludes, "Disney World is indeed splendid—though I could not stand more than one hour of it" (*TS*, 337).

But it is Father Smith rather than Dr. More who says no in thunder to contemporary America. He is the Jeremiah crying out in the wilderness—in this case from atop a fire tower overlooking Feliciana. Ironically, his confession seems at first to have nothing to do with America in the 1990s, since it concerns his memory of a visit to Germany in the 1930s. Yet interspersed with that account are *Lancelot*-like denunciations of "local village atheists, professor philosophers, ACLU zealots, educated Episcopal-type unbelievers, media types, NBC anchormen, *New York Times* pundits, show-biz gurus" (*TS*, 243). Criticizing a French family he met on his trip, Father Smith complains that "they were like my mother's family in Thibodaux. They knew nothing, cared about nothing except business and eating and politics" (*TS*, 245). When he finally recounts the amazing story of his having met the most prominent psychiatrists and eugenicists of the Weimar Republic while in Tübingen —the cultivated, scholarly men who in a few years would preside over the murder of countless numbers of the "unfit" in Hitler's hospitals and death camps—the priest does so with the aim of posing a single question to his lone listener, Dr. More: "Do you think we're different from the Germans?" (*TS*, 256). Percy, then, actually uses Father Smith's account of his trip to Germany for the traditional purposes of the jeremiad—to berate America for failing to live up to its moral mission as the New Jerusalem.

In an early interview, Percy admitted that "a good deal of my energy as a novelist comes from malice—the desire to attack things in our culture."[2] To an increasing degree, from Aunt Emily to Sutter Vaught to Lancelot Lamar, Percy has included characters in his fiction who embody that idea. In *Lancelot*, in my judgment one of Percy's best novels, Percy found a way to unleash the rage inherent in the American jeremiad without finally identifying himself with it: Lance's tirade cries out against the failure of the American mission, while Percival's final "yes" holds out hope for its eventual success. The tension between Lance and Percival is almost palpable, and it charges the novel with the ambivalence of denunciation and affirmation so characteristic of the jeremiad. Likewise, in *The Thanatos Syndrome*, Father Smith identifies himself as "a spiteful man" who sees those around him as "either victims or assholes" (*TS*, 243), and the sheer force of his anger stands in sharp contrast to the moral enervation of the rest of the novel's characters. Unfortunately, though, the parts of *The Thanatos Syndrome* exclusive of "Father Smith's Confession" seem flat. As John Edward Hardy observes, dramatic tension is lacking in the main plot because Dr. More never seems "in much real danger of losing out to the likes of Van Dorn or Comeaux."[3] Further, the intense internal conflict the reader has come to expect in Percy's protagonists simply is not there. In "Father Smith's Confession," then, Percy used the effective strategies of his fourth novel, perhaps consciously so, in order to energize an otherwise flagging narrative—to rescue an intellectual thriller that had run out of thrills.

Parallels between the confession and *Lancelot* are easy to uncover. In both cases, a half-mad, alcoholic Jeremiah figure "confesses" to a psychiatrist in a small room. Similar to what Bercovitch says of the jeremiad, the discourse of Lance and Father Smith links "social criticism to spiritual renewal, public to private identity, the shifting 'signs of the times' to certain traditional metaphors, themes, and symbols" (*L*, xi). And in such signs as X-rated movie theaters and Qualitarian Centers for euthanasia both see evidence of impending apocalypse. The difference, of course, is that Lance's vision of history is the Gnostic one of secular apocalypse followed by a ruthless "new order," while Father Smith's is the Christian design of man's fall, the possibility of his salvation through God's grace, and the climax of time with the second coming of Christ.

Yet in terms of their early character formation, Father Smith and Lancelot are alike in one crucial respect: they had a weak father whom they resented. In contrast to Percy's typically benign priest figures, such as Fathers Boomer and Weatherbee, Father Smith possesses a large measure of purely personal (as opposed to prophetic) anger of the kind found in such characters as Sutter Vaught and Lancelot. His confession that disgust with his ineffectual, "second-rate," "romantic" father led him to idolize the iron-willed young Nazi Helmut Jäger is a continuation of a familiar pattern in Percy's work. As I have suggested in *Walker Percy: A Southern Wayfarer*, a troubled father-son relationship has been one of the major concerns of Percy's fiction.[4] An alcoholic, a cuckold, a bribe taker, the father of each protagonist either tries to or succeeds in killing himself, leaving his son to struggle with a heritage of suicide. The well-known facts of Percy's biography—the suicides of his paternal grandfather and father—help explain both the persistence of this theme in Percy's writing and the forcefulness with which he treats it. So important has this generational struggle been to Percy that he has Will Barrett realize in *The Second Coming*, when thinking of his father's suicide, that "nothing else had ever happened to him" (*SC*, 52)—and "him" refers not to Ed Barrett but to Will himself. Thus "Father Smith's Confession" is charged with the central psychic conflict that has generated much of Percy's fiction.

Percy's writing has its sources in his ambivalent feelings not only toward his literal, suicidal father but also toward a series of father figures: his literary, stoical adopted father, William Alexander Percy; literary fathers on both sides of the Atlantic, such as Kierkegaard and Faulkner; and the father of psychology, Sigmund Freud, with whom he has quarreled in the past (in *The Last Gentleman* and in his essays) but finally comes to acknowledge in *The Thanatos Syndrome*. Lastly, there is Percy's relationship to God the father, which has arguably been the most significant of all in terms of shaping his fiction. But perhaps these fathers come full circle: Freud famously theorized that the God and Satan of Christianity have their origins in the love-hate relationship between father and son. Though Percy praises Freud throughout the novel, he rejects Freud's theological position—even while his fictional obsession with the Oedipal struggle ironically supports it.

"Father Smith's Confession" seethes with conflicts over familial and national loyalty, sexual identity, and the fear of death. Just out of high school, with his mother recently having died, Rinaldo Smith finds himself for the first time in a foreign culture, comparing his parents to their German relatives, the highly accomplished Jägers. Dr. Jäger, "a distinguished child psychiatrist," musician, and "courageous foe of the Nazis," far outshines Rinaldo's father, whom Rinaldo characterizes as "second-rate, not really first-class at playing [music], not really first-class at teaching, not really a scholar" (*TS*, 240). Rejecting not only his parent but his native region, Rinaldo complains that his father was "a type familiar in the South, not successful in life but an upholder of culture, lofty ideals, and the higher things" (*TS*, 241). He admits that in rejecting his father's self-indulgent romanticism and his mother's vengeful Catholicism he had turned in high school to sports and science: "I played tackle and we beat Jesuit, who thought they were the hottest stuff in town. I liked to hit, as they say. And I liked the science courses —no bull, just the facts and verifiable theory, no praying for anyone's 'intentions,' no swooning over Puccini" (*TS*, 243). It is small wonder that this young athlete-scientist would be attracted to Helmut Jäger, the embodiment of modern, "hard" German culture.

The young Walker Percy had felt the same attractions to Germany on his visit there in 1934, the summer after his first year at the University of North Carolina. In a recent interview Percy recalls that he and his German professor had stayed with the professor's relatives in Bonn, and that Percy had met a young man

> who was about fifteen and in the Hitler Jugend, and I got to know him real well. I got to know the family, and I'm not going to say the family Father Smith was talking about was drawn from them, but this youth was the one who made an impression on me. . . . He was dead serious, with his impressive uniform, and he was graduating from the Hitler Jugend and going to Schutzstaffel. I remember he talked about the Teutonic knights, and taking the oath at Marienberg, the ancient castle. And there was a tremendous mystique there. I don't remember the Jews being mentioned the whole time.[5]

As Hardy observes, however, "In 1933, the year before Percy's visit, Jews were officially banned from government service, the universities, and many professions, and Hitler's uniformed thugs were already in the streets proclaiming a boycott of Jewish businesses. Of course, it is easy to understand how an idealistic, eighteen-year-old visitor from the United States, charmed by the 'verve and vitality' of his forward-looking Aryan hosts, might not have noticed all these unpleasant goings on."[6]

I would suggest that Percy's youthful attraction to Nazi Germany was in part a reaction to his family situation and to his upbringing in the South. In the interview just quoted, Percy admits that he had gone to Germany despite Uncle Will's advice that he go to France. Father Smith's diatribe against the French and his comparison of them to Louisianians perhaps reflects this conflict. While Percy has written a good deal about his intellectual relationship to Will Percy—especially in his introduction to the 1973 edition of Will's autobiography, *Lanterns on the Levee*[7]—he has remained largely silent about the more personal aspects of his life with the man who acted as his father during his teenage years. The major reason for this reticence, I suspect, was Will Percy's uncertain sexual orientation. In *A Southern Renaissance*, Richard King notes the presence of "several fleeting and apparently unfulfilled homoerotic encounters" in *Lanterns on the Levee*, and he characterizes the lifelong bachelor as "a man divided within himself and unable to express openly his essential sexual desires."[8] It is revealing that the young Walker Percy distanced himself from Will in space by going to college in relatively far-off Chapel Hill and distanced himself from his poetic adopted father in temperament by concentrating on science rather than literature. Coming to adulthood in the 1940s, after the death of Will Percy and his marriage to Mary Bernice Townsend and their conversion to Catholicism, Walker Percy could begin to make his internal peace with the man he had deeply cared for but who nevertheless had been a problematic father figure.

But it is not difficult to understand how, back in 1934, the impressionable and emotionally conflicted young man was temporarily seduced by the hypermasculine fantasies of scientific and martial omnipotence being acted out before his eyes in Nazi Germany. Years later, "Father Smith's Confession" would be a way for Percy to give an account of his singular experience while disclaiming it, to confess his attraction to aspects of what he saw in Germany while reasonably excusing that attraction as the error of judgment of a young man troubled by his weak father. Speaking of Germany as perceived in the 1930s by most Americans, Rinaldo remarks that "Fascism was then thought of as a bundle of sticks, fasces, stronger than one stick and not necessarily a bad thing." Hitler was "simply a strong man whom the Germans had in fact elected" (*TS*, 241). Percy himself says much the same thing: "No one [in America] thought much of the Nazis. Hitler had just come in during the early thirties; he had been elected, after all, and there was no great thought of the Nazis."[9]

In hindsight, one might judge Percy harshly for not perceiving the sinister aspects of the Nazis, even in 1934. But I believe his emotional conflicts with his two weak fathers—the biological one suicidal, the adopted one of questionable masculinity—do much to explain why he failed to see the perversion in the Nazi ideal. Tellingly, the underlying sexual conflict in Rinaldo's account becomes more and more apparent as his confession progresses. Above all, the quality he admires in German culture, and especially in its leader, is strength. Fascists are sticks that cannot be broken. Young Helmut faces his *mutprobe* (test of courage) by jumping off a twenty-foot tower in full battle gear. In contrast, Rinaldo's father is all melting *gefühl* (feeling) at cathedrals and concerts. Recalling one decisive moment, Rinaldo says, "I remember hearing *Tristan and Isolde* with him. He had graduated from Puccini to Wagner. His eyes were closed during the entire second act. I confess I felt contempt for him and admiration for Helmut" (*TS*, 251). As in *Lancelot*, Rinaldo's emblematic gift, the object he perceives as liberating him from the latent homosexuality of his father, is the phallic knife. Rinaldo recounts with awe how Helmut had presented him with his bayonet: "He handed it to me in a kind of ceremony, with both hands. On the shining blade was etched *Blut und Ehre* [Blood and Honor]. I took it in silence. We shook hands. I left" (*TS*, 248). Here "Father Smith's Confession" reaches its climax: Rinaldo admits that had he been German rather than American, "I would have joined him" (*TS*, 249). But had he joined Helmut, he would, of course, have been caught up in the Nazi nightmare of Fascism breaking down into its component parts: narcissism, sadomasochism, homophobia, and the desire for death. Instead of contributing to the Holocaust, Rinaldo comes home to become a priest—and eventually to try to stop what Percy believes is the Holocaust's modern equivalent, abortion and euthanasia.

As Dr. More listens to Father Smith's story, Percy does not have him recall his own conflicts with his weak father—conflicts that form an important motif in *Love in the Ruins*. Perhaps since Will Barrett so thoroughly worked through the father-son problem in *The Second Coming*, Percy believed he had nothing more to say on the subject, at least in terms of his protagonists. While many readers would agree, the problem is that the new fictional strategies on which Percy relied in *The Thanatos Syndrome*—especially combining the thriller mode with the farcical ending of "mating" Van Dorn with a gorilla—simply do not work well enough to make up for the loss of what has been the sine qua non of his fiction. As if Percy himself sensed this problem, he tried to link Dr. More to Father Smith through the curious device of letting them have eerily similar dreams about Germany—even though Dr. More realizes afterward that he has never been there (*TS*, 162–63, 166). Since there is no explanation for this odd phenomenon within the novel, one must look outside of it, to the complex relationship of the author to his real "fathers" and to their fictional counterparts.

Yeats famously remarked that quarreling with others makes rhetoric, while quarreling with oneself makes art. In Percy's best novels—*The Moviegoer, The Last Gentleman,* and *Lancelot*—his quarrel appears to have been mostly with himself. His early protagonists seem to be on an authentic search, on a personal quest to sort through the various internalized voices competing for their allegiance: the Stoic, the existentialist, the scientist, the potential suicide, the potential Christian. But in later novels Percy has begun to quarrel more with others, to the detriment of his art. Moreover, the positions he takes in these quarrels are hard to defend. The message of *The Thanatos Syndrome*—it is impossible to call it anything else—is Father Smith's paradoxical assertion that "tenderness leads to the gas chamber" (*TS*, 360)—that the attempts by secular scientists to better society will inevitably end up where the German eugenicists did during the war. Percy's evidence for this claim is almost solely based on the existence of legalized abortion in the United States. In a recent interview dealing with *The Thanatos Syndrome*, Percy said that in writing the majority decision on abortion in 1973, Justice Harry Blackmun "helped to legalize the murder of 20 million unborn human beings."[10] In another interview, Phil McCombs remarks that Percy has been surprised "that most reviewers don't seem to have come fully to grips with the implications of the book's profoundly illiberal message," and McCombs goes on to quote Percy as worrying that "I'm gonna get it eventually! . . . They're gonna link me with the right wing."[11] The change in Percy's recent fiction becomes clear when one realizes it would be impossible to imagine Percy expressing such political anxieties about, say, *The Moviegoer*.

The Thanatos Syndrome implies that abortion exists because an ill-defined group of male scientists is out to restructure society according to their perverse design. In fact, abortion exists because women in sufficient numbers in America and elsewhere have demanded control over their reproductive lives. Moreover, many of those same women have been active in working to reduce the rate of abortions in America by addressing the underlying social problems of poverty, unemployment, poor education, and the like that contribute to unwanted pregnancies. While *The Thanatos Syndrome* depicts those problems, it rejects the only solution to them it considers—the manipulation of behavior with drugs. Of a political rather than a medical reshaping of a more just America, Percy says nothing. His hopes, like those of the early jeremiadists, lie solely with Christian religious revival. But the earth has many religions; and in just forty years it will have a population of ten billion. We are only now beginning to realize how difficult it is to support just half that number. Given these facts, can the polemical assertions of *The Thanatos Syndrome*—that we must outlaw abortion and, presumably, other methods of birth control—make any sort of sense? Ironically, in a dangerously overcrowded world, Percy's position on human reproduction is an anachronism that has itself become an aspect of the Thanatos syndrome.

Elzbieta H. Oleksy

Walker Percy's Demonic Vision

In his essay on Herman Melville, published six years after
the publication of *Lancelot*, Walker Percy marvels at what it felt like
to have written *Moby-Dick*, "an experience which Melville called being
broiled in hellfire, and which was surely a triumphant taking on of
hell and coming through."[1] Was it the same for Percy, one wonders,
after writing his "wicked book"? Did Percy feel, as he writes of Melville,
"spotless as a lamb, happy, content"?

Even a cursory reading of *Lancelot* reveals striking parallels with *Moby-
Dick*. Belle Isle is as much a self-contained entity as the microcosm
of Melville's Pequod. Lance's relationship with Elgin echoes the marriage of white and black in *Moby-Dick* (Ishmael and Queequeg, Ahab
and Pip), and the merging of whiteness and blackness in the whale
is reenacted in Lance's encounter with the convulsed bodies of Margot
and Jacoby as "the strangest of all beasts, two-backed and pied, light-
skinned and dark-skinned" (*L*, 239). Like Ahab's (and Hamlet's),
Lance's madness has a method in it, or, as Matthiessen says of Ahab's,
is a "sanity of controlled madness."

Percy too, moreover, draws upon the biblical Ahab as a prototype,
and in fact Percy's Lance exhibits even more remarkable affinities with
the biblical source than Melville's does. In his portrayal of Lance, Percy
alludes to the episodes in the biblical text which present Ahab not as
a popular and apt ruler but as a kind of ill-starred buffoon who not
only topples from his high place as the king of northern Israel (by the
prompting of this corrupt, licentious, wicked hussy of a wife, Jezebel)
but also brings about the decline of his entire dynasty. There is a direct
allusion to the biblical story when Lance asks Percival why anyone
should take the matter of fidelity seriously if "even the ancients didn't

seem to dwell on it too much; even the Bible is rather casual. Your [Percival's] God seemed much more jealous of false idols, golden calves, than his people messing around with each other" (*L*, 16). But then, of course, he takes pains to demonstrate that what he calls "sexual offence" is the mark and religion of the new age, which, to Lance's obsessive mind, has replaced Christianity.

The story of Ahab and Jezebel belongs to what Northrop Frye calls the Bible's demonic vision.[2] He distinguishes two types of vision revealed in the biblical narrative, both of which are conveyed in terms of the female figure: the apocalyptic (to Frye, ideal) vision and its parody, the demonic vision. Frye's categories, if only in this particular case, seem somewhat confusing, for if *apocalypsis* is the Greek word for revelation in the metaphorical sense of disclosing the truth, then both visions (ideal and demonic) inhere in the meaning of apocalypse. Nonetheless, Frye's schema appears to be useful, especially when we approach what he calls the "human" element of the Bible and, specifically, when we explore biblical female figures. Maternal presentations of the Virgin Mary and Rachel, as well as marital or bridal figures, symbolically represented by Jerusalem, Christ's "spouse," belong to the ideal vision, whereas the demonic counterpart of the mother figure is Lilith, the mother of demons, and the demonic bride is, for instance, Jezebel, Ahab's queen, whose demonic character the narrator of 1 Kings conveys in both theological and sexual terms, though prevalently in the former.

The crucial episode in *Lancelot* where the maternal and bridal figures merge to create a single demonic image of womanhood is during Lance's hallucination concerning the Lady of the Camellias. Lance is drugged, and he finds it difficult to establish the identity of the woman he sees. He first seems to recognize her as one of the women he and Percival used to know in their adolescence. He then perceives a camellia pinned at her shoulder, and the apparition begins to talk. She mentions Lance's mother, Lily, who was "a lovely delicate creature. Like a little dove" (a traditional attribute of ideal womanhood). Of herself she says that she is "more a sparrow. Plain but tough" (more like Margot, in fact). She then speaks about Lily's relationship with Harry and (the father) Lamar's resigned acceptance of their liaison. She alludes to Lily and Harry as "Camille and Robert Taylor," which of course provides the final clue (*L*, 212). The very heading of this part of the narrative, "Our Lady of the Camellias," bluntly reveals the demonic parody of the apocalyptic, or ideal, vision. "Our Lady," of course, refers to the Virgin Mary, whereas "Lady of the Camellias" is the courtesan Marguerite Gautier (or Margot) from Dumas's *La dame aux camélias*. The figure of the mysterious woman therefore signifies a merging of the mother (Lily) and the wife (Margot) figures.

Even though the name Lily suggests purity, there is virtually nothing in Lance's recollections of his mother to support such an identification. On the contrary, the more details we receive, the more supportive they become of the mother's mythological function as Lilith. The name Lilith evokes the powers of the night. Early Semitic folklore believed Lilith to be a female demon, or vampire, who inhabited ruins. She was reputed to haunt such desolate places during storms, and men, especially young men, were vulnerable to her playful charm. Lilith enjoyed a splendid career in European romanticism. For instance, Goethe refers to Lilith's demonic charm when he has Mephisto tell Faust:

> The first wife of Adam.
> Watch out and shun her captivating tresses:
> She likes to use her never-equaled hair
> To lure a youth into her luscious lair,
> And he won't lightly leave her lewd caresses.[3]

Percy draws on a similar fund of imagery when he has Lance allude to his mother's mischievous manner, recalling "a kind of nervous joking aggressiveness about her." She used to "get" Lance in this playfully aggressive way: "On cold mornings when everyone was solemn and depressed about getting up and going off to work or school, she would say, 'I'm going to get you,' and come at me with her sharp little fist boring away into my ribs. There was something past joking, an insistence, about the boring. She wouldn't stop" (L, 215). It is, tellingly, the Lady of the Camellias, as his mother, who hands Lance the bowie knife during the hurricane in the same playfully aggressive fashion: "It was then she gave me the sword—*The sword*? Ha ha. It was the Bowie knife. Then she looked like my mother again, and when she gave me the Bowie knife, she picked it from the desk and thrust it at me point first in the same insistent joking way my mother would bore her sharp fist into my ribs" (L, 226).

The bowie knife is an important requisite in the novel. Lance alludes in the passage to the Arthurian source because Sir Lancelot received his sword from his foster mother, the Lady of the Lake, who kidnapped him when he was an infant. More importantly, however, the knife functions as one of several phallic attributes in the novel. When Lance first meets Margot on the occasion of the Azalea Festival held at Belle Isle, she invites herself to the pigeonnier. Then, again taking the initiative, she requests that Lance bolt the door, and, when he obliges, she wants to see the key he has just turned in the lock: "I lay down and gave her the iron key. She held it in one hand and me in the other and was equally fond of both" (*L*, 80). In Lance's recollection of another erotic scene, Margot grabs the bedpost, not as "a point of anchorage or leverage in the storm-tossed sea of love," but to explore "the delicate fluting of the heavy columns" (*L*, 119). This iconography reminds one of the way the term "phallus" was used in classical antiquity, as the figurative representation of the male organ: a simulacrum. Jacques Lacan uses the term "phallus" in much the same fashion, indicating that the anxiety of castration (the discovery that the mother lacks a penis) makes the phallic function into the symbolic function, thus detaching the subject from its dependence on the mother.[4] In Lance's case, however, castration anxiety is transferred from the mother to the wife (Margot). In the Lacanian dialectic of desire, generic relationships revolve around the "to be" or "not to be" and the "to have" or "not to have" of the phallus. We well remember the cryptic sign from the beginning of the book, which reads: "*Free &/Ma/B*" (*L*, 4).

Notwithstanding what the complete sign says, which Lance plans to find out upon leaving the asylum, it possibly communicates a vital message: Free of mother in order to be. Thus Lance's anxiety of castration becomes resolved in Oedipal violence, but not in the Freudian sense reserved for the father of a male child, but rather directed at the "phallic" mother-wife. Here ensues one further analogy with Lacan's argument. In one of his earliest articles, "Aggressivity in Psychoanalysis," Lacan notes that "the structural effect of identification with the rival is not self-evident, except at the level of fable."[5] We can indeed leave the fable aside, for what we have in *Lancelot* is rather a post-Freudian identification of the father as a disgraced rival; there is no question of his being a venerated model, a distinction that Freudian psychoanalysis maintained. The figure of the father becomes compromised by two discoveries Lance makes. One, when still a child, he accidentally came upon a cache of ten thousand dollars hidden in his father's bureau—evidence of his father's corruption. The second discovery Lance also made as a child, but he did not realize its full import until much later: his father's resigned or, as Lance believes, cowardly acceptance of Lily's liaison with the jovial Uncle Harry. The irony of Lance's situation is that even though he knows the reasons for the old Lamar's gradual decline, he ultimately falls into his cuckolded father's footsteps, impotent, drinking, and apathetically watching life go by. And one day, in the pigeonnier, he makes another chance discovery, this time of Margot's infidelity, with which disclosure comes the disconcerting realization that he cannot possibly be the father of his second daughter. He now becomes a Raymond Chandler character, a Marlowe (his own analogy), or a Chillingworth, and he proves not only that Margot was unfaithful to him but also that she still is, whereupon he systematically plans his bloody vengeance.

The fallacy of Lance's quest (a monstrously twisted quest for love) is that he does not understand any of the women he loves or, as he obsessively repeats, "loves." Lance wants Percival to believe that Lucy was part and parcel of his romantic dream ("a slim brown dancer in a bell jar spinning round and round in the 'Limelight' music of old Carolina long ago") (*L*, 119). However, this portrayal of womanhood ultimately becomes ambivalent when Lance speaks of Lucy's legs, which "scissored and flashed under her white skirt" (*L*, 82). We need only recall Faye Greener's "scissoring" legs to realize the full import of Lance's description. He dismisses all of his first marriage with a single sentence ("We were married, moved to Belle Isle, had two children" [*L*, 84]), and he reports that when Lucy had died he felt neither sad nor bereft but "simply curious." Not even female children are spared in Lance's paranoid vision of womanhood. The "scissoring" legs and "boring" fists are tokens of his "daughter" Siobhan's demonic, Lance believes, nature (*L*, 195).

It should be apparent by now that in Lance's account of any woman in his life we cannot see the "real" woman but only his own story or metaphor for this woman. Margot is the case most in point. When Lance first meets Margot, she is one of the belles in hoop shirts who show Belle Isle to rich tourists, and Lance intimates his first impression —namely, that Margot was not "like Scarlett." A casual remark, true, but it becomes meaningful as we pursue the analogy a little further. What Lance apparently has in mind is that Margot is not pretty. She is nevertheless remarkably like Scarlett in her practicality, her lust for life, her lack of moral scruples, her "male" ways, her self-confidence, willfulness, even her healthy appetite. Lance reports that Margot eats "like a horse," drinks from the bottle, drives a car "like a man . . . not push-pulling with two hands but palming the wheel around with one hand" (*L*, 33). She knows what she wants and she pursues it determinedly. She first wants Lance and Belle Isle, and even though Lance likes to think that at their first meeting he took the lead, it is entirely on her own initiative that Margot secures both. Moreover, Lance, needless to say, is no Rhett Butler. The fact is that Margot and Lance are as androgynous a couple as any one could find. She is strong, possessed of iron will, demanding, loud, resourceful, brimming with energy and initiative. He is weak, quiet, and passive. In an odd way, they resemble the marriage of "énergie femelle et . . . faiblesse masculine" of Bette and Steinbock in Balzac's *La Cousine Bette*. Consider, for instance, this litany of explicitly masculine features of Margot's physical portrait: "Her face was shiny and foreshortened . . . her mouth too wide . . . her coarse stiff hair invited the hand to squeeze it to test its spring . . . her back was strong and runneled. . . . She . . . had voluptuousness, the boyishness being just a joke after all when it came to her looking straight at me" (*L*, 74). A difference between the couples is that Balzac's Bette, who is described in very much the same fashion (large feet, strong arms, warts), never marries Steinbock, and so the androgynous couple never really forms.[6]

With Margot, Lance makes another puzzling discovery: a "lustful woman." Their relationship appears to be successful for a number of years, but when she completes the restoration of Belle Isle and when Lance "takes to the bottle" and becomes an incompetent lover, she turns to other jobs and other men. Lance's impotence typically originates in his fear of the castrating mother of pre-Oedipal fantasy, which becomes reactivated by what Christopher Lasch perceives as "apparently aggressive overtures of sexually liberated women."[7] To Lance, Margot epitomizes the characteristics of the "she-man," a female type emerging from the ruins of the chivalric code. But this discovery comes too late: had he really known Margot he would either have not married her or have not lost her. Margot pertinently sums up Lance's dichotomized conscience regarding womanhood in her last utterance in the novel: "With you I had to be either—or—but never a—uh—woman"(*L*, 245). Lucy, who was a virgin when he married her, had incarnated Lance's dream of the southern past, and Lance imagines that he can recapture this dream with Anna, since "the violation she suffered has in some sense restored her virginity, much as a person recovering from the plague is immune to the plague" (*L*, 86). What Lance covertly tries to sell to Percival is the notion that the very fabric of civilization depends upon there being a sweet helpless woman, like Anna, in the house to minister to the physical as well as psychical well-being of her husband. Her very presence maintains the generic equilibrium. This generic tension in Lance is nowhere more evident than in the passage where he relates to Percival his dream in which Anna played the "New Woman": "There was perfect quiet. Yet I was not alone in the house. There was someone else in the next room. A woman. There was the unmistakable sense of her presence. How did I know it was a woman? I cannot tell you except that I knew.

Perhaps it was the way she moved around the room. Do you know the way a woman moves around a room whether she is cleaning it or just passing time? It is different from the way a man moves. She is at home in a room. The room is an extension of her" (*L*, 36).

Upon surveying Percy's fiction, we find a considerable group of psychotic, helpless women who are almost invariably marital candidates for his males. There is Kate in *The Moviegoer*, whom Binx has to "hand along" and tell what to do and say. There is a mute girl in *The Last Gentleman*, with whom Will Barrett recalls playing Chinese checkers in the hospital when he was treated for amnesia. There are the psychotic mute Anna in *Lancelot*, schizophrenic Allison in *The Second Coming*, who can hoist an iron stove but cannot make herself comprehensible, and any number of psychotic women with speech disorders in Percy's last novel, *The Thanatos Syndrome*. The idea of a mute girl may be traced biographically to Percy's own traumatic discovery that his first daughter was born deaf and mute. But the curious mating in Percy's novels has yet another significance. When we look at his central male figures, what we invariably find is an unaccommodated man with all sorts of psychic problems. It is therefore only natural that he find a suitable partner in a woman who reflects his mental condition, and, though certainly nothing guarantees that such an accord will last, most of Percy's novels end with a promise of a lasting relationship.

Inevitably, however, *Lancelot* is an exception. Annoyingly judgmental, confused, raging with hatred, and sanguinely convinced of his own salvation, Lance propounds his theory of *felix culpa* to Anna, whose repudiation is outright and complete: "'Are you suggesting,' she said to me, 'that I, myself, me, my person, can be violated by a *man*? You goddamn men. Don't you know that there are more important things in this world? Next you'll be telling me that despite myself I liked it'" (*L*, 251). Lance's misogyny reaches its peak when he reflects upon Anna's words and remembers Saint Augustine's account of the Visigoths' rape of the nuns, who "enjoyed it despite themselves"—"no doubt howled with delight," he adds. In Lance's recollection of his hallucination, the figure who hands him the bowie knife is fantasized into Joan of Arc, a militant virgin. Is, then, Anna another version of an archetypal feminist, Ann Lee, a victimized woman, founder of the Shakers?[8] Lance's vision gains momentum when, just before the explosion of the house, he looks at Margot lying on her side and imagines not his mother but Anna. Thus, in remembering this scene, he kills them all.

Women, to borrow a phrase from Hélène Cixous, "function within"

Lance's discourse: he either patronizes or demonizes them. Hence, we are back at Frye's schema, where the differences between the apocalyptic, or ideal, vision and its demonic counterpart are conveyed primarily through the presentation of female figures. Frye notes, however, that the term "whoredom," as used in the biblical narrative, denotes not so much sexual irregularities as theological ones. This connotation derives from the practice of maintaining cult prostitutes in Canaanite temples, both female and male, the latter known as "sodomites" (1 Kings 14:24). We may recall that Lance uses this antecedent several times in reference to the Hollywood group (Margot included). Jezebel, Ahab's wife, incarnates both sexual and theological evil, not only because she cuckolded Ahab, which appears to be of slight importance to the narrator of Kings, but also, and primarily, because she introduced the worship of Baal, the "false god," into northern Israel. The reality of a "false god" is a devil, Frye maintains, the word "Baal" appearing in several concatenations suggestive of this meaning, such as "Beelzebub." Baal functioned among ancient Semitic people as a god of fertility, or a sun god, the meaning associated also with Lucifer ("light bringing"). It remains to be said that Lance's ascent from the inferno of Belle Isle, after the explosion, is conveyed as the upward movement of Lucifer ("I was wheeling slowly up into the night like Lucifer blown out of hell, great wings spread against the starlight" (*L*, 246).

One of the rites that the worshipers of the god Baal introduced was the fertility rite, whereby they "gashed themselves with swords and spears until the blood ran" (1 Kings 8:28). The significance of the rite is not only to express the desire for fertility but also to identify the worshiper's body with that of the fertility god. Frye cites a similar rite, known as the "garden of Adonis," where plants in pots, which were symbolically associated with female sexual organs, were dipped in water by a group of females as a rain charm. A female counterpart of Baal was a fertility goddess, Asherah, whose emblems were carved wooden poles and a star (*stella maris*). And the Bible makes reference to the prophets of Baal and Asherah as Jezebel's "pensioners."

It is impossible to ignore the structural and symbolic parallels between *Lancelot* and the biblical text. The god of fertility becomes the god of sexual sin, who is worshiped by Margot and the Hollywood moviemakers (Margot's "pensioners"). Margot does not "carry" a star but is one and her special dedication in restoring wooden surfaces of antiques at Belle Isle are both suggestive of Percy's source. Sex, or what Lance obsessively calls the sexual sin (the unholy grail he seeks), is time and again conveyed in religious terms. Having first commissioned and then viewed the video recordings of the sexual antics of his wife and daughter, Lance, puzzled and hurt into cynicism, asks "A prayer?" And in the scene during the hurricane, just before the explosion of the house, Lance conceives of the two bodies, Margot's and Jacoby's, on a Calhoun bed, as his encounter with the "beast" which held "discourse with itself in prayers and curses" (*L*, 239).

What role, in the above scheme, can we then assign to the silent addressee of Lance's confession? Percival's "religious" name, the name he adopted after ordination, is John, and, at one point, Lance wonders: "Is it John the Evangelist who loved so much or John the Baptist, a loner in the wilderness?" (*L*, 10). He himself suggests the answer when he says that Percival *was* a "loner." In the gospel, the prophecy of Elijah's return fulfills itself in the figure of John the Baptist (Matt. 11:14). According to the biblical account, when Elijah flees from the priests of Baal, he hears the noise of earthquakes, thunder, and fire, after which "a still small voice" speaks. It tells Elijah that he need not worry because the followers of the god Baal will be slaughtered in due time. The weaving of this context together with its wonderful phrase into the ending of Percy's text undoubtedly constitutes a masterstroke. Percival, like Elijah in the biblical account, has envisaged the thunder and fire of Lance's apocalyptic story, and his tacit "Yes," with which the book ends, parallels the biblical "still small voice." What his inner voice, the voice of God, tells him he is ready to pass onto his raging patient. Whether Lance is ready to hear this message remains a question. Having just given Percival his mad rant, Lance paradoxically says that there is no confession "forthcoming." What he surely means, and what the priest awaits, is an act of penance. The reader, and Percival too, may hope in vain that the message will disclose the "secret" Lance has taken so much pain to search for elsewhere. Though, arguably, at the end of *Lancelot*, there resonates a note of reintegration of human and divine love, the reader must wait until Percy's next novel for its realization.

It is thus apparent that *Lancelot*, like *Moby-Dick*, works on a cathartic principle. The analogy with *Moby-Dick* seems all the more pertinent as in both books the meaning of catharsis is experienced not by respective protagonists (Ahab, Lance) but rather by the books' authors, perhaps also by Ishmael and Percival. Even though the final chapter of *Lancelot* begins with a Wordsworthian "tranquil restoration," there can be no doubt that purgation does not transform Lance—at least, not in the text. He complains to Percival of the numbness and chill he feels, and once again with cold logic he outlines his plan ("We know what we

want. And we'll have it. If it takes the sword, we'll use the sword"
[*L*, 256]).

To say that the ending of the novel poses a binary choice (either
Percival's way of divine love or Lance's way of secular wrath) and that
Percival's unspoken words after the novel ends will lead Lance to faith
would surely hackney what no doubt still remains Percy's most complex
novel. Some readers assign to Percival the role of a final resolver of
the book's contextual tensions. They see Percival as their friend, rather
than Lance's. They acknowledge the irreconcilable polarities of the
book, but they claim that its system is sustained by some final assertion
that gives *Lancelot* its aesthetic wholeness.

But Percival is more than a moral nucleus of the novel; he is a literary
device. His presence, like Ishmael's in *Moby-Dick*, not only organizes
Lancelot but, in so doing, purges it of Lance's demonism. He patiently
bears Lance's vision, yet without, as Murray Krieger says of Ishmael,
"denying an affirmative power to the universe and its Author."[9] Like
Ishmael, he understands the moral integrity of Lance's quest, but he
does not accept its immoral perpetration. Lewis A. Lawson seems to
hit the mark in claiming that both Lance and Percival are parts of Walker
Percy. Hence the polarities they embody are irreconcilable; no synthesis
can be reached without what Krieger calls a "newly disruptive synthesis." What Krieger says of Gide, which in his scheme applies also to
Conrad and Melville, we may say of Percy—namely, that he "does not
exhaust himself even in his most intensely created character but creates
such a character as but one extreme of the dialogue the self conducts
with the soul, an extreme that the very act of dialogue—so long as
it is a disciplined act—manages partly to tame. The author is more
than his creature . . . and proves it by the mere fact that he has created
him, and has created him within a larger aesthetic whole that contains
him as but a part of it."[10]

In his essay on Melville, Percy says that a writer's satisfaction comes
from the "ineffable socialities" and that is when "the writing works and
somebody knows it." Conceivably every professional writer creates with
this belief. Melville's joy at getting his vision across to reticent Hawthorne, whom he ranked with Shakespeare, was ecstatic. Like
Melville's, Percy's vision in *Lancelot* passes through the hellfire of its
antithesis, but there always remains a chance that the reader will go
with this vision and become chastened by its extremity. And many have
confessed this. How meaningful is the fact that many a Melville reader
finds the neat moral solutions in *Billy Budd* disturbing, just as we have
criticism to similar effect of Percy's *The Second Coming*.

And thus, rather than seek for a principle of cohesion in *Lancelot*, we may concede with Harold Bloom that confusion is beautiful because it cannot be resolved or, as Gabriel Marcel says, because it remains a mystery. Percy's vision in *Lancelot*, moving heaven and earth and descending into hell, terrifies us, but it returns us, purged by its extremes, to our midearth existence.

Patricia Lewis Poteat

Pilgrim's Progress;
or, A Few Night Thoughts
on Tenderness
and the Will to Power

*Love yourself through grace—was his solution—then you are no longer
in need of your God, and you can act the whole drama of Fall and
Redemption to its end in yourself.*

FRIEDRICH NIETZSCHE

Tenderness leads to the gas chamber.

WALKER PERCY

Near the end of Walker Percy's *Love in the Ruins*, Father
Rinaldo Smith quietly admonishes Tom More to set aside his "middle-
aged daydreams" and devote himself instead to being a better father,
husband, and doctor. He will for his part try to be a better priest (*LR*,
397). After all, Smith reminds More, Jesus teaches us that the first two
commandments are greater than all the rest.

When Father Smith reappears in *The Thanatos Syndrome*, however,
it seems that he has forgotten his own excellent advice. Following the
example of his patron saint, Simeon the Stylite, who spent twenty years
atop a tower praying for the forgiveness of his and the world's sins,
Father Smith has abandoned his hospice and retreated to a one-
hundred-foot-tall fire tower where he looks out for fires and rambles
on about the Germans, the Jews, and "the Depriver." He is also given
to dark utterances such as "Tenderness leads to the gas chamber." Psychiatrist More's diagnosis: "a true nut" (*TS*, 359, 128, 120).

Nutty or no, Father Smith sees much from his fire tower. Indeed, it is he who proves the better diagnostician in this last and surely the grimmest of Percy's novels. Like Binx Bolling in *The Moviegoer*, Father Smith is "onto something." What he is onto is not simply the machinations of the dangerously tenderhearted Comeaux and the demonically sensuous Van Dorn. Rather, in his own addled way, Father Smith diagnoses a complex cultural pathology of which the plots of Comeaux and others are but one outward and visible sign. The Holocaust, aimed at wiping out "the only sign of God which has not been evacuated," is another (*TS*, 123). This pathology is nothing less than the death of spirit in Western culture. This is the subject of *The Thanatos Syndrome*.

The death of spirit—what it means and how it manifests itself—is not an original theme. Pascal, Kierkegaard, and Nietzsche struggle with it. In a different but complementary vein, Eric Voegelin's work on modern gnosticism likewise wrestles with the consequences of, as he puts it, drawing God into man.[1] This is distinguished company, and each can help us measure the depth of Percy's novel. In taking up this theme, however, Percy has one unique advantage: he is a master storyteller. In this tale of a failed priest and an alcoholic psychiatrist who no longer knows what he believes, the religious situation that follows upon the "evacuation" of the transcendent is illumined with subtlety and grace. In this story of criminal acts committed in the name of "ultimate goals" and "the greatest good," the anthropological situation that follows upon the death of spirit is conveyed with devastating clarity. More's patients, abstracted and utterly lost to themselves; Comeaux, secure in his vision of earthly salvation with himself as savior; and Father Smith's Dr. Jäger, lover-theorist of mankind, who has nothing but contempt for the Nazis but who readily accepts an assignment in the "special department" of their children's psychiatric hospital—all these wear the death of spirit like the mark of Cain.

The Thanatos Syndrome presents an astute analysis of the consequences of the death of spirit. Father Smith is the key. However, Percy's analysis has implications far beyond the novel itself, implications for the role of the philosophical novel as an instrument for cultural criticism. Indeed, in *The Thanatos Syndrome*, we have the means of illuminating one of the darkest episodes to mark the face of modern Western culture; we have, that is, the means of illuminating the intimate bond between tenderness and the will to power.

"Small disconnected facts, if you take note of them, have a way of becoming connected" (*TS*, 67). With this simple but prescient observation, Tom More sets out to connect "a few disconnected facts, as untidy as these pesky English sparrows buzzing around the martin house" (*TS*, 68). Just home from a two-year stay in the minimum security prison at Fort Pelham, Alabama, More finds that some curious changes have occurred in his absence. His wife, Ellen, for instance, has been transformed from "a thrifty albeit lusty, abstemious albeit merry, Presbyterian girl to a hard-drinking, free-style duplicate-bridge fanatic" (*TS*, 68). She also exhibits a positively spooky ability to calculate the distribution of the cards with computerlike precision. Moreover, several of Tom's patients, each of whom had previously suffered from depression, anxiety, phobias, and the like, now display a "curious flatness of tone;" or, as he says at one point, "They've all turned into chickens" (*TS*, 68, 90). No more night exaltations and morning terrors for them. Each shows changes in sexual habits, the women "presenting" and exhibiting other signs of estrus behavior. Their use of language is limited to short, declarative sentences of the sort one hears from a three-year-old. They will answer any question no matter how weirdly out of context. Finally, like an idiot savant, each has perfect recall of any information he or she ever received. When asked a question, they respond like so many computers, rolling their eyes up behind their lids, scanning their memory banks, and "reading" the information. "Is this a syndrome?" More asks. "If so, what is its etiology? Exogenous? Bacterial? Viral? Chemical? In a word, what's going on here?" (*TS*, 69). He hasn't a clue, but aims to find out.

Thus with characteristic directness does Dr. More turn his considerable skills to the business of diagnosing both wife and patients, all of whom are clearly in a predicament. As a self-described "psyche-iatrist . . . a doctor of the soul," he assumes there is more to this than meets the eye: "There's more to it than neurones" (*TS*, 88). Even so, the situation is much more complex than More realizes. The syndrome exhibited by Ellen, his patients, and others in the community is not the only peculiar thing in Feliciana. Bob Comeaux wants something. Max Gottlieb is worried. And then there is the matter of Father Smith. Tom's old friend is among those whom he finds changed upon his return home. Father Smith has "conked out" and retreated to the top of his fire tower. He refuses to come down. He refuses to preach. According to Father Placide, he claims to have "discovered a mathematical proof of what God's will is, that is, what we must do in these dangerous times" (*TS*, 111). When Tom first sees him, he refuses to speak and behaves very strangely. Is it depression? A mild stroke? Worse? In any case, the prognosis is not encouraging.

This initial encounter between physician and priest introduces into what has been shaping up as a kind of psychiatric detective story a whole set of new and disconcerting issues. At first glance, these issues seem as disconnected from More's concerns as does Father Smith from the affairs of the world one hundred feet below. What do these ramblings about the Depriver, the Jews, and the Holocaust have to do with More's patients? What is the point of Father Smith's refusal to preach and his claim that the words have been "evacuated" and no longer "signify"? Most puzzling of all, why does he describe More as an "able psychiatrist, on the whole a decent, generous, humanitarian person in the abstract sense of the word" and, in the next breath, declare that he will end up killing Jews (*TS*, 127–28)? We might well echo Tom's question: What's going on here?

We can get our bearings by recalling the scene from *Love in the Ruins* alluded to earlier. By drawing More back from his "middle-aged daydreams" and directing him to his responsibilities as father, husband, and doctor, Father Smith turns him away from (as he puts it here) his "demonic hurry," his "grandiose, even Faustian" schemes to save mankind. Instead, he comes to know the joys and sorrows of "living a small life" (*TS*, 67). This is not to say More is without his problems. He still finds it necessary to knock back a few fingers of Jack Daniels from time to time. It is clear, however, that Father Smith's admonishment took hold and has been strengthened by two years of living a very small life indeed at Fort Pelham. In a word, More has come to know and value the ordinary goodness of things, the ordinary goodness of creation.

This is not merely incidental. Rather, it is this very affinity for the ordinary and the concrete as well as his gift for tending the psyche ("a doctor of the soul") that enable More to identify a syndrome that cannot be, as Father Smith might put it, "subsumed" under the category "cortical deficit" ("there's more to it than neurones") and that make him, eventually, the foil of Comeaux's and Van Dorn's schemes to do that to which More himself had aspired in his previous life, namely, to save mankind. It is also this affinity and this skill that provide the key to the complex conceptual business being transacted in Father Smith's otherwise inexplicable discourse. To put it in terms that will be important later on, the priest sees the peril in which we stand when the transcendent is made immanent and we are left with no alternative but to, as Nietzsche puts it, act the whole drama of Fall and Redemption to its end in ourselves. Without even knowing it, More stands with Father Smith against the nihilism and despair played out in that drama. As we shall see, he does so by resisting the temptations of both tenderness and sensuousness. Resistance is not a matter of belief or unbelief because, as the priest says, either way, "the words don't signify" (*TS*, 118). Rather, it is a matter of refusing to be ruled by what Percy, in "The Delta Factor," calls "the spirit of the age which was informed by the spirit of abstraction" (*MB*, 26). Father Smith understands this. More does not.

For the priest, this refusal hinges upon a steadfast search for some "sign" of the transcendent, which, unlike the words of the Mass, does signify; which does give indisputable testimony to God's presence in the world. Why is this search necessary? When he claims that the words of the Mass "no longer signify," Father Smith means that transcendent spirit has disappeared from the world; the transcendent spirit, that is, of Yahweh, God of Abraham, Isaac, and Jacob, who has his being outside the world but who enters into history, into a covenant with men, and before whom all are accountable. Unlike the spirit that infuses and thereby imparts an eternal, finite order to the cosmos of the ancient Greeks, transcendent spirit is the very breath of God's world-creating speech, "Let there be light." This is the breath that, breathed into Adam, makes him a living soul. It is the breath in which Yahweh addresses Abraham and by means of which Abraham answers. It is limited only by his never-failing faithfulness.

God's transcendent spirit is ordinate because he is always who he is and always faithful to his covenant with men. As Martin Buber translates the enigmatic "I am that I am" of Exod. 3:14, "I am the one who will always be there." But unlike smoke, which is an unambiguous sign of fire, "word signs," which in an earlier time were taken to signify the faithfulness of God and the ordinance of transcendent spirit, have been deprived of meaning. What we have in their place are word signs signifying the transcendent spirit of man, inordinate and potentially demonic once severed from God's presence. Whereas before, the signal story of the West was that of Abraham standing "before God" (Kierkegaard's language), it is now that of restless, demonic spirit: Faust, Don Juan, the Wandering Jew. Whereas before, the words of the Mass embodied transcendent spirit in the midst of immanent creation, we are now left to say, after Pascal, "I have tried to find out if God has left any traces of himself."[2]

In Father Smith's view, God has in fact left one trace of himself, the Jews: "Since the Jews were the original chosen people of God, a tribe of people who are still here, they are a sign of God's presence which cannot be evacuated" (*TS*, 123). Moreover, they resist abstraction. When asked to "free associate" with the word "Jew," Tom can think in terms of only particular Jews, not vague abstractions or stereotypes. Nor can they be subsumed, made a subordinate part of a larger class. Jews are Jews, "the beloved, originally chosen people of God," period (*TS*, 124). As such, they stand as the one inescapable sign of the action of God in history, a constant reminder of the covenant in which the self is grounded and the fallen creature, body and spirit, redeemed. Perhaps most important, however, the Jews are a stumbling block to the spirit of the age, which is the spirit of abstraction. They remind us that to stand "before God" is to be held accountable, accountable to the transcendent God *and therefore* to men. Simply put, the covenant makes it incumbent upon us to acknowledge our fellows as neighbors who, like ourselves, are accountable to God. This acknowledgment is not an abstract exercise but implies responsible action toward particular, historical others, each of whose face is a "sign" of the covenant. Ellen. Chandra. Hudeen. Max Gottlieb. By contrast, when the covenant becomes so attenuated that it no longer "signifies," the imperative for responsible action is radically undermined and no longer governs our relation to our neighbor. What we have in its place is abstract feeling. What we have in its place is tenderness.

Under the governance of tenderness, our fealty is no longer to God and neighbor but to "culture, lofty ideals, and the higher things"—abstractions all (*TS*, 241). No longer bonded to others by our common predicament as fallen creatures and our common hope of redemption through God's grace, we are bonded to them by tenderness infused not with the transcendent spirit of God but with the transcendent spirit of man, a demonic spirit that is at once abstracted from and rampant in the world. Against this demonic spirit, the creature cannot stand. No longer a person "before God," our fellow becomes an abstraction and, in a profound sense, disappears—*just as* Ellen and More's patients have disappeared. Vacant, abstracted, absent from themselves, "they're somehow—diminished," Tom says. "The old ache of self is gone," replaced by "a certain curious disinterest . . . a flatness of affect . . . unfocused animal good spirits" (*TS*, 85, 21).

This state of affairs does not necessarily result in great harm. Tom's earlier misadventures with his Qualitative Quantitative Ontological Lapsometer is a good case in point. As Father Smith puts it, one can be either "a lover of Mankind in the abstract . . . [or] a theorist of Mankind . . . who believes he understands man's brain," and, chances are, nothing really terrible will happen. But "if you put the two together . . . what you've got now is Robespierre or Stalin or Hitler and the Terror, and millions dead for the good of Mankind." Thus tenderness that bears no relation to any *particular* person or act can be used to "diminish" *any* person or justify *any* act. Thus does tenderness serve as "the first disguise of the murderer" (*TS*, 128, 129).

As Father Smith observes, to be constantly reminded of God's presence in history and the responsibilities it places upon us "offends people, even the most talented people, people of the loftiest sentiments, the highest scientific achievements, the purest humanitarian ideals" (*TS*, 126). It offends all those tenderhearted souls, lovers of mankind and theorists of mankind, who are decent, generous, and humanitarian, *"in the abstract sense of the word"* (*TS*, 127; emphasis mine). Why? By their very existence, the Jews repudiate tenderness. By their very existence, they mitigate against the "evacuation" of the transcendent and the consequent transformation of man into his own god. They mitigate against acting out the drama of Fall and Redemption within oneself. To the lover-theorist of Mankind who glories in this transformation and this drama, this is anathema. Thus was the Holocaust "a consequence of the sign which could not be evacuated" (*TS*, 126).

Tom More is not convinced, of course. He leaves the fire tower more certain than ever that his old friend has gone round the bend. Even so, the priest does, as he claims, know more than Tom thinks. What he says, fragmentary and cryptic as it is, gives us our first real inkling of what is at stake in this psychiatric detective story. The affliction of Ellen, More's patients, and others and the peculiar behavior of Comeaux and Van Dorn now appear as "signs" of a deep cultural pathology. At the root of this pathology is the death of spirit. When the transcendent is "evacuated" and the covenant fails, the spirit that had its life and its home "before God" is evacuated from the world. As Kierkegaard puts it, in its place there comes a "restlessness, tumult, and infinity" as spirit is transformed into a homeless, self-absolutizing demon. Thus is spirit at once dead and rampant in the world. The import of this death is not yet fully apparent, but thanks to Father Smith, firewatcher and latter-day stylite, we now know what More is really up against. *"Gefühl! Gefühl!"* (*TS*, 240).

Unlike Tom More, Bob Comeaux has no difficulty diagnosing and treating all manner of pathologies, psychiatric and otherwise. Mickey LaFaye is "neurological and not psychiatric" and will be fine once committed to Comeaux's program at NIMH. Father Smith's "behavior" is a "problem" that is sure to go away as soon as he agrees to turn the hospice into a Qualitarian Center. The inconvenience of Tom's probation will be remedied once he joins Comeaux's team. He also has the solution to the burden of unwanted infants and old people: a tender release from life via "pedeuthanasia" and "gereuthanasia." Best of all, the seemingly intractable social pathologies of teen pregnancy, street crime, drug abuse, and AIDS will be taken care of by dumping a little heavy sodium in the public water supply. No doctor of the soul he. Comeaux prefers to go straight for the neurones: "Cortical control has unlimited possibilities, once cortical hang-ups are eliminated" (*TS*, 195). All this is in the service of "lofty ideals," of course: "the greatest good, the highest quality of life for the greatest number" (*TS*, 346). As Father Smith says with irony, "Not bad reasons, are they? They make considerable sense, wouldn't you agree?" (*TS*, 116).

Bob Comeaux is a man consumed by a soteriological passion. This passion is fueled by secret knowledge, by gnosis—not merely a vision of the eschaton but a plan to bring it about. He is both prophet and leader. The telos of his salvific activity is nothing less than halting "the decay of the social fabric" and instituting a happy world in which teenagers cheerfully apprentice themselves as mechanic's helpers, gardeners, and the like; AIDS disappears due to "lack of interest"; and black felons are transformed into mild-mannered "darkies" who serve out their sentences picking cotton and singing "Swing Low, Sweet Chariot." In this new and improved world (in Gnostic parlance, the Third Realm), reading books and writing sentences will be superseded by "graphic and binary communication—which after all is a lot more accurate than once upon a time there lived a wicked queen." Last but certainly not least, LSU will never lose a football game again (*TS*, 196–97, 266). There are, Comeaux admits, a few "bugs" in the scheme, such as acts of gratuitous violence by some experimental subjects. Mickey LaFaye did shoot all of her thoroughbreds and set fire to the stable. Tom's role is to help get these bugs out; as Comeaux puts it, "Both my colleagues and I need some dialoguing on the subject and we think you could contribute a very creative input" (*TS*, 194). Right.

It is by no means an overstatement to say that if the pilgrim's progress is the sanctification of life and its goal is a state of perfection, then Bob Comeaux is the consummate pilgrim. For him, however—and this point is critical—sanctification has nothing to do with even a tacit or de facto (let alone explicit) sense of himself as "before God." Likewise, the state of perfection has nothing to do with the reconciliation of the world to the transcendent God who made it. Rather, salvation is an entirely intramundane affair; or, to use an apposite phrase of Eric Voegelin's, his energy is directed toward achieving "the miracle of self-salvation . . . by extending grace to [himself]"—and, we might add, *through* himself to the rest of society by creating a "terrestrial paradise."[3]

Consequently, Comeaux is ruled not by the covenantal imperative for responsible action implicit in Father Smith's discourse but rather by that abstract feeling, tenderness, before which persons disappear. What we have instead are (Comeaux's language) superegos to be "cooled," natural highs to be "induced," the family to be "improved," and, of course, the social fabric to be saved. Every detail of Comeaux's conversations with More point to this—the abstract (but tender) language he uses to justify what goes on in the so-called Qualitarian Centers; his willingness to overlook Van Dorn's "eccentricities" because of his usefulness to his (Comeaux's) world-saving project; his unwillingness to consider the "technicality of civil rights" vis-à-vis his hapless experimental subjects; and, not least, his great fondness for German romantic music, which positively carries him away in a rapture. Moreover, this way of thinking, Comeaux assures Tom, is "gaining ground among psychologists, anthropologists, neurologists, to mention a few disciplines —as well as among academics and in liberal arts circles—even among our best novelists!"(*TS*, 194–95). Clearly, the eschaton is near at hand.

Comeaux is not alone in his soteriological ambitions and eschatological lust. His sometime collaborator, John Van Dorn, is likewise bent upon intramundane redemption. According to the local paper, Van Dorn is a Renaissance man: computer wizard, world-class contract bridge player, headmaster of an exclusive school modeled after a rigorous European Gymnasium-Hochschule ("We work their little asses" [*TS*, 219], a nicely ambiguous turn of phrase, as we discover). Van Dorn's heroes are Einstein and Don Juan (a "sexual genius"), and his "ultimate goal" is to "get past the mental roadblocks of human relationships—namely, two thousand years of repressed sexuality." "We call him," says Comeaux, "our Dr. Ruth of the bayous" (*TS*, 302, 200). To Tom, he more closely resembles an Afrika Corps officer complete with what could pass for a saber scar on his cheek.

As the supplier of the heavy sodium isotope for Comeaux's "pilot," Van Dorn is essential to its success. Even so, he is scornful of his coconspirators, who remind him of the "guilt-ridden Puritan transcendentalist assholes who wanted to save their souls by freeing the slaves and castrating the planters"—not to put too fine a point upon it (*TS*, 217). No tender talk for Van Dorn. What Comeaux politely refers to as "the decay of the social fabric," Afrika Corps officer Van Dorn bluntly calls war. He does not fault Comeaux for his "short-term goals" but despises him for having no clear vision of "the ultimate goals of being human." Naturally, Van Dorn has such a vision informed by his own theory of the nature of man. More, who can barely stand to listen at this point, says, "It has something to do with science and sexuality, how the highest achievements of man, Mozart's music, Einstein's theory, derive from sexual energy, and so on" (*TS*, 218–19). This is highfalutin talk from a pedophile who systematically and repeatedly molests children of both sexes.

It is of no small importance that Don Juan and "Mozart's music" (the opera *Don Giovanni* comes to mind) occupy a central place in Van Dorn's eschatological vision and in his image of himself as leader and prophet of the new age. Don Juan is the very essence of the sensuous as it emerges in the world upon the death of spirit. As Kierkegaard puts it, "As spirit disengages itself from the earth, the sensuous shows itself in all its power. . . .The whole world on all sides becomes a reverberating abode for the worldly spirit of sensuousness, whereas spirit has forsaken the world."[4] Earlier, I suggested that More stands with Father Smith against nihilism and despair because he resists the temptations of both tenderness and sensuousness. Whereas Comeaux is the harbinger of tenderness, Van Dorn plays a similar role for its ontological complement, sensuousness. Like tenderness, no longer subject to Yahweh's sovereignty, sensuousness is abstract, worldless, and infused with a demonic energy which attaches itself to everything and to nothing. In the idiom of Kierkegaard, sensuousness is musical eroticism, and as such, it lacks the formal means that language has—demonstratives, personal pronouns, tenses, and moods—for connecting itself to the actual world of creatures. Kierkegaard could have had Van Dorn's school in mind when he writes: "In the Middle Ages, much was told about a mountain that is not found on any map; it is called Mount Venus. There sensuousness has its home; there it has its wild pleasures for it is a kingdom, a state. In this kingdom, language has no home, nor the collectedness of thought, nor the laborious achievements of reflection; there is heard only the elemental voice of passion, the play of desires, the wild noise of intoxication. There everything is only one giddy round of pleasure. The first born of this kingdom is Don Juan."[5]

Like Comeaux, Van Dorn dresses up his real interests in abstract finery: "Once we get past the mental roadblocks of human relationships . . ."; "Tom, we're talking about caring"; "We have to . . . achieve the ultimate goals of being human" and so on (*TS*, 302, 303, 219). This is not, however, a cynical strategy. Again like Comeaux, he is ontologically incapable of doing otherwise. Emulating his spiritual forebear, Don Juan, Van Dorn rushes headlong from one seduction to the next ("in Spain one thousand and three"), propelled by and intent only upon the fulfillment of erotic desire abstracted from the joys and sorrows of ordinary love and sex. For Van Dorn, this is heaven on earth.

Comeaux and Van Dorn are lovers-theorists of Mankind. Through a combination of speculative gnosis and activist redemption, each is determined to bring about a state of earthly perfection. For them, profane history is "divinized" and becomes the locus of eschatological fulfillment. Both would no doubt be in accord with Feuerbach and Marx, who, as Voegelin observes, "interpreted the transcendent God as the projection of man into the hypostatic beyond; for them the great turning point in history, therefore, would come when man draws his projection back into himself, when he becomes conscious that he himself is God, when as a consequence man is transfigured into superman." From this, we are only a hair's breadth away from the "world-immanent Last Judgement of Mankind," with the lover-theorist of Mankind "deciding on immortality or annihilation for every human being."[6] We are only a hair's breadth away from killing Jews.

The divinization of profane history and the consequent death of spirit are achieved only at a great price. Father Smith knows this and is determined that More know it, too: "I'm afraid this concerns you. I didn't want to tell you but I'm afraid I have to. There is something you need to know" (*TS*, 238). This is Father Smith's confession. In his recollection of the time he and his father spent in Germany in the 1930s in the company of the spiritual descendants of Feuerbach and Marx, the extreme consequences of the death of spirit are clear. The perils at which he hinted in his earlier discourse take shape and form in the persons of the Weimar psychiatrists who loved German romantic music and spoke often of Goethe but never of Hitler; his cousin, Helmut, an SS cadet ready to die for the fatherland and captivated by the prospect of taking his oath at the ancient castle at Marienburg; his own father, "a romantic . . . not successful in life but an upholder of culture, lofty ideals, and the higher things"; and, finally, perhaps most important, the young Father Smith himself, who, he admits, had he been German, would have joined Helmut at the Junkerschule and sworn the oath at Marienburg—"*Blut und Ehre*" (*TS*, 239 ff).

Father Smith's confession is a story of the triumph of intelligence unaffiliated with responsibility to the created world and innervated by mysticism, an abstract longing for totality. Contrary in every way to the desire to stand, after Abraham, in a personal relation to the transcendent God, this longing catapults the mystic beyond the sovereignty of Yahweh, past any imperative for responsible action toward particular, historical others, and into, in Voegelin's phrase, a "hypostatic beyond" in which there is no transcendence greater than that within oneself. Man becomes God and profane history the locus of his salvific activity. He can and will do as he pleases. Rampant in the German romantic music beloved by his father and the Weimar psychiatrists, Dr. Jäger in particular, this abstract longing for totality shows itself in the world in benign ways (the psychiatrists reciting Schiller and Rilke and singing student drinking songs, "*Trink, trink, trink*") and in demonic ones (their easy enthusiasm for the practice of eugenics and euthanasia, an enthusiasm riddled with talk about "reverence for nation" and "reverence for life") (*TS*, 247, 246). Most important, however, the distance between these manifestations, benign and demonic, is but a hair's breadth. Dr. Jäger's history bears bleak testimony to this. Moreover, both betray the same intramundane soteriology and eschatology we have seen in the spiritual heirs of the Weimar group, Comeaux and Van Dorn. Lovers-theorists of Mankind, each is Judge and Redeemer on the brink of the new age.

This is a powerful vision indeed. It must be to have tempted even Father Smith, who did not like his German relations, Helmut excepted, and was put off by the romanticism of father and psychiatrists alike. The hold of this vision upon the world is not complete, however, as Helmut unwittingly attests. "Not much interested" in the Jews (nor were the others in the group), he does refer to the "Judaic conspiracy" and pointedly includes the Catholic church in this ill-defined plot (*TS*, 250–51). This was completely beyond Father Smith's ken at the time, but he now observes, "Of course, in his own mad way he was right, but not quite in the way he meant" (*TS*, 250). We know already that, according to Father Smith, the Jews are the one sign of God which cannot be evacuated and, as such, are a constant irritant to the tender-hearted. Now the Catholic church is allied with the Jews. Why? What the church brings to this alliance becomes clear later when Tom remarks the newly Pentecostal Ellen's aversion to his Catholicism. Particularly horrified by the Eucharist ("*Eating* the body of Christ"), Ellen takes great exception to "the mixing up of body and spirit, Catholic trafficking in bread, wine, oil, salt, water, body, blood, spit—things. What does the Holy Spirit need with things? Body does body things. Spirit does spirit things" (*TS*, 353). The church's insistence upon the union of body and spirit, upon the fundamental goodness of the created order, flies in the face of the abstracting tendencies of both tenderness and sensuousness, before which both persons and things disappear. Thus is the conspiracy of the Jews and the Catholic Church a conspiracy against the nihilism and despair embodied in the distinguished Weimar physicians and their Nazi brothers, for whom they feel only contempt but to whom, as the priest remarks, they taught a thing or two. In a word, theirs is a conspiracy of life against death. As Father Smith says, in answer to More's question, "Why did you become a priest?": "'In the end, one must choose . . .' 'Choose what?' 'Life or death. What else?'" (*TS*, 257).

The warning in the priest's confession, the thing which Tom must know, is that he too is vulnerable to the suasions of tenderness and sensuousness, to the suasions of making oneself over into God. The only armor is to choose life over death and to make that choice again and again. Much later, after Comeaux's little experiment is ended and Van Dorn's school is closed, Comeaux says to Tom, "You and I are more alike than most folks think. . . . The only difference between us is that you're in good taste and I'm not. You have style and know how to act, and I don't" (*TS*, 347). This is a typically self-serving remark, of course, and it would reduce the whole controversy to a mere disagreement over aesthetics. Even so, rather like the young Helmut, he is right but not quite in the way he means. He and More are different, but the difference, like that between the SS cadet and his American cousin, is but a hair's breadth.

With the help of some unlikely accomplices, More finally scuttles the ambitions of Comeaux and Van Dorn. Father Smith, apparently in his right mind and spry as ever, descends from the fire tower to run the hospice, now reopened to care for the sick and the dying. Even Ellen, Pentecostalism aside, gradually returns to her old tart, Presbyterian self. As for More, he reaches for the Jack Daniels less often, but his practice is still shot. The relative peace that descends at the novel's end is not seamless, however. On the occasion of the reopening of the hospice, Father Smith, rather like an Old Testament prophet, manages to offend everyone, "even those most disposed to help him and the hospice . . . decent, tenderhearted, unbelieving, philanthropic people." He detects, he says, "a benevolent feeling here." It is, he declares, "the Great Depriver's finest hour" (*TS*, 357, 360). Foiling the plans of Comeaux and Van Dorn did not restore the transcendent that was evacuated. It did not resurrect the spirit, which has long since fled the world. It did not restore significance to words of belief or unbelief. Tenderness and sensuousness, handmaids of the Great Depriver, are still rampant.

Comeaux and Van Dorn only reminded us of their demonic power when embodied in a lover-theorist of Mankind.

What then are we to do? Speaking with the authority of Kierkegaard's apostle or Percy's newsbearer, Father Smith tells the assembly the one thing he can tell them: send the suffering, the afflicted, the dying, to the hospice. Do not kill them. Choose life over death. His advice to More: "It is only necessary to wait and be of good heart. . . . Do what you are doing. You are on the right track. Continue with the analysis and treatment of your patients" (*TS*, 363, 366). As for himself, Father Smith eventually returns to the fire tower, where he "watches the horizon, mainly in the east, like a hawk"—watching for fires or for a sign of God, no one can say for sure (*TS*, 367).[7]

The Thanatos Syndrome is a sad and funny story. As we know, the best, the most enduring stories tell us something deep and abiding about who we are and where home is: Faust, Don Juan, the Wandering Jew; forbidden fruit eaten; an exodus from desert to promised land; a story of birth, death, and resurrection. It is doubtful that *The Thanatos Syndrome* will attain the status of these, times being what they are. Nonetheless, it does tell us something deep and abiding about who we are as denizens of the postmodern age. It may, if we pay attention, give us a clue as to where home is.

The evacuation of the transcendent, the death of spirit, and the transfiguration of man into God: in the twentieth century, these have ravaged the human heart and left their mark, the mark of Cain, upon every one of us. That this situation is conveyed so clearly and powerfully in the context of a story (as distinct from, say, a philosophical treatise) is itself worth noting. More important, however, Percy displays profound insight into what is surely the most vexed question in modern history: how did national socialism get such a death grip upon the most cultured people of Europe, and what does that have to do with us? The answer Percy gives us is stark: tenderness is but a hair's breadth from the will to power. The pilgrim's progress is a journey more hazardous than we knew.

The Thanatos Syndrome, then, is a cautionary tale. Against the seduction of the will to power, however, there is still a choice to be made, the choice between life and death. It is as Father Smith suggests when, at the novel's end, he tells More about the reported appearance of the Virgin—not as the Queen of Heaven but as "an ordinary, red-cheeked Jewish girl"—to a group of little children some years earlier: "But you must not lose hope, she told the children. Because if you keep hope and have a loving heart and do not secretly wish for the death of others, the Great Prince Satan will not succeed in destroying the world. In a few years this dread century will be over. Perhaps the world will end in fire and the Lord will come—it is not for us to say. But it is for us to say, she said, whether hope and faith will come back into the world. What do you think?" (*TS*, 365).

Sue Mitchell Crowley

The Thanatos Syndrome: Walker Percy's Tribute to Flannery O'Connor

In 1960, just four and a half years before she died of lupus at the age of thirty-nine, Flannery O'Connor wrote what is in fact an essay on the problem of suffering. She agreed to write the introduction to *A Memoir of Mary Ann*, penned by a group of Dominican sisters in memory of the child who had died in their midst at the age of twelve of a grotesque facial tumor.[1] The heart of O'Connor's extraordinarily forthright statement has often been cited, but since it becomes the primary motif in Walker Percy's last novel, *The Thanatos Syndrome*, I will quote it here:

> One of the tendencies of our age is to use the suffering of children to discredit the goodness of God, and once you have discredited his goodness, you are done with him. . . . Ivan Karamazov cannot believe, as long as one child is in torment; Camus' hero cannot accept the divinity of Christ, because of the massacre of the innocents. In this popular pity, we mark our gain in sensibility and our loss in vision. If other ages felt less, they saw more, even though they saw with the blind, prophetical, unsentimental eye of acceptance, which is to say, of faith. In the absence of this faith now, we govern by tenderness. It is a tenderness which, long since cut off from the person of Christ, is wrapped in theory. When tenderness is detached from the source of tenderness, its logical outcome is terror. It ends in forced-labor camps and in the fumes of the gas chamber. (*MM*, 226–27)

A number of Percy critics who had recognized his source immediately were quite surprised to learn that the author did not realize that he was quoting O'Connor almost verbatim in *The Thanatos Syndrome*.

When Scott Walter, interviewing him for *Crisis*, asked him how he happened to use her words as "the leitmotif" for the novel, Percy responded: "I'm amazed. I would happily admit that I did that consciously because I'd love to give her credit."[2] (And, indeed, he often credits her in interviews for certain ideas.) Percy then explains that the "romantic" concept of "*Gefuel*, tenderness or openness to feeling," comes from the Germans and may paradoxically lead to countless horrors, and he names many that readers will recognize in *The Thanatos Syndrome*.

One may find it deeply significant that Percy has so absorbed O'Connor's ethical attitudes and apocalyptic vision, and the actual language in which she couches these, that they have become his own. This is now a habit of mind with Percy: we may also witness him weaving into this work allusions from a number of other figures in whose Catholic tradition he stands, such as Hopkins and Eliot. The tribute to O'Connor, as well as to them, exists, even if it surprises and delights its author. He has interwoven her words ever so quietly into the fabric of his own fiction and, at the same time, has accepted the theological challenge inherent in her statement. Percy, too, raises that most difficult of all questions: why does an all-good and all-powerful God allow children to suffer? And further, why do the well intentioned of the twentieth century, in inflicting their ideologies on others, so often commit what Hawthorne calls the unforgivable sin: "The violation of the sanctity of the human heart"?

In her novel, *The Violent Bear It Away*, O'Connor places Bishop, the retarded child, as a sacred symbol at the center of a radial structure of other characters, each of whom must react to his existence. Both Rayber, his father, and Tarwater, O'Connor's backwoods young hero, feel threatened by intimacy with this creature of God; each fears that if he looks too long at Bishop he will be captured by him. Rayber, the man of reason, sees his son as a "freak of nature" and responds to his condition in the mode of Ivan Karamazov: how can one believe as long as one—even one—child suffers?[3] But at the same time Rayber is always tempted to a love of his only begotten son, a love "without reason . . . that appears to exist only for itself" (*TFO*, 372). Tarwater, who is fleeing from his prophetic vocation, fears the touch of the little boy, fears he will succumb to Old Mason Tarwater's command to baptize Bishop. In the penultimate scene, Rayber, looking on in silence at the two boys in a boat on a lake, understands intuitively that Tarwater has "baptized the child even as he drowned him" (*TFO*, 423). Finally, realizing that he will not feel the pain that is his due, Rayber collapses. The "nit wit" child, in dying, "has made the capture" (*TFO*, 419) of young Tarwater, who is ultimately destined to go off to preach "THE TERRIBLE SPEED OF MERCY " to the sleeping city (*TFO*, 447).

The influence of O'Connor's fiction on Percy's has been growingly evident as each of his novels is published: the linguistic coincidence of opposites; the jeremiad against contemporary secularism; the comic, grotesque exaggeration that covers a deeply theological subject matter; and perhaps, most importantly, the symbolism that emerges from a sacramental sense of the world. Like O'Connor, Percy realizes that a writer cannot use the language of religion, words such as "sin" and "salvation," but must rather make his message apparent by shock. You must shout at the hard of hearing, and, O'Connor writes, "for the almost-blind you draw large and startling figures" (*MM*, 34). Now *The Thanatos Syndrome* seems suddenly to invite the reader to consider how the presence of O'Connor's "Mary Ann theme" has been present in Percy's thought from the beginning. This theme seems to culminate in his last novel, which is dedicated, quite significantly, to Robert Coles, author of both *Flannery O'Connor's South* and *Walker Percy: An American Search*.[4] Coles is one of the saviors of the children in our own time.

In his first novel, *The Moviegoer*, Percy employs O'Connor's symbolic mode creating the crippled and dying child Lonnie, like Bishop a personified hierophany, to be the occasion of faith for his half brother, Binx Bolling. In *The Last Gentleman* the young Will Barrett realizes, in the words of an O'Connor hero, that "something has happened" (*LG*, 407) in the baptism of Jamie Vaught, who is dying of leukemia, and he determines to find out what does happen in a sacramental act. In *Love in the Ruins* Dr. Tom More's daughter is horribly disfigured by her "blastoma," is, in fact, almost identical to O'Connor's description of Mary Ann as she appears in her first communion picture. Tom ponders that his first wife, even in leaving him, had never forgiven him for their daughter's death. "'That's a loving God you have there,' she told me toward the end, when the neuroblastoma had pushed one eye out and around the nosebridge so that Samantha looked like a two-eyed Picasso profile"(*LR*, 72).

In Percy's fourth novel, *Lancelot*, the issue shifts to the terrifying abuse inflicted on children by other human beings in their God-given freedom. Lancelot's daughter, Lucy, is seduced in her father's house by both male and female members of a film crew. Lancelot, having blown up the group, is incarcerated in a mental hospital, where he communicates with Anna, the young autistic victim of a mass rape. In *The Second Coming* it is Allie's own parents who, so that they may control her large inheritance, will have her committed. In the apocalyptic "Space Odyssey," the final chapter of *Lost in the Cosmos*, the children who survive the nuclear holocaust of A.D. 2069 are genetically malformed. *The Thanatos Syndrome*, as its Freudian title implies, is concerned with the postmodern world's fascination with, and lust for, death in all its forms. Dr. Tom More, returned and continuing his "Adventures of a Bad Catholic at a Time near the End of the World," now believes that the syndrome, the beginning of "the age of thanatos," can be traced to those extraordinary examples of human aggression, the battles of Verdun and the Somme, which resulted in the deaths of two million young men. And now, somewhat closer to the end of the world, Eros and Thanatos have merged so that the syndrome takes the form of both chemical manipulations of the population and scientifically regulated child abuse.

Dr. Thomas More is Percy's most cinematic hero, and he must discover, as did his sixteenth-century namesake, and define his very self in authentic action against powerful forces in the secular world. Unlike the more self-reflective Binx Bolling and Will Barrett, Tom wastes little thought upon himself but sets to work like some middle-aged catcher in the rye to save his patients and the children. He believes that prison has restored his humanity, if not his faith: "I still don't know what to make of God, don't give Him, Her, It a second thought, but I make a good deal of people, give them considerable thought" (*TS*, 81). Though flawed by a love for Early Times and lusty women, as well as the occasional bad judgment that has sent him to federal prison for selling uppers and downers to keep truck drivers safer on the highway, he is as a veritable John Wayne, deliberate, decisive, and utterly decent in his pursuit of the bad guys.

It is, however, to the classic existential hero of Camus, Dr. Rieux, the man of simple decency who shuns heroics and knows that curing is the first order of business, that Percy alludes in the opening of *The Thanatos Syndrome*. Following his release from Fedvillle, More notices that "strange events" are occurring in Feliciana Parish (*TS*, 1). As Percy himself was to have been, More is a physician of the soul; he believes, with Freud, in the existence of the human psyche. His patients are exhibiting a peculiar "loss of self" characterized by attenuated speech patterns and comically overt and animal-like sexual behavior. More recalls a physician he once knew, "a natural diagnostician," who discovered a "dead rat with a drop of blood hanging like a ruby from its nose" (*TS*, 4) and, acting on a hunch, confirms, just as Rieux did, the diagnosis of plague in his patients. "There they were, sure enough, the little bypolar dumbbells of Pasteurella pestis." Many readers will recall Walker Percy's diagnosis of his own particular plague when he discovered the tuberculosis bacillus under a microscope.[5] "This is not to suggest," More continues, "that I have stumbled onto another black plague. But if I am right I have stumbled onto something. It is a good deal more mysterious and perhaps more ominous." Percy seems to indicate that the plague, Camus's allegory for evil in the universe, may well be increasing in intensity. But it is in regard to secular humanism's response to the plague that he and O'Connor stake their claims against Camus.

The central event of Camus's *The Plague* is, of course, the horrible death of Monsieur Othon's son and the ensuing debate between Father Paneloux and Dr. Rieux. The priest believes that he must see in the suffering of innocence the love of God which surpasses all understanding; the doctor, in the manner of Ivan Karamazov, "will refuse to love a scheme of things in which children are put to torture."[6] Samantha More is as much M. Othon's son as she is Mary Ann. The points of view represented by Camus's rejection of Christianity as in its very inception based on the death of innocence, on the one hand, and O'Connor's acceptance, like Paneloux's, of suffering as mysteriously redemptive, on the other, once again form the underlying dialectic in Percy's antic satire on American culture.

For Percy, as for O'Connor, however, evil may take a truly demonic form, and the artist must find a means to incarnate that demon: "Our salvation," Flannery writes, "is a drama played out with the devil, a devil who is not simply generalized evil, but an evil intelligence determined on its own supremacy. I think that if writers with a religious view of the world excel these days in the depiction of evil, it is because they have to make its nature unmistakable to their particular audience" (*MM*, 168).

The first of Percy's demons is the scientific establishment led by Dr. Bob Comeaux. The group adds heavy sodium to the water supply in order to control the human neocortex and thus cool the superego (consciousness itself being an aberration of evolution). Tom enlists the help of his cousin Lucy, an epidemiologist, and her vast array of federally connected computer terminals to fight this plague. Referring to herself as "a strong girl," Lucy is, indeed, a "works person," totally concerned, like Tom, at Kierkegaard's ethical level. She continually asks him if everything is "all right." Lucy is named for one of Dante's three ladies called by Mary to aid the poet, who has "need" of her. She is characterized by Dante as "Lucy, the enemy of all cruelty" (*Inferno* 2:97–100). Percy's heroine in turn "summons" Vergil Bon, a transformation of Dante's guide and also the very model of Stoical reason, a black engineering graduate student who will be their resource person in pipes.

In Faulkner's *Absalom, Absalom!* the mixed-blood Bons evolve tragically until only the retarded Jim Bond is left. Percy's Bons, on the other hand, are thought to be descended from "the freejacks," so called because they were freed by Andrew Jackson for services rendered in the Battle of New Orleans. Vergil has American Indian blood as well, and, like his ancestors, he has chosen not to pass. The Bons embody Percy's idea of beginning to begin again in America, and their name signifies the ethical, as does Lucy's. Vergil and Lucy, the new scientists, are ideal guides for Tom in the hell of contemporary America.

Meanwhile, another plot, another plague, has been developing. Percy's second demon, the headmaster of the segregated school, John Van Dorn, dreams of genetically combining Don Juan and Einstein, "without the frivolity of the Don or the repressed Jewish sexuality of Einstein" (*TS*, 220). Tom and Lucy discover that the children in the school are not only being given the treated water but also being sexually abused. They discover, too, the child pornography that Van Dorn and his curious band of associates have produced. In what must be the funniest scene in Percy's fiction, More, the good cowboy, forces them all to drink the modal sodium, and they immediately revert to ape behavior, going about on all fours, picking lice, and grooming one another. (Critics may wonder if Percy is alluding here, as well as in the scene with the lonely ape Eve, sitting on the riverbank in Zaire, to the story of Enoch Emory in O'Connor's *Wise Blood*). To further his own grotesque method, Percy directly borrows O'Connor's apocalyptic emblem: Old Tarwater, in an effort to protect his great nephew from Rayber, has shot off the schoolteacher's ear, as if to say, in that refrain from Revelation, "He who has an ear, let him hear." Tom More touches his ear, giving Lucy's Uncle Hugh a sign to shoot the pedophiles if they try to escape. The school coach makes a move, and the uncle takes his Woodsman and shoots him in the ear. "'O, my God,'" screams coach in a perfect O'Connoresque coincidence of opposites,[7] "'Jesus, he's shot me in the head'" (*TS* 304). O'Connor's even more prevalent theme of the quality of vision is continually reflected in the eyeglasses of her characters. Rayber's metal-rimmed spectacles signify his blindness to the sacred. Uncle Hugh next takes on Mr. Brunette, whose vision is pornographic, and knocks his glasses "awry" in the rather significant act of shooting out the seat of his pants. On the other hand, Milton, who assists at mass, has omega-shaped glasses which "flash in the sun" (*TS*, 130).

Still a third and interrelated form of plague has been indigenous in Feliciana Parish, and in describing it Percy places his most O'Connoresque jeremiad on twentieth-century culture at the very heart of his novel. Saint Margaret's hospice, founded by Tom's old friend from *Love in the Ruins*, Father Simon Rinaldo Smith, has been closed down by Comeaux and company. All the dying old people and children have been sent to one of the many Medicare-supported Qualitarian Centers, where, as euthanates and neonates, they will experience gereuthanasia and pedeuthanasia with the joy and exultation induced by THC, the active constituent in marijuana (*TS*, 351). The landmark case, *Doe v. Dade*, now the law of the land, has, on the best scientific evidence, decreed "that the human infant does not achieve personhood until eighteen months" (*TS*, 333). In protest, Father Smith, who thinks that the social engineers will end by killing the Jews (*TS*, 351), has, like his patron saint, Simon the Stylite, ascended to a watchtower and re- fused to come down until the hospice is reopened. Living atop his pillar for more than twenty years, the stylite was intent on doing penance for the sins of the world. Father Smith's parishioners also recall that the penance of the fourteenth-century desert fathers put a stop to the Black Plague in one village. It is not clear, Percy writes, whether the priest watches for "brushfires or God" (*TS*, 367), but it is clear that, true to the gospel writers, he understands that you must "watch and wait" because "you do not know on what day your Lord is coming."[8]

The old priest, like his creator, is fascinated with words as signs, and on one of Tom's visits he proclaims that the word "Jew" is the only word that cannot be subsumed under a class, a word that cannot be "evacu- ated" of its significance or turned into an abstraction (*TS*, 123–25). He believes that the Holocaust was the consequence of a sign that could not destroyed. Percy has repeatedly made clear in both his fiction and his essays that he believes that the endurance of God's chosen people is a sign of the existence of God himself. Quietly—ever so quietly— Percy, however unconsciously, makes O'Connor's statement on the new barbarism of the twentieth century a refrain in the novel: "'Do you know where tenderness always leads?' asks Father Smith. 'To the gas chamber. . . .Tenderness is the first disguise of the murderer'" (*TS*, 128). The priest continues this musing: If you put together "'a lover of Man- kind and a theorist of Mankind, what you've got now is Robespierre or Stalin or Hitler and the Terror, and millions dead for the good of Mankind'" (*TS*, 129).

A concomitant theme in *The Thanatos Syndrome*, one deeply related to the title, involves repeated allusions to German militarism. Lucy's uncle holds that Germans, along with the Roman legions and the Con- federates (both from civilizations often rejected by Percy), were the greatest soldiers in history. Van Dorn, headmaster of Belle Ame, an academy that he describes as a Gymnasium-Hochschule, looks like a Prussian general. Strauss waltzes form a leitmotif for More's auto trip with Comeaux, the heavy sodium expert. More dreams of a Wehrmacht officer and a Tiger tank in a Panzer division in Freiburg, only to awaken to the curious and certain knowledge that he has never been in Freiburg. On the other hand, the possibility of the victimization of an innocent German is repeatedly pointed out as various characters demand to know why Tom's only clothing is his old rumpled "Bruno Hauptmann suit," which makes him look like the man who, though executed fifty years ago, many suspect was not the Lindbergh kidnapper.

Tom—and Percy—seem to stand against death in all its forms. The full meaning of the German-Jewish theme and its relation to O'Connor is very gradually revealed in More's long encounter with Father Smith in the fire tower. Tom arrives fearing the old priest has had a stroke. The latter's arm and hand are frozen in a gesture as if he has been signaling someone to approach him. Now the prophet's voice is stilled, and "Father Smith is sitting at the high table, temple propped on three fingers" (*TS*, 234). (Percy's word picture, with its Trinitarian implications, is almost identical to Rembrandt's *Old Man Thinking*.) Something has happened to this man who looks like an elderly Ricardo Montalban, something very like a Percyan repetition.

In the interview with Walter, Percy makes clear that his source is his recollection of his trip to Germany in 1934 and his later sense of the mystery of the "apposition of that German tenderness and the gas chambers." Tom gradually gets Simon to explain: it is not a dream but "the memory of an experience which is a thousand times more vivid than a dream but which happens in broad daylight when you are wide awake" (*TS*, 235). He recalls two perceptions from his boyhood: lying in bed in his cousin's house in Tübingen and waking to the sound of silvery church bells, like crystal striking crystal, and the smell of red geraniums. The first reference is, of course, to the initial Nazi attack on Jewish homes on Kristallnacht. Percy's second allusion has, I believe, two sources: the first, altogether conscious, and the second, probably unconscious. One of the most chilling statements in the novel, the reader later comes to see, is Percy's declaration in his preface: "All the people of Feliciana have been made up. The only real persons are the German and Austrian professors and physicians who were active in both the Weimar Republic and the Third Reich"—and he names them (*TS*, 2). Percy concludes his preface, "For this information about the Nazi doctors and their academic precursors in the Weimar Republic

I am indebted to Dr. Fredric Wertham's remarkable book, *A Sign for Cain*.[9] But the other source derives, I would like to believe, from those recesses of Percy's creative imagination occupied by the person and work of Flannery O'Connor, whose first story is entitled "The Geranium."[10]

Percy, with great skill, distances his central fiction—the heart of his fiction, if you will—which is itself a reference to works of fact and fiction, by creating inside the novel "Father Smith's Confession" and inside that fiction "Father Smith's Footnotes." All of these are fictions about historical facts more terrifying than any fiction.

The lengthy story of the aged priest, the teller, comes pouring forth once Tom, the hearer, now *his* confessor, has induced him to speak. It is a moment of perfect, if unconscious, intersubjectivity, a reversal of, and somehow a perfecting of, the Lancelot-Percival confession. The priest discovers himself in the intersubjective *telling* and *listening* that Tom has long understood to be proper psychiatry. Simon realizes that during a visit to Germany in the 1930s he would himself have joined his cousin in the Hitler Jugend, with its romantic fascination with "the flag and death," with *"Blut und Ehre"* (TS, 248), with the Teutonic oath at Marienberg. Percy's point is that the Thanatos syndrome infused not only a nation at a moment in history, but also a young American visitor as well.

In that same house lived Simon's cousin's father, Dr. Jäger, a member of a group of charming and cultured psychiatrists and eugenicists who were arguing the merits of a new book, *The Release of the Destruction of Life Devoid of Value (TS*, 246). (The book was actually published, Wertham explains, in Leipzig in 1920 by a jurist, Karl Binding, and a psychiatrist, Alfred Hoche.) Percy will then paraphrase Wertham's exacting description of the children's hospital at Eglfing-Haar in 1945 from his chapter entitled, "The Geranium in the Window: The Euthanasia Murders."

Percy recounts that when Simon Smith returned to Germany with the seventh army, he went to the same hospital from which Dr. Jäger had been "transferred" a few days earlier.

But one nurse showed me where he worked. It was the Kinderhaus, the children's division, a rather cheerful place which had a hundred and fifty beds for child psychiatric cases. There were only twenty children there, most in bad shape, though nothing like what I saw at Dachau. I asked the nurse what had happened to the others. She didn't say anything, but she took me to a small room off the main ward. She said it was a "special department."

It was a very pleasant sunny room with a large window, but completely bare except for a small white-tiled table only long enough to accommodate a child. What was notable about the room was a large geranium plant in a pot on the windowsill to catch the sunlight. It was a beautiful plant, luxuriant, full of bloom, obviously very carefully tended. The nurse said it was watered every day. . . . I asked her what the room was used for. She said that five or six times a month a doctor and nurse would take a child into the room. After a while the doctor and nurse would come out alone. The "special department" room had an outside door. (*TS*, 253–54)

Flannery O'Connor rewrote that first story, "The Geranium," shortly before she died. The geranium is no longer in the story, but the themes of racism, aging, and violence and the problem of suffering still are. Both ethical choice and eternal life are implied in the new title, "Judgement Day." Tom More has struggled with his little band to hold the line against the new barbarisms for which the Holocaust is an ongoing metaphor. But Tom is a creature of Walker Percy's imagination—a deeply Catholic imagination which understands itself as gifted by grace—and only works *and* faith will make him once again, like Walker Percy himself, a true physician of the soul.

Percy's verbs, his continuous repetitions of one-syllable verbs, contain much of his theology and may provide clues to what he sees as still lacking in his hero. Tom believes that he must do no as well as say no to the demons. Father Smith encourages him: "Do what you are doing" (*TS*, 266). As Camus's man in revolt, More knows that one cannot both cure and know at the same time: he is a works man. He chooses to become director of the hospice, taking in the victims of Alzheimer's and AIDS, as well as *all* the dying children, thus undoing the Qualitarian Program.

True to the O'Connoresque tone and content of his prophetic novel about works, Percy has repeatedly employed forms of the verbs "say" and "tell" as well as "do." But words in themselves have not been adequate to the problem of the culture. More complains that the words of the mass do not signify. Percy the semioticist seems to ask: How does one "do" faith? Must Marcelian intersubjectivity go beyond speech? What is the true nature of creative fidelity?

In *Love in the Ruins*, Tom More began his adventures of a bad Catholic by proclaiming his belief in the Holy Roman Catholic Church and the election of the Jews. He also acknowledged that he had left off "eating Christ in communion" (*LR*, 24), but at the end of the novel he has gone to communion at Father Smith's Christmas mass. At the conclusion of the sequel, during the dedication of the hospice, the priest seems to have lost the words of the mass and begins to declaim prophetically and plead, like the Stylite, for penance. He accuses the little congregation of "tenderness," of the benevolence that "leads to the gas chamber" (*TS*, 360). "Everyone here," he declares, "is creaming in his drawers from tenderness," and meanwhile "the Great Prince has pulled off his masterpiece." Finally, having offended everyone (as O'Connor thought herself wont to do), he asks that Tom "assist" him at mass. Tom, Percy says, will "Do Mass" (*TS*, 355). He will in fact "do Mass" for the feast of Saint Thomas More, who wrote a lengthy disquisition on the Eucharist during his imprisonment in the Tower,[11] and he serves again for "Christ-mass." His second wife, Ellen, once a Presbyterian, then an Episcopalian, and now a Pentecostal, is "horrified by the Eucharist: *Eating* the body of Christ." But Tom seems, like Tarwater, all unconsciously to be "hungry for the bread of life." For O'Connor and for Percy, the Eucharist is the "doing" that is beyond the Kierkegaardian ethical and is a *work* of faith. It is to "do yes."

If one must watch and wait, as Father Smith does for the Second Coming, one has meanwhile the seven sacraments, but one has also those other signs, those meanings that have come to live in the body of the world. Such an incarnational vision of the universe, as itself redeemed, may well be Percy's most important debt to O'Connor. They both seem to pay fictional tribute to a common mentor, that nineteenth-century convert to Catholicism, who counterpoints to the horrors of "the black West," his inscape, his sense of "the dearest freshness deep down things,"[12] the gift of hierophany. Not only do Bishop, the sacred child, and O'Connor's "artificial nigger" figure forth Christ; even the beasts do. The gentleman-lover, the bull who pierces the heart of Mrs. May in "Greenleaf" (*CS*, 311–48), and the transfigurational and apocalyptic peacock with his tail full of suns in "The Displaced Person" (*CS*, 194–235) point to the spiritual reality of Hopkins's Christ, who "plays in ten thousand places" (*HR*, 19). Percy's christological hierophanies are less obvious, as easy, it seems, to overlook today as the one they signify. Colley Wilkes, near the Christmas ending of *Love in the Ruins*, reports two signs. The first is "a great unclassified beast of a fish" (*LR*, 387), which has returned after a long absence, of whom Colley says, "I thought of Christ coming again at the end of the world and how it is that in every age there is the temptation to see signs of the end and that, even knowing this, there is nevertheless some reason, what with the spirit of the new age being the spirit of watching and waiting, to believe that." The second is an ivory-billed woodpecker, almost extinct in North America (*LR*, 388). Colley insists that they must again find him, this great bird who wears a flaming crest and haunts deep forest solitudes.

The same pattern of bird and fish recurs in *The Thanatos Syndrome* and is even more reminiscent of O'Connor. As any reader of her stories knows, O'Connor's persistent images of the sun and its reflection in the people, places, and things of the physical world point to the pervasive presence of the Son of Man. Sunlight surrounds Bishop's head like a halo in the eyes of the secularist Rayber, and the sun pursues the child Bevel, struggling even to penetrate the dirty windows of his parents' desacralized apartment. In much the same manner, Percy's Will Barrett in *The Second Coming* creates his own metaphor for the salvific Allie: "In the darkness of the pine and spruce there grew a single gold poplar which caught the sun like a yellow-haired girl coming out of a dark forest" (*SC*, 297).

As Tom More and the scientific engineer Bob Comeaux look across Grand Mer at the wasteland panorama of Fedville and the nuclear cooling tower, both signifying crimes against nature, they also see the "wings of the ibis," which flash sunlight, in Hopkins's very words, like "shook foil" (*TS*, 190; *HR*, 13). Percy, quietly but consistently placing himself in the great tradition of literary converts to Catholicism, has already introduced "pied beauty" into *Love in the Ruins*. Now Hopkins's sense of "dappled things" merges with an extraordinarily complex set of images from twentieth-century writers. And, insofar as *The Thanatos Syndrome* has asked us to recall the great religious poets of the past, it is not altogether surprising to discover Eliot's fisher king theme, with all its attendant grail implications.[13] Tom protests that Father Smith does not have his "hooks" in him, though, in fact, he does (*TS*, 355). The demonic Van Dorn demands that Tom take him fishing. They proceed down Percy's own Bogue Falaya into Pontchatolawa Swamp, which is reminiscent of so many of O'Connor's remote, sacred places: "The silence is sudden. There is only the ring of a king fisher. The sun is just clearing the cypresses and striking shafts into the tea-colored water. Mullet jump. Cicadas tune up. There is a dusting of gold on the water. The cypresses [like Gironella's, they seem "to believe in God,"[14]] are so big their knees march halfway across the bayou" (*TS*, 57). As Hopkins (and Eliot and Robert Lowell after him) knows, released from Noah's ark the legendary "kingfishers catch fire" as they fly toward the setting sun. With his scorched scarlet breast, the kingfisher may be the healer of the wounded fisher king's twentieth-century wasteland, what Percy calls "the Christ-forgetting Christ-haunted death-dealing Western world" (LR, 3).

Suddenly Tom and Van Dorn spot a sunfish. Tom wants only to "watch" him. Surprisingly, Van Dorn catches the fish, which "feels like a marlin"—perhaps Hemingway's christological marlin—on a fly line" (TS, 59). For a moment the pornographer feels like a child, but he responds in the manner of one of O'Connor's anti-Christ figures who unknowingly speaks the truth: "Well, I be god damned." Then Tom's apocalyptic vision of the grail becomes ours: "We gaze at the fish, fat, round as a plate, sinewy, fine-scaled, and silvered, the amazing color spot as his throat catching the sun like a topaz set in amethyst. The colors will fade in minutes, but for now the fish looks both perfectly alive yet metallic, handwrought [like O'Connor's Christ on Parker's back (CS, 510–30)] in Byzantium and bejeweled beyond price, all the more amazing to have come perfect from the muck" (TS, 58–59). Tom More is a just man, a healer, but in transcending Rieux's ethical imperative, he seems to be on the verge of understanding that there is no answer to the deaths of M. Othon's son and Mary Ann and Samantha unless it lies in Christ's own knowledge of suffering, of what it means to be a Jew and truly chosen. The final events of The Thanatos Syndrome take place at Epiphany, the feast of the revelation of Christ, the source of tenderness, to the Gentiles. First Flannery O'Connor and then Walker Percy, both "newsbearers," understand their fictions as works whose ultimate intention is just such revelation.[15]

Notes

Lewis A. Lawson, "The Cross and the Delta: Walker Percy's Anthropology"

1. James Barr, *The Semantics of Biblical Language* (London: Oxford University Press, 1961), 1–20. See also Thorleif Boman, *Hebrew Thought Compared with Greek*, trans. Jules L. Moreau (New York: W. W. Norton, 1970).

2. Walter Kaufmann, trans., *I and Thou*, by Martin Buber, (New York: Charles Scribner's Sons, 1970), 33–34.

3. Don Ihde, *Listening and Voice* (Athens: Ohio University Press, 1976), 177.

4. See Walter Ong's *Interfaces* and *The Presence of the Word* and Edward Schillebeeck's *The Eucharist*.

5. J. N. Sanders, *The Gospel According to John*, ed. and completed by Brian A. Mastin (New York: Harper and Row, 1968), 67–68.

6. Victor Warnach, "Symbol and Reality in the Eucharist," trans. Clement Dunne, in *The Breaking of Bread*, ed. Pierre Benoit, Roland E. Murphy, and Bastiaan Van Iersel (New York: Paulist Press, 1969), 103–4.

7. Harold Stahmer, *Speak That I May See Thee* (New York: Macmillan, 1968).

8. Quoted in Martin Heidegger, *Poetry, Language, Thought*, trans. Albert Hofstadter (New York: Harper and Row, 1971), 191.

9. Quoted in Terence J. German, *Hamann on Language and Religion* (London: Oxford University Press, 1981), 64.

10. Stahmer, *Speak That I May See Thee*, 123.

11. Linda Hobson, "'A Sign of the Apocalypse': Walker Percy," *Horizon* 23 (Aug. 1980): 60.

12. John M. Lincourt and Paul V. Olczak, "C. S. Peirce and H. S. Sullivan on the Human Self," *Psychiatry* 37 (Feb. 1974): 78–87.

13. Arthur Koestler, *The Act of Creation*, (New York: Macmillan Company, 1964), 222.

14. Quoted in James Feibleman, *An Introduction to Peirce's Philosophy* (New York: Harper and Row, 1946), 417.

15. Quoted in Donna M. Orange, *Peirce's Conception of God* (Lubbock, Tex.: Institute for Studies in Pragmaticism, 1984), 21–22.

16. *Writings of Charles S. Peirce*, ed. Edward C. Moore, (Bloomington: Indiana University Press, 1982), 2:168–69.

17. Linda Hobson, "An Interview with Walker Percy," *Xavier Review* 4 (1984): 6.

18. Phil McCombs, "Century of Thanatos: Walker Percy and His 'Subversive Message,'" *Southern Review* 24 (1988): 812.

Gary M. Ciuba, "Walker Percy's Enchanted Mountain"

1. Shelby Foote, letter to Walker Percy, 6 Apr. 1978, Shelby Foote Papers, Southern Historical Collection, University of North Carolina at Chapel Hill.

2. For grants that supported my research for this essay, I wish to thank Kent State University, the National Endowment for the Humanities, and the American Council of Learned Societies. I am especially grateful for Walker Percy's permission to quote from "The Gramercy Winner," Walker Percy Papers, Southern Historical Collection, I, F:1. University of North Carolina at Chapel Hill (hereafter cited as "GW").

3. *Letters of Thomas Mann, 1889–1955*, trans. Richard and Clara Winston (New York: Alfred A. Knopf, 1971), 641.

4. Thomas Mann, "The Making of *The Magic Mountain*," in *The Magic Mountain*, trans. H. T. Lowe-Porter (New York: Vintage Books, 1969), 725.

5. Thomas Mann, *The Magic Mountain*, trans. H. T. Lowe-Porter (New York: Vintage Books, 1969), 496 (hereafter cited as *MM*).

6. Walker Percy, "From Facts to Fiction," *Writer* 80 (Oct. 1967): 28.

7. Susan Sontag, *Illness as Metaphor* (New York: Farrar, Straus, and Giroux, 1977), 26, 37.

8. Lewis A. Lawson, *Following Percy: Essays on Walker Percy's Work* (Troy, New York: Whitston, 1988), 231.

9. Mann, "Making of *The Magic Mountain*," 725, 727.

Patrick Samway, S. J., "Two Conversations in Walker Percy's *The Thanatos Syndrome*: Text and Context"

1. On 18 May 1989, Percy deposited the manuscript and typescripts of *The Thanatos Syndrome* in his possession in the Southern Historical Collection of the University of North Carolina at Chapel Hill (phone conversation with Tim West of the Southern Historical Collection, 7 July 1989). Since a definitive listing of this material has not yet been completed by the library, I am presuming that it is identical to the material that Percy allowed me to study. My essay is based on this premise. Should new material come to light, then my analyses would be subject to change and modification.

2. A. The holograph manuscript (hm). In all, there are 907 pages, many of which have writing on the versos. Included in this material are notes and various drafts of situations and episodes, indicating clearly that Percy had not conceived the novel fully from the outset, but allowed it to develop as he wrote.

B. The first typescript (t1). In all, there are 368 pages of typescript and manuscript material in a large three-ring Wilson James binder, excluding blank sheets, with some holograph writing especially on some of the versos. The last page has a typed number "287." This typescript does not contain the entire novel.

C. The second typescript (t2). In all, there are 516 typed pages with holographic corrections throughout, some on the versos. Pages 311–15 are missing. Also, there is the title page and dedication page, three variants of the introduction, and three pages that are substitutes for pages 311–15:

    1. Two typed pages with holographic corrections.

    2. Three typed pages with holographic corrections.

    3. The same three typed pages as (t2/B) but with different holographic corrections, plus a new concluding sentence, which is the one found in the first edition.

    4. Three pages, which are substitutes for pages 311–15.

D. The typescript setting copy (tsc). This is the same typescript as (t2) except that there are the copyeditor's marks plus holographic corrections and additions throughout.

There are some changes: page 313 is numbered pages 313–15. In addition to the "Short Run Classified Customer Material Transmittal" notice dated 5 May 1987, there are twenty-three pages of front matter, most of it already set in type.

E. The unbound master galleys (umg). According to the number stamped on the final galley, there are 188 galleys. Throughout there are corrections made by one of the editors, plus questions.

In an interview with Zoltán Abádi-Nagy published in the *Paris Review* 103 (Summer 1987), a photographic copy of a manuscript page is reproduced on page 50. Dr. Percy told me on 17 July 1989 that he probably sent Mr. Abádi-Nagy this page only, which he had written out, not the entire manuscript. Excluding foreign-language editions, the following are versions and various editions of the novel: (1) the blue copy, whose pages represent a final proof of the novel, indicating that the corrections in (umg) have been made; (2) the bound, unrevised, uncorrected proofs, whose pages, on the last of which is written in hand "388," are not numbered in type; (3) the first (signed) edition (the Franklin Library); (4) a signed, limited edition (250 copies) published by FS&G; (5) the first trade edition published by FS&G; (6) the edition for the Quality Paperback Book Club (paperback); (7) the edition for the Book-of-the-Month Club (hardback); (8) the Ivy Books paperback edition (Ballantine Books [May 1988]).

3. In addition to the interview with Zoltán Abádi-Nagy, see Phil McCombs, "Century of Thanatos: Walker Percy and His 'Subversive Message,'" *Southern Review* 24 (1988): 808–24.

4. Mikhail Bakhtin, "Discourse in the Novel," in *The Dialogic Imagination: Four Essays by M. M. Bakhtin*, ed. Michael Holquist, trans. Caryl Emerson and Michael Holquist (Austin: University of Texas Press, 1981), 281.

5. I have counted the pages of the holographic manuscript and the first typescript; the pages of the manuscript are not numbered, while those of the typescript have unnumbered pages interspersed among typed numbered pages. The page numbers cited in parentheses refer to my own sequential pagination; this was done for the purpose of identification. In some cases, especially where the notes seem hastily scrawled, I have regularized Percy's phrases and sentences.

6. The reverse side of the stone supporting the statue has the following inscription: "They out talked thee hissed thee / Tore thee / Better men fared thus before thee / Fired their ringing shot and passed / hotly charged—and sank at last / Charge once more then and be dumb / Let the victors when they come / When the forts of folly fall / Find the body by the wall."

7. Walker Percy, phone conversation with author, 17 July 1989.

8. Interview with Mrs. Percy, 7 May 1988.

W. L. Godshalk, "The Engineer, Then and Now; or, Barrett's Choice"

1. "Reentry by travel . . . nearly always takes place in a motion from a northern place to a southern place, generally a Mediterranean or Hispanic-American place, from a Protestant or post-Protestant place stripped by religion of sacrament and stripped by the self of all else, to a Catholic or Catholic-pagan place, . . . vividly informed by rite, fiesta, ceremony, quaint custom, manners, and the like" (*LC*, 149).

2. Sutter's thinking closely parallels that of *Lost in the Cosmos*, and it is not too fanciful to think of Sutter (or someone like him) as the narrator of that "Self-Help Book," the concepts of which help us to understand the engineer who is surely lost in the cosmos, orbiting and trying to find reentry into the "world" (see *LC*, 96).

3. See *LG*, 372, for further discussion.

4. See *LG*, 353, where Sutter indicates that the engineer's "posture is self-defeating." Barrett wants "to locate a fellow transcender (e.g., me) who will tell him how to traffic

with immanence (e.g., 'environment,' 'groups,' 'experience,' . . .) in such a way that he will be happy."

5. See *LG*, 354, for the failure of Christianity with the engineer.

6. Falling becomes a pattern throughout the narrative and takes on multiple meanings.

7. Barrett comes "to see [the slice] as an emblem of his life, a small failure at living, a minor deceit, perhaps even a sin" (*SC*, 45).

8. We remember the engineer's comic attempt to get Farther Boomer to baptize Jamie. It seems significant that the first narrative ends with Jamie's death and the second with Will's impending marriage to Allie.

Joseph Schwartz, "Will Barrett Redux?"

1. Walker Percy, "From Facts to Fiction," *Book Week*, 25 Dec. 1966, 9.

2. Henry James, *The Art of the Novel*, ed. R. P. Blackmur (New York: Scribner's, 1937), 5.

3. Whitney Balliet, "Will and Allison," *New Yorker*, 1 Sept. 1980, 86; Richard Gilman, "Review: *The Second Coming*," *New Republic*, 5 and 12 July 1980, 30; Gene Lyons, "Deep Hidden Meaning," *The Nation*, 16 and 23 Aug., 1980, 157; Thomas Williams, "A Walker Percy Novel Puzzles over the Farce of Existence," *Chicago Tribune Book World*, 29 June 1980, 1.

4. Joseph Schwartz, "Questioning Mr. Percy," *Chronicles of Culture* 4 (1980): 8.

5. Fyodor Dostoevsky, *Crime and Punishment*, ed. George Gibian (New York: W. W. Norton, 1975), 464–65.

6. Scott Walter, "Out of the Ruins," *Crisis* 7 (1989): 13.

7. Dostoevsky, *Crime and Punishment*, 465.

8. Leo Tolstoy, *Anna Karenina*, trans. David Magashack (New York: New American Library, 1961), 803.

9. Ibid., 807.

10. *The Rhetoric and Poetics of Aristotle*, ed. Friedrich Solmsen (New York: Modern Library, 1954), 204.

Bertram Wyatt-Brown, "Percy Forerunners, Family History, and the Gothic Tradition"

1. James T. Lloyd, ed., *Lives of Mississippi Authors, 1817–1967* (Jackson: University Press of Mississippi, 1981), 452–54; Mary T. Hardy, *The Living Female Writers of the South* (Philadelphia: Claxton, Remsen, and Haffelfinger, 1872), 74–80.

2. Anthony Storr, *Churchill's Black Dog, Kafka's Mice, and Other Phenomena of the Human Mind* (New York: Grove Press, 1988), 3–51.

3. Anthony Storr, *The Dynamics of Creation* (New York: Atheneum, 1972), 79.

4. Elizabeth McAndrew, *The Gothic Tradition in Fiction* (New York: Columbia University Press, 1979), 8.

5. Hardy, *Living Female Writers*, 21.

6. William Patrick Day, *In the Circles of Fear and Desire: A Study of Gothic Fantasy* (Chicago: University of Chicago Press, 1985), 23.

7. Catherine Ann Warfield, *The Household of Bouverie; or, the Elixir of Gold*, 2 vols. (New York: Derby and Jackson, 1860), 1:154.

8. Charlotte Brontë, *Villette* (New York: Bantam, 1986), 154.

9. Hardy, *Living Female Writers*, 21.

10. Sarah Anne Ellis Dorsey [Filia, pseud.], *Agnes Graham: A Novel* (Philadelphia: Claxton, Remsen, and Haffelfinger, 1869); Hardy, *Living Female Writers*, 79–80; Lloyd, *Lives of Mississippi Authors*, 139–40.

Susan V. Donaldson, "Tradition in Amber: Walker Percy's *Lancelot* as Southern Metafiction"

1. Quoted in J. P. Telotte, "Charles Peirce and Walker Percy: From Semiotic to Narrative," in *Walker Percy: Art and Ethics*, ed. Jac Tharpe (Jackson: University Press of Mississippi, 1980), 76.

2. Walker Percy, "The Diagnostic Novel: On the Uses of Modern Fiction," *Harper's*, June 1986, 43.

3. Richard Malcolm Johnston, "Middle Georgia in Rural Life," *Century* 43 (1892): 740.

4. Hennig Cohen and William B. Dillingham, introduction to *Humor of the Old Southwest*, ed. Cohen and Dillingham (Boston: Houghton Mifflin, 1964), xiii; James Justus, "Poe's Comic Vision and Southwestern Humor," in *Edgar Allan Poe: The Design of Order*, ed. A. Robert Lee (London and Totowa, N.J.: Vison Press and Barnes and Noble, 1987), 76.

5. Jacques Derrida, *Of Grammatology*, trans. Gayatri Chakravorty Spivak (Baltimore: Johns Hopkins University Press, 1976), 136.

6. Walker Percy, "Naming and Being," *The Personalist* 41 (1960): 153.

7. Frederic Jameson, "Reification and Utopia in Mass Culture," *Social Text* 1 (1979): 135.

8. See Lewis Lawson, "The Fall of the House of Lamar," in *The Art of Walker Percy: Stratagems for Being*, ed. Panthea Reid Broughton (Baton Rouge: Louisiana State University Press, 1979), 238.

9. See Walker Percy, "Stoicism in the South," *Commonweal*, 6 July 1956, 342–44.

10. Sigmund Freud, *Beyond the Pleasure Principle*, trans. and ed. James Strachey (New York: W.W. Norton, 1961), 12.

Jan Nordby Gretlund, "On the Porch with Marcus Aurelius: Walker Percy's Stoicism"

1. Lewis A. Lawson, "*The Moviegoer* and the Stoic Heritage," in *The Stoic Strain in American Literature: Essays in Honour of Marston LaFrance*, ed. Duane J. MacMillan (Toronto: University of Toronto Press, 1979), 180–82.

2. *Literary Criticism: Essays on Literature, American Writers, English Writers*, ed. Leon Edel and Mark Wilson (New York: Library of America, 1984), 12.

3. William Alexander Percy, *Lanterns on the Levee: Recollections of a Planter's Son* (Baton Rouge: Louisiana State University Press, 1984), 313 (hereafter cited as *LOL*). This edition has an introduction by Walker Percy.

4. William Alexander Percy, *"Enzio's Kingdom" and Other Poems* (New Haven: Yale University Press, 1924), 112.

5. Walker Percy, "If I Were King," *The Pica*, 22 Feb. 1933, 8.

6. Walker Percy, "Stoicism in the South," *Commonweal*, 6 July 1956, 344.

7. Ibid., 343.

8. Walker Percy, interview with author, Covington, La., 29 Jan. 1985.

9. Brainard Cheney, "To Restore a Fragmented Image," *Sewanee Review* 69 (Autumn 1961): 691–700. Walker Percy's letter to Brainard Cheney, dated 30 Oct. 1962, is located in the archives at the Alexander Heard Library, Vanderbilt University.

10. Ellen Douglas, *Walker Percy's "The Last Gentleman": Introduction and Commentary*, Religious Dimensions in Literature, no. 11 (New York: Seabury Press, 1969), 8.

11. Marc Kirkeby, "Percy: He Can See Clearly Now," *Los Angeles Times Calendar*, 3 Aug. 1980, 52.

12. Zoltán Abádi-Nagy, "The Art of Fiction XCVII: Walker Percy," *Paris Review* 103 (Summer 1987): 69.

13. Walker Percy, "The Fateful Rift: The San Andreas Fault in the Modern Mind," Eighteenth Jefferson Lecture in the Humanities, 3 May 1989, transcript from the National Endowment for the Humanities, 2.

Peggy Whitman Prenshaw, "Elegies for Gentlemen: Walker Percy's *The Last Gentleman* and Eudora Welty's 'The Demonstrators'"

1. Eudora Welty, "Must the Novelist Crusade?" collected in *The Eye of the Story* (New York: Random House, 1978), 147 (hereafter cited as *ES*).

2. *Conversations with Eudora Welty* (Jackson: University Press of Mississippi, 1984), 259 (hereafter cited as *EW*).

3. Eudora Welty, "The Demonstrators," in *The Collected Stories of Eudora Welty* (New York: Harcourt Brace Jovanovich, 1980), 610 (hereafter cited as *CS*).

4. Richard King, *A Southern Renaissance: The Cultural Awakening of the American South, 1930–1955* (New York: Oxford University Press, 1980), 9.

5. Albert Devlin, *Eudora Welty's Chronicle: A Story of Mississippi Life* (Jackson: University Press of Mississippi, 1983), 146.

Marion Montgomery, "Kierkegaard and Percy: By Word, *Away from* the Philosophical"

1. Søren Kierkegaard, *Point of View for My Work as an Author: A Report to History*, trans. Walter Lowrie, Benjamin Nelson (New York: Harper and Brothers, 1962). Page references in parenthesis, after quotations, are to this edition.

2. Kierkegaard's master's thesis, a truculent and fascinating work that defied the establishment, was translated by Lee. M. Capel and published by Indiana University Press in 1965. Of it, Kierkegaard says he welcomes judgment, "modestly and without any demands," but, he adds, *"by boys I will not be judged."* If his intellectual antagonists entrenched in the Danish academy were, in his view, largely "boys," not so was Paul Martin Møller, who, it is said, let it be known he wished Kierkegaard to succeed him as professor of philosophy at the University of Copenhagen. Møller will figure in some of my argument to follow, so the relationship is worth remembering.

3. The question of multiple presences in words almost obsesses Kierkegaard. He remarks in a journal entry (*Papirer*, I A, 2 Dec. 1837), "Each time I wish to say something there is another who says it at the very same moment. It is as though *I thought double*, and my other self continually stole a march on me; or while I am standing and speaking everyone thinks it is another." One little knows how to take a public Kierkegaard, then, as his academic patron Møller discovered to his grief. Kierkegaard, by revealing Møller's editorial relation to the controversial political journal *The Corsair*, ruined Møller's academic career and in effect sent him into exile.

4. Phil McComb, "Century of Thanatos: Walker Percy and His 'Subversive Message,'" *Southern Review* 24 (1988): 821.

5. On this general concern for the *intuitive*, we might say that since Descartes the rational has increasingly been divorced, with a growing internecine war in the intellectual community, one leading to the divisive "Two Cultures" that C. P. Snow laments. We might remember attempts in this century to recover the authority of the intuitive to rational respectability, no attempt so conspicuous as that by Freud, with whom Walker Percy carries on a respectful quarrel. More recently, such thinkers as Michael Polanyi, in his *Personal Knowledge* and *Tacit Dimension*, have explored the mind in pursuit of the intuitive as rationally demonstrable in relation to the inadequacies of language to say what is known. Such attempts, independent of Thomistic metaphysics, seem to me to lead us back toward Thomas's metaphysical inclusiveness, and Etienne Gilson's *Linguis-*

tics and Philosophy strongly supports my own intuition about the considerable rational arguments out of science about the nature of man and his relation to the signs he makes. One might say that work by Gilson could be subtitled "From Thomas to Chomsky and Back Again," paralleling Gilson's own companion to the consideration, *From Aristotle to Darwin and Back Again.*

6. Paul Martin Møller, *En Dansk Students Eventyr* [The Adventures of a Danish Student] (Copenhagen: Gyldendal, 1980), 73–74. The unfinished novel was published upon the author's death in 1838, but the manuscript had circulated in Copenhagen as early as 1824.

Kathleen Scullin, *"Lancelot* and Walker Percy's Dispute with Sartre over Ontology"

1. William Barrett, *Irrational Man* (New York: Doubleday, 1962), 253.

2. Ibid., 247.

3. For a lucid discussion of the Sartrean ways in which one can submit to or dominate the other, see Thomas J. Owens, "Absolute Aloneness or Man's Existential Structure," *New Scholasticism* 40, no. 3 (July 1966): 341–60.

4. Thomas Anderson, *The Foundation and Structure of Sartrean Ethics* (Lawrence: Regents Press of Kansas, 1979), 63–64.

Linda Whitney Hobson, "The 'Darkness That Is Part of Light': *Lancelot* and 'The Grand Inquisitor'"

1. Phil McCombs, "Century of Thanatos: Walker Percy and His 'Subversive Message,'" *Southern Review* 24 (1988): 816.

2. Fyodor Dostoevsky, *The Brothers Karamazov*, trans. Andrew H. MacAndrew (New York: Bantam Books, 1981), 296 (hereafter cited as *BK*).

3. Wylie Sypher, "The Meanings of Comedy," in *Comedy*, ed. Wylie Sypher (Garden City, N.Y.: Doubleday, 1956), 234, quoting Søren Kierkegaard.

4. Ibid., 215–18.

5. Ibid., 220.

6. Ibid., 220–21.

7. Ibid., 231.

8. Ibid., 231–34.

9. Geir Kjetsaa, *Fyodor Dostoyevsky: A Writer's Life* (New York: Viking Penguin, 1987), 339.

10. Sypher, "Meanings of Comedy," 231.

11. Robert Coles, *Walker Percy: An American Search* (Boston: Little, Brown, 1978), 184.

John F. Desmond, "Language, Suicide, and the Writer: Walker Percy's Advancement of William Faulkner"

1. Percy states this position on southern literature and Faulkner in several places through the interviews.

2. Søren Kierkegaard, *Fear and Trembling and the Sickness unto Death* (New York: Doubleday, 1954), 150–65. All further references to this edition are cited in the text.

3. See especially Louis D. Rubin, Jr., "William Faulkner: The Discovery of a Man's Vocation," 43–68, and Lewis P. Simpson's "Faulkner and the Legend of the Artist," 69–100, in *Faulkner: Fifty Years after "The Marble Faun,"* ed. George H. Wolfe (Tuscaloosa: University of Alabama Press, 1980).

4. Lance's statement that the past is "feckless" echoes *in extremis*, of course, Percy's

own claim about his unconcern with storytelling the past. Yet like Quentin's monologue, Lance's is obsessed with the past. The force of Lance/Percy's argument suggests, however, that on one level the novel is about the uselessness of trying to come to terms with the past through autonomous self-scrutiny. If so, this amounts to a critique from a religious perspective of Faulkner's general practice, because the only way from a religious point of view to "escape" the past and live freely in the present is through repentence and forgiveness, the conversion to a new life achieved paradoxically by admission of one's "noughtness" under God.

5. Lewis P. Simpson, "What Survivors Do," in *The Brazen Face of History* (Baton Rouge: Louisiana State University Press, 1980), 233–55.

6. In "Faulkner and the Legend of the Artist," Lewis P. Simpson also sees Hamlet as an early embodiment of the predicament of the modern writer.

John Edward Hardy, "Man, Beast, and Others in Walker Percy"

1. See Lev. 16:7–26 and John Edward Hardy, *The Fiction of Walker Percy* (Urbana: University of Illinois Press, 1987), 243–44, 294–95 n. 16, 295 n. 17.

2. See Sarah L. Marshall, "A World of Birds: Walker Percy's Aviary," *New Orleans Review* 15, no. 2 (Summer 1988): 48–52.

3. Concerning associations of Christ with big cats, see the Middle English bestiary on the panther and the reference to "Christ the tiger" in T. S. Eliot's "Gerontion."

4. Phil McCombs, "Century of Thanatos: Walker Percy and His 'Subversive Message,'" *Southern Review* 24 (1988): 811.

Robert H. Brinkmeyer, Jr., "*Lancelot* and the Dynamics of the Intersubjective Community"

1. Walker Percy, "The Diagnostic Novel: On the Uses of Modern Fiction," *Harper's* June 1986, 45.

2. For further discussion of Percy's ideas on "news" and "knowledge," see Percy, "The Message in the Bottle" (*MB*, 119–49).

3. For further discussion of Percival, see especially Deborah Barrett, "Discourse and Intercourse: The Conversion of the Priest in Percy's *Lancelot*," *Critique, Studies in Modern Fiction* 23 (Winter 1981–82): 5–11; Robert H. Brinkmeyer, Jr., "Walker Percy's *Lancelot*: Discovery through Dialogue," *Renascence* 40 (Fall 1987): 30–42; Lewis A. Lawson, "Walker Percy's Silent Character," *Mississippi Quarterly* 33 (Spring 1980): 123–40; and Simone Vauthier, "Story, Story-Teller, and Listener: Notes on *Lancelot*," *South Carolina Review* 13 (Spring 1981): 56–66.

Ashley Brown, "Walker Percy: The Novelist as Moralist"

1. Walker Percy to Caroline Gordon, 6 Apr. 1962, in the possession of the author.

2. Herbert Marshall McLuhan, "The Southern Quality," in *A Southern Vanguard*, ed. Allen Tate (New York: Prentice-Hall, 1947), 102.

François Pitavy, "Walker Percy's Brave New World: *The Thanatos Syndrome*"

1. Flannery O'Connor, *Mystery and Manners*, ed. Sally Fitzgerald and Robert Fitzgerald (New York: Farrar, Straus, and Giroux, 1957), 35.

2. Ibid., 44.

William Rodney Allen "'Father Smith's Confession' in *The Thanatos Syndrome*"

1. Sacvan Bercovitch, *The American Jeremiad* (Madison: University of Wisconsin Press, 1978), 6 (hereafter cited as *J* in the text).

2. Ashley Brown, "An Interview with Walker Percy," *Shenandoah* 18 (1967): 8.

3. John Edward Hardy, *The Fiction of Walker Percy* (Urbana: University of Illinois Press, 1987), 235.

4. William Rodney Allen, *Walker Percy: A Southern Wayfarer* (Jackson: University Press of Mississippi, 1986).

5. Phil McCombs, "Century of Thanatos: Walker Percy and His 'Subversive Message,'" *Southern Review* 24 (1988): 809.

6. Hardy, *Fiction of Walker Percy*, 287 n. 14.

7. Walker Percy, introduction to William Alexander Percy, *Lanterns on the Levee* (Baton Rouge: Louisiana State University Press, 1973).

8. Richard King, *A Southern Renaissance* (New York: Oxford University Press, 1980), 97.

9. McCombs, "Century of Thanatos," 809.

10. Robert Cubbage, "A *Visitor* Interview: Novelist Walker Percy," *Our Sunday Visitor*, 1 Nov. 1987, 5.

11. Phil McCombs, "Walker Percy and the Assault on the Soul," *Washington Post*, 14 May 1987, C2.

Elzbieta H. Oleksy, "Walker Percy's Demonic Vision"

1. Walker Percy, "Herman Melville," *New Criterion* 213 (Nov. 1983): 39.

2. Northrop Frye, *The Great Code: The Bible and Literature* (San Diego: Harcourt Brace Jovanovich, 1982), 140–42.

3. Goethe, *Faust*, trans. Walter Kaufman (Garden City, N.Y.: Doubleday, 1961), 381.

4. See Jacques Lacan, *Écrits: A Selection*, trans. Alan Sheridan (New York: W. W. Norton, 1977), 289.

5. Ibid., 22.

6. See Dorothy Kelly, *Fictional Genders: Role and Representation in Nineteenth-Century French Narrative* (Lincoln: University of Nebraska Press, 1989), 1–2.

7. Christopher Lasch, *The Culture of Narcissism: American Life in an Age of Diminishing Expectation* (New York: W. W. Norton, 1979), 346.

8. The figure of Lilith, as seen by most contemporary feminist theologians, is also approached as a viable archetype of a liberated woman. See, for instance, Barbara Hill Rigney, *Lilith's Daughters: Women and Religion in Contemporary Fiction* (Madison: University of Wisconsin Press, 1982), 93–94.

9. Murray Krieger, *Visions of Extremity in Modern Literature*, vol. 1, *The Tragic Vision* (Baltimore: Johns Hopkins University Press, 1973), 250.

10. Ibid., 253.

Patricia Lewis Poteat, "Pilgrim's Progress; or, A Few Night Thoughts on Tenderness and the Will to Power"

1. Eric Voegelin, *The New Science of Politics* (Chicago: University of Chicago Press, 1952). This image appears several times in chapters 4 and 5, 107–61.

2. Blaise Pascal, *Pensées*, trans. A. J. Krailsheimer (London: Penguin Books, 1966), 88.

3. Voegelin, *op. cit.*, 129.

4. Søren Kierkegaard, *Either/Or: Part 1*, ed. and trans. Howard V. Hong and Edna H. Hong (Princeton: Princeton University Press, 1987), 89.

5. Ibid., 90.

6. Voegelin, *New Science of Politics*, 125, 131.

7. On the apostle and the newsbearer, see Percy's essay, "The Message in the Bottle," in *MB*, 119–49, and Søren Kierkegaard, *On the Difference between a Genius and an Apostle*, trans. Alexander Dru (New York: Harper and Row, 1962).

Sue Mitchell Crowley, "*The Thanatos Syndrome*: Walker Percy's Tribute to Flannery O'Connor"

1. Flannery O'Connor, Introduction to *A Memoir of Mary Ann*, in *Mystery and Manners*, ed. Sally Fitzgerald and Robert Fitzgerald (New York: Farrar, Straus, and Giroux, 1961) (hereafter cited as *MM* in the text).

2. Scott Walter, "Out of the Ruins," *Crisis: A Journal for Catholic Laymen* 7, no. 7, (July–August 1989): 12–18.

3. *Three by Flannery O'Connor* (New York: Signet, 1962), 386 (hereafter cited as *TFO* in the text).

4. Robert Coles, *Flannery O'Connor's South* (Baton Rouge: Louisiana State University Press, 1980), and *Walker Percy: An American Search* (Boston: Little, Brown, 1978).

5. Walker Percy, "From Facts to Fiction," *Writer* 80 (Oct. 1967): 27–28.

6. Albert Camus, *The Plague* (New York: Modern Library, 1948), 197.

7. See Nathan A. Scott, Jr., "Flannery O'Connor's Testimony: The Pressure of Glory," in *The Added Dimension: The Mind and Art of Flannery O'Connor*, ed. Melvin J. Friedman and Lewis A. Lawson (New York: Fordham University Press, 1966), 138–56.

8. Matt. 24 and 25; see also Mark 13 and Luke 21.

9. Frederic Wertham, *A Sign for Cain: An Exploration of Human Violence* (New York: Macmillan, 1966), 153–91.

10. "The Geranium" is the opening story in the typescript of O'Connor's master's thesis at Iowa. It was published prior to this in *Accent* 6 (Summer 1946) and is printed at the beginning of her *Collected Stories* (New York: Farrar, Straus, and Giroux, 1971), 3–14 (hereafter cited as *CS* in the text).

11. Thomas More, *The Tower Works: Devotional Writings*, ed. Garry E. Haupt (New Haven: Yale University Press, 1980).

12. Gerard Manley Hopkins, "God's Grandeur," in *A Hopkins Reader*, ed. John Pick (New York: Oxford University Press, 1953) (hereafter cited as *HR* in the text).

13. See J. Donald and Sue Mitchell Crowley, "Walker Percy's Grail," in *Arthur through the Ages*, vol. 2, ed. Valerie Lagorio and Mildred Day (New York: Garland Press, 1990).

14. José Maria Gironella, *The Cypresses Believe in God* (New York: Knopf, 1955).

15. See "Revelation" in *CS*, 488–509.

Contributors

William Rodney Allen teaches English at the Louisiana School for Math, Science, and the Arts. He is the author of *Walker Percy: A Southern Wayfarer* and *Understanding Kurt Vonnegut* and the editor of *Conversations with Kurt Vonnegut*.

Robert H. Brinkmeyer, Jr. is a professor of American literature and southern studies at the University of Mississippi. He is the author of *Three Catholic Writers of the Modern South* and *The Art and Vision of Flannery O'Connor*.

Ashley Brown is a professor of English at the University of South Carolina. He has contributed many essays, reviews, and translations to journals in the United States and England and has edited several books, most recently *The Poetry Reviews of Allen Tate, 1924–1944*.

Gary M. Ciuba is a professor of English at Kent State University and has written articles on Percy for *American Literature, Mississippi Quarterly, New Orleans Review, Thought,* and others. His *Walker Percy: Books of Revelations* will be published in 1991.

Sue Mitchell Crowley is lecturer in religion and literature in the Department of Religious Studies and coordinator for the Humanities Sequence in the Honors College at the University of Missouri, Columbia. She is coeditor of *Critical Essays on Walker Percy* and coauthor of "Walker Percy's Grail" in Vol. II of *King Arthur Through the Ages*.

John F. Desmond is professor of English at Whitman College and the author of *Risen Sons: Flannery O'Connor's Vision of History*. He has published articles on Walker Percy in the *Southern Review, Mississippi Quarterly, New Orleans Review,* and the *Flannery O'Connor Bulletin.*

Susan V. Donaldson teaches American literature and American studies at the College of William and Mary. She has published articles on Nathanael West, Robert Penn Warren, William Faulkner, and Eudora Welty.

W. L. Godshalk is a professor of English at the University of Cincinnati where he teaches courses on Renaissance English drama and contemporary fiction. He has written on various authors, including Shakespeare, Marlowe, James Branch Cabell, Lawrence Durrell, and Walker Percy.

Jan Nordby Gretlund is a professor of American literature at Odense University, Denmark. He is a contributor to *American Literary Scholarship* and coeditor of *Realist of Distances: Flannery O'Connor Revisited.*

John Edward Hardy is professor of English at University of Illinois at Chicago and the author of *Certain Poems, The Curious Frame, Man in the Modern Novel, Katherine Anne Porter,* and *The Fiction of Walker Percy.*

Linda Whitney Hobson of New Orleans is the author of *Understanding Walker Percy* and *Walker Percy: A Comprehensive Descriptive Bibliography.* Her articles on southern fiction have appeared in the *Georgia Review,* the *Southern Literary Journal,* the *South Atlantic Review* and the *Mississippi Quarterly.*

Lewis Lawson teaches at the University of Maryland, College Park. He is the author of *Another Generation: Southern Fiction Since World War II* and *Following Percy: Essays on Walker Percy's Work* and the coeditor of *Conversations with Walker Percy.*

Marion Montgomery is professor emeritus of English at the University of Georgia and has published fiction, poetry, and criticism. His most recent books are *Liberal Arts and Community: the Feeding of the Larger Body, Virtue and Modern Shadows of Turning,* and *The Men I Have Chosen for Fathers: Literary and Philosophical Passages.*

Elzbieta H. Oleksy is a professor at the Institute of English Studies, University of Lodz. Her major publications include *Battle and Quest: The American Fable of the 1960s* and *Plight in Common: Hawthorne and Percy.*

François Pitavy is professor of American literature at the University of Burgundy and specialist of southern literature and particularly of William Faulkner. His most recent book is *Oublier Jerusalem: The Wild Palms de William Faulkner.*

Patricia Lewis Poteat is associate vice chancellor for academic affairs at the University of North Carolina at Chapel Hill and the author of *Walker Percy and the Old Modern Age.*

Peggy Whitman Prenshaw is dean of the Honors College and professor of English at University of Southern Mississippi, and general editor of the University Press of Mississippi's Literary Conversations series. She is also editor of *The Southern Quarterly.*

Patrick Samway, S.J. is the literary editor of *America* magazine. He is the author of a book on Faulkner and coeditor with Ben Forkner of four anthologies on southern literature. He has also edited a forthcoming volume of Walker Percy's uncollected prose and interviews.

Joseph Schwartz is professor of English at Marquette University and is the editor of *Renascence: Essays on Values in Literature.* He is the bibliographer of Hart Crane, the author of nine books, many articles, and numerous reviews.

Kathleen Scullin is a professor at Mount Mary College and has published on Walker Percy.

Karl-Heinz Westarp is a professor of English at University of Århus, Denmark and has published on Joyce, modern British drama, Flannery O'Connor, and Walker Percy. He is coeditor of *Realist of Distances: Flannery O'Connor Revisited.*

Bertram Wyatt-Brown is Richard J. Milbauer Professor of History at the University of Florida and the author of numerous articles and books, including *Southern Honor: Ethics and Behavior in the Old South, Yankee Saints and Southern Sinners,* and *Honor and Violence in the Old South.*

Index

Allen, William Rodney, 193
Anderson, Thomas, 117
Antoninus, Marcus Aurelius, 74–80, 83
Aquinas, Thomas, 4, 99, 106
Aristotle, 103, 121
Atlas, James, 45
Augustine, St., 4, 205

Bakhtin, Mikhail, 25
Baldwin, Joseph Glover, 66
Balliet, Whitney, 43
Balzac, Honoré de, 204
Barth, Karl, 7
Baudrillard, Jean, 69
Benjamin, Walter, 66
Bercovitch, Sacvan, 189, 190
Berdyaev, Nicholas, 7
Blackmun, Harry, 197
Bleich, David, 8
Bloom, Harold, 209
Bohr, Niels, 106, 109
Braden, Waldo W., 66
Brontë, Charlotte, 62; *Villette*, 62
Browning, Robert, 174
Buber, Martin, 7, 10, 214
Buckley, William, 92
Bunting, Charles T., 173
Burgess, Anthony, 191
Byrd, William, 75
Byron, George Gordon, 173

Camus, Albert, 120, 169, 174, 228, 234
Carr, John C., 160

Cassirer, Ernst, 7, 8
Catholicism. *See* Percy, Walker
Chandler, Raymond, 203
Cheever, John, 175–76
Chekhov, Anton, 173, 176
Cheney, Brainard, 79
Churchill, Winston S., 56
Cixous, Hélène, 205–06
Claudel, Paul, 178–79
Clemens, Samuel, 107
Coles, Robert, 227
Conrad, Joseph, 80, 208
Cotton, John, 190
Cremeens, Carlton, 86, 160, 164

Dante, Alighieri, 174–75, 229
Darwin, Charles R., 145
Derrida, Jacques, 66–67
Descartes, René, 6–8, 9, 89, 106, 158
Devlin, Albert, 92
Dorsey, Sarah A., 55, 63
Dostoevsky, Feodor, 16, 51, 124, 173–74;
    The Brothers Karamazov, 28, 45–46,
    119–30, 226, 229; *Crime and
    Punishment*, 46–48; *The Idiot*, 44;
    "Notes from Underground," 172–74
Douglas, Ellen, 80
Dumas, Alexandre, 186, 200

Ebner, Ferdinand, 7
Ehrenberg, Hans, 6–7
Eliot, George, 170
Eliot, T.S., 107, 226, 236
Epictetus, 75, 77, 78, 80, 82

Faulkner, William, 66, 67, 73, 85, 131–40, 169, 171, 178, 186, 193, 230; *Absalom, Absalom!*, 181, 230; *The Sound and the Fury*, 132–35
Feuerbach, Ludwig Andreas, 220
Fitzgerald, F. Scott, 178, 190
Flaubert, Gustave, 169, 175
Foote, Shelby, 13, 131
Forrest, Nathan Bedford, 73
Freeman, Douglas Southall, 79
Freud, Sigmund, 12, 43, 72, 156, 179, 193, 202, 228
Frye, Northrop, 174, 200, 206–07

Gide, André, 208
Gilman, Richard, 44
Giroux, Robert, 24
Glasgow, Ellen, 171
Goethe, Johann Wolfgang von, 122, 128, 201, 220
Gordon, Caroline, 169, 171, 173, 175
Grant, Ulysses S., 84
Gray, Richard, 71
Green, Julien, 179
Greene, Graham, 169

Hamann, Johann Georg, 5–6
Hardy, John Edward, 190, 194
Harris, George Washington, 66
Hawthorne, Nathaniel, 179, 201, 208, 226
Heidegger, Martin, 7
Heisenberg, Werner, 109
Hemingway, Ernest, 237
Hobson, Linda, 7, 11
Hopkins, Gerard Manley, 145, 226, 235, 236
Huxley, Aldous, 61, 177

James, Henry, 75; *Roderick Hudson*, 42, 47, 52
Jameson, Frederic, 69
Jefferson, Thomas, 75, 182
Jeremiad, 81, 102, 189–93, 231
Johnson, Dale, 7
Johnston, Richard Malcolm, 66
Jones, John Griffin, 119, 161
Jones, Madison, 172

Joyce, James, 169
Jung, Carl, 59, 62–63

Kaplan, Bernard, 8
Kaufmann, Walter, 4
Keller, Helen, 6–8, 138, 156
Kierkegaard, Søren, 5, 51, 72, 99–109, 121, 132, 169, 193, 211, 214, 216, 219, 229, 235
King, Richard, 89, 195
Kisor, Henry, 7
Koestler, Arthur, 8
Krieger, Murray, 208

Lacan, Jacques, 202
Langer, Susanne, 7, 8
Lasch, Christopher, 204
Lawrence, D.H., 169
Lawson, Lewis A., 21, 208
Lee, Ann, 205
Lee, Eleanor Percy. *See* Percy, Eleanor
Lee, Robert E., 75, 81, 84
Little, John, 87
Lowell, Robert, 236
Lumpkin, Grace, 171
Lyons, Gene, 43

McAndrew, Elizabeth, 57
McCombs, Phil, 105, 153, 194, 197
McLuhan, Marshall, 171–72
Madox, Lucy Percy, 26
Mann, Thomas, 13–15, 23; *Magic Mountain*, 13–23
Marcel, Gabriel, 7, 45, 50, 172, 209, 234
Maritain, Jacques, 7–8
Marx, Karl, 220
Matthiessen, Francis Otto, 199
Mauriac, François, 169, 178
Mead, George Herbert, 9, 158
Melville, Herman, 208; *Moby Dick*, 199, 207–08
Meredith, James, 90
Merton, Thomas, 27
Mitchell, Margaret, 82, 181, 184, 203
Mitgang, Herbert, 174
Møller, Poul Martin, 107–09
Moliére, Jean Baptiste, 175
Morris, Willie, 84

Nietzsche, Friedrich, 211, 213
Novel. *See* Percy, Walker

O'Connor, Flannery, 47, 171, 178,
    188, 225–37; *A Memoir of Mary Ann*,
    225
Olsen, Regine, 105
Orwell, George, 31, 61, 174

Pascal, Blaise, 169, 211, 214
Patmos Circle, 7
Peirce, Charles Sanders, 7–10, 141, 156,
    158
Pelham, John, 82
Percy, Charles, 58, 62–63
Percy, Eleanor, 55, 58, 63
Percy, LeRoy (Senator), 26
Percy, LeRoy Pratt, Jr., 76
Percy, Mary Bernice ("Bunt"). *See*
    Townsend, Mary Bernice
Percy, Phinizy Billups, 76
Percy, Sarah Ellis, 58, 59
Percy, Walker: and the novel, 46–47, 57,
    61–62, 66–70, 92, 93, 100, 119, 155,
    160, 165, 169, 171, 172–76, 208; and
    religion, 44; *Old Testament*, 3–5, 47, 51,
    78, 103, 126–27, 145, 190, 200–01,
    206, 207, 230; *New Testament*, 3–4, 47,
    51, 76, 106, 125, 190, 207; and
    Catholicism, 3, 26–27, 35, 47, 62–63,
    79–80, 90, 114, 121, 129, 146–47,
    165, 178–79, 194, 221–22, 234–35;
    and other Christian denominations,
    75–77, 105, 189–90; and science, 7,
    30, 83, 156–57, 187, 197–98, 220–21;
    and the South, traditional values, 6, 58,
    73, 162; Southern society 66–68, 74,
    75–76, 84–85, 91, 93–94, 166, 169–70,
    187, 231
    Works: *Conversations*, 46, 51, 63–64,
    65, 66, 67, 86, 87, 105, 107, 120,
    129, 131, 143, 160, 161, 162, 164;
    "The Failure and the Hope," 78;
    "The Fateful Rift: The San Andreas
    Fault in the Modern Mind," 82; "The
    Gramercy Winner," 13–23; "If I
    Were King," 77; *Lancelot*, 26–27, 46,
    55, 57, 60, 62, 65, 67–73, 81–82,
    110–18, 119–30, 133–38, 153–54,
    161–65, 174–76, 189, 192–93, 196,
    199–209, 227; *The Last Gentleman*,
    17, 20, 27, 33–36, 40, 42–45, 48–
    49, 51, 56, 72, 80, 84, 87, 89–92,
    93–94, 145, 148, 173, 193, 196,
    205, 227; *Lost in the Cosmos*, 69, 82,
    132, 138, 141–42, 158, 161–62,
    227–28; *Love in the Ruins*, 25, 27, 45,
    83, 120, 145, 147, 152–53, 166,
    173–74, 190, 196, 210, 213, 227,
    234–36; *The Message in the Bottle*, 3,
    5–12, 14, 18, 23, 67, 105–06, 110,
    113–15, 118, 148–49, 155–59, 178,
    214; "Mississippi: The Fallen
    Paradise," 84; *The Moviegoer*, 16, 27,
    42, 45, 58, 72–73, 75, 79, 108, 142–
    47, 154, 169–72, 173, 178, 181,
    184, 187, 197, 205, 211, 227; *The
    Second Coming*, 27, 33, 36–41, 42–47,
    59, 60, 73, 80–81, 82, 94, 132–34,
    136–40, 145, 148–50, 151–53, 193,
    196, 205, 208, 227, 236; "Stoicism
    in the South," 78; *The Thanatos
    Syndrome*, 12, 20, 24–25, 46–47, 50,
    58, 82–83, 107–09, 121, 144, 149–
    51, 153, 177–88, 189–98, 205, 210–
    24, 225–37; manuscript versions,
    24–32
Percy, William Alexander, 25–26, 58, 75–
    78, 81, 193, 194–95,
Pica, The, 77
Picht, Werner, 6
Pinckney, Josephine, 171, 172
Plato, 104
Poe, Edgar Allan, 60, 61
Pratt, Alice, 26
Proust, Marcel, 170
Pushkin, Alexander, 173

Religion. *See* Percy, Walker
Rhodes, Richard, 107
Rilke, Rainer Maria, 221
Rosenstock-Hussey, Eugen, 6
Rosenzweig, Franz, 7
Royals, Tom, 87
Rubin, Louis D., Jr., 132
Rumbaugh, Duane, 141–42

Sagan, Carl, 141–42
Sartre, Jean-Paul, 110–18, 158, 169
Scheler, Max, 7
Schiller, Friedrich, 221
Science. *See* Percy, Walker
Scott, Walter, 80, 186
Seneca, 77
Shakespeare, William, 43, 44, 82, 122, 175, 199, 208
Siegle, Robert, 65
Simms, William Gilmore, 171
Simpson, Lewis P., 132
Skinner, B.F., 141–42, 156
Socrates, 100, 104
Sontag, Susan, 14
South, The. *See* Percy, Walker
Spencer, Elizabeth, 172, 176
Stahmer, Harold, 7
Stoicism, 71–73, 74–83, 131–34, 135, 170, 229
Storr, Anthony, 56
Strauss, Johann, 184
Stuart, J.E.B., 82
Styron, William, 187
Sullivan, Harry Stack, 8, 121
Swift, Jonathan, 175
Sypher, Wylie, 121–22

Tate, Allen, 66, 93
Taylor, Peter, 172, 176

Telotte, J.P., 65
Thorpe, Thomas Bangs, 66
Tolstoy, Leo, 143; *Anna Karenina*, 44, 49–50; *War and Peace*, 143
Townsend, Mary Bernice (Mrs. Walker Percy), 195

Voegelin, Eric, 211, 217, 220
Voting Rights Act, 85

Walter, Scott, 47, 226
Ware, Nathaniel, 58
Warfield, Catherine Ann, 55, 57–64; *The Cardinal's Daughter*, 63; *The Household of Bouverie*, 55, 60–63
Warren, Robert Penn, 171, 190
Waugh, Evelyn, 173–74
Weismantel, Leo, 6
Welty, Eudora, 84–95, 131, 172–73; "The Demonstrators," 84, 87–90, 94
Werner, Heinz, 8
Wertheim, Fredric, 233; *A Sign for Cain*, 233
Whitman, Walt, 107
Williams, Thomas, 44
Winthrop, John, 190–91
Woodward, C. Vann, 93

Yeats, William Butler, 89, 145